1

RECONSTRUCTION IN TEXAS

RECONSTRUCTION IN TEXAS

BY

CHARLES WILLIAM RAMSDELL

PUBLISHED IN COOPERATION WITH

THE TEXAS STATE HISTORICAL ASSOCIATION

UNIVERSITY OF TEXAS PRESS, AUSTIN & LONDON

Standard Book Number 292-70031-8
Copyright 1910 by Charles William Ramsdell
Original hardcover edition published by the
Columbia University Press, 1910
Texas History Paperback, 1970
Printed in the United States of America

To
My Mother
AUGUSTA HALLEY RAMSDELL

PREFACE.

In narrating the process of reconstruction in any of the Southern States, one is naturally drawn into a sympathetic attitude toward the people whose social and political system was being "reconstructed." But, though this is essential to a clear understanding and a just portrayal of their problems, their motives, and their acts, it is equally necessary to keep in mind the great and pressing problems that confronted the national government and the forces that determined its policies. An exposition of the national point of view is, of course, precluded here by the character and limitations of the subject, but the author has been careful to keep it in a corner of his mind, and has often found it a valuable corrective. It is hoped that this monograph may present in fairly clear outline a period that has left a deep impress upon the later history, the political organization and the public mind of Texas.

Chapters III to VI, with slight modifications, are reprinted from the *Quarterly of the Texas State Historical Association*, with the kind permission of the editor, Professor George P. Garrison. The author is especially indebted for information and suggestions to Mr. and Mrs. W. W. Mills, General Webster Flanagan, Major Ira H. Evans and Judge A. W. Terrell, of Austin, Texas; to Mr. P. H. Windsor, formerly Librarian of the University of Texas; Mr. E. W. Winkler, Librarian of the Texas State Library; Mr. Worthington C. Ford, formerly of the Library of Congress; and to Professor A. C. McLaughlin, formerly of the Carnegie Institution. Professor Wm. A. Dunning of Columbia University has generously given valuable time to reading the manuscript and preparing it for the printer, and has made many helpful criticisms and suggestions. Above all the author is indebted to his wife for faithful assistance and constant encouragement.

CHARLES W. RAMSDELL.

AUSTIN, TEXAS. *November 22, 1909.*

CONTENTS

INTRODUCTION

CHAPTER I

PART I—PRESIDENTIAL RECONSTRUCTION

CHAPTER IV

PART II—CONGRESSIONAL RECONSTRUCTION

CHAPTER VII

CHAPTER VIII

CHAPTER IX

CHAPTER X

CHAPTER XI

EPILOGUE

CHAPTER XII

INTRODUCTION

CHAPTER I

THE SECESSION MOVEMENT

FOR nearly a decade after the annexation of Texas to the Union the questions uppermost in the public mind of the state were the local issues growing out of the days of the Revolution and the Republic. The heavy state debt, the ravaged frontier, and the boundary dispute determined the complexion of the party platforms and measures and furnished the staple subjects of political discussion. Issues of national politics held second place until after the Compromise of 1850, which settled the boundary question, and at the same time provided the means of paying off the state debt. The protection of the frontier was to be a problem for twenty-five years more.

Gradually, the questions involved in the great dispute over slavery forced themselves upon the immediate attention of the people of Texas. Slavery had existed in the state ever since the Anglo-Americans had first pushed their way into the wilderness; and climatic conditions, agricultural development, and constant immigration from the older southern states had contributed to the spread of the institution. It had rooted itself most firmly in the populous eastern and southeastern counties, along the Sabine, Trinity, Brazos, and Colorado rivers, where the plantation system was in almost exclusive possession of the country and conditions, social and economic, were practically identical with those existing in the older slave states. In the other regions there were fewer slaves and correspondingly more free labor. The northern counties contained a large number of settlers from Illinois, Indiana, and Kentucky who were mostly non-slaveholding; the frontier counties, running south through the middle of the state, had only a small proportion of slaves, and the southwest, with a heavy German population, had fewer still. However, in these districts, except, possibly, the last—for the Germans were still segregated and unfamiliar with the institution—the absence of slaves argued no hostility to the ownership of human chattels, but simple inability to own them. Texas was still a new country, half covered with savages, and most of the people were poor after the manner of pioneers. Standing between the old South and the new West, partaking of the character of both, every year of slavery saw her drawn closer to the former; and it was inevitable that she should soon find herself in the political current setting so strongly toward secession.

It was the fight over the Kansas-Nebraska Bill that first drew Texas into the arena of national politics. Sam Houston, then United States Senator, opposed the bill and lost much of his popularity thereby; for most of the voters and political leaders were state-rights Democrats. Nevertheless, he was backed by a strong following of independent Democrats, old line Whigs, Know-Nothings, and others who deprecated agitation of the slavery question as dangerous to the peace and permanence of the Union. The feeling aroused in the contest over Douglas's bill was intensified by the quarrels over the Fugitive Slave Law and particularly by the outbreak of the border war in Kansas. In 1857, after an exciting canvass, Houston was defeated for the governorship by H. R. Runnels, the Democratic nominee and an extreme state-rights man. However, Texas had not yet given permanent adhesion to extreme measures

and the strong conservative element became alarmed at the
disquieting utterances of some of the radical Democrats,
who were now advocating the purchase of Cuba, the pro-
motion of filibustering in Central America, and the re-
opening of the African slave trade. These propositions
were never popular in Texas and the Democratic organization never championed them; but because of a few inconsid-
erate and hot-headed leaders, the party fell under suspicion,
and in 1859 conservatism was able to administer a severe
rebuke by reversing the decision of two years before. Runnels and Lubbock, again the Democratic nominees for the
chief state offices, were defeated by Houston and Clark, and
T. N. Waul, Democratic candidate for Congress from the
western district, was beaten by A. J. Hamilton, who ran
on the Houston or Independent ticket. In the eastern district, John H. Reagan, Democrat, was successful.

In October, John Brown made his raid on Harper's
Ferry. The effect in Texas was to neutralize the results
of the recent conservative victory, and to place the fire-
eating section of the Democracy in the ascendancy. When
the legislature met in November it elected to a vacancy in
the United States Senate, Louis T. Wigfall, the most rabid
state-rights man in Texas and one particularly obnoxious
to Houston. The course of the debates in Congress and
the speeches of Republican leaders were followed with the
liveliest apprehensions, and talk of secession as the only
way to safety from abolitionist aggression became common.
In the national Democratic convention at Charleston in
April, 1860, the Texas delegates bolted along with those
from the other southern states, and at Baltimore helped
nominate the ticket headed by Breckenridge and Lane. The
situation was far beyond the control of Governor Houston,
but he made tremendous efforts to still the rising storm.
Under his leadership the Unionists gathered to the support

of Bell and Everett, in the vain hope that evasion of the great issue would bring peace. When the state-rights extremists declared that the election of the " Black Republican " candidate, Lincoln, would be a declaration of war upon the South and would necessitate secession, he denounced them as traitors, and insisted that secession was an unconstitutional and revolutionary measure and could be justified only after the federal government should begin aggressions upon the slave states. Until that time should come, he pleaded for caution and for confidence in the government.

When the result of the election was positively known, the secessionist leaders determined to act. In nearly all parts of the state mass-meetings were held and resolutions passed, requesting the governor to assemble the legislature at once in extra session in order that it might provide for a convention to act for the state in the emergency. In most cases it was clearly intended by the agitators that the convention should frame and pass an ordinance of secession; but there were some who wished it to go no further at first than to appoint delegates to consult with the other slave states and seek from the free states a renewal of the constitutional guarantees of property in slaves.[1] The plan for a state convention was checked for a time by the refusal of Governor Houston to convoke the legislature; and despite a flood of letters, editorials, and resolutions conveying entreaties and threats, he held firm. But the men with whom he had to deal were as determined as he, and if they could not secure the convention in a regular way they would have it in another. On December 3, 1860, a group of secession leaders at Austin drew up an address " to the people of Texas " suggesting that the voters of each repre-

[1] Lubbock, *Six Decades in Texas,* p. 299.

sentative district hold an election on January 8th, under the order of the chief justice of the district or of one or more of the county commissioners or at the call of a committee of responsible citizens, vote for twice as many delegates as the district had representatives in the legislature, and make returns of the election to the persons ordering it. The delegates were to meet in Austin on January 28, 1861.[1] Extra-legal and revolutionary as the plan was, it won the endorsement of the secessionists everywhere, and by its very audacity at once gave them a great advantage over the Unionists, whose defensive and negative opposition only assured the election of secessionist delegates.

Outflanked, Houston now called the legislature to meet one week before the convention. Soon afterward came the news that South Carolina, Georgia, Florida, Alabama, and Mississippi were already out of the Union. Not all of the counties held elections for the convention—for some districts were too strongly Unionist and others lacked organization—but of the delegates elected nearly all were secessionists. To the objection that it was an assemblage without authority under the law, the followers of Houston now added another—that it represented only a minority of the people. When the legislature met the governor sent in a message in which he still insisted that the rights of the people could best be maintained in the Union, advised against hasty action, and intimated that the approaching convention was an illegal body. The legislature, however, displayed little sympathy with his views, and passed a resolution recognizing the full authority of the convention to

---

[1] *Comprehensive History of Texas*, II, 87 *et seq.* The address was drawn up by O. M. Roberts, George M. Flournoy, W. P. Rogers and John S. Ford. Roberts was then associate justice of the supreme court and Flournoy was attorney-general.

act for the people, except that its action upon the question
of secession should be submitted to a vote of the people.[1]
The convention met on January 28th, as arranged. Associate Justice O. M. Roberts, one of the authors of the
call, was elected president; a committee was appointed to
wait upon the governor, and another to draft an ordinance
of secession. The first found Governor Houston willing
to concede the authority to secure " an expression of the
popular will ", because of the action of the legislature, but
reserved as to other powers. The second committee reported an ordinance setting forth the reasons for secession,
namely, that the Federal government had failed to give
protection to the persons and property of citizens of Texas
upon the frontier, that the northern states had violated the
compact between the states and the guarantees of the constitution, and that the power of the Federal government
was now sought as a weapon to strike down the interests
and prosperity of the people of Texas and of her sister slave-
holding states. It was, therefore, declared that the ordinance of annexation of 1845 was repealed and annulled;
that all the powers which had been delegated by Texas to
the Federal government were revoked and resumed; that
Texas was of right absolved from all restraints and obligations incurred by the Federal compact, and was a separate
sovereign state; and that all her people were absolved
from allegiance to the United States. The ordinance was
to be submitted to the people for ratification or rejection
on February 23d, and, if carried by a majority of the votes
cast, should take effect March 2, 1861. A resolution was
offered to strike out the clause submitting the ordinance to
a popular vote, but it was voted down. On February 1st,
in the presence of crowded galleries and hall and a number

---

[1] *Comprehensive History of Texas,* II, 296-99.

of invited guests, including the governor, the vote was taken and the ordinance passed overwhelmingly, 166 to 7. Among those voting "no" was J. W. Throckmorton, of Collin, afterwards reconstruction governor.

The convention did not stop here, but took it upon itself to transact a vast amount of business not even hinted at in the call under which its delegates were elected. Commissioners from the other seceded states were present urging participation in the general government being organized at Montgomery, Alabama; and the convention, anticipating the popular adoption of the secession ordinance, elected seven delegates to Montgomery.[1] At the same time the senators and representatives at Washington were informed of the action of the convention. A "committee of public safety" of nineteen members was appointed and endowed with extensive powers for the defense of the state. Among other things it was authorized to remain in session during recess, to appoint officers and commissioners to carry out its plans, and to keep its operations secret. On February 5th the convention adjourned until March 2d.

One of the first projects of the committee of public safety was to secure the munitions of war in the possession of the United States troops in western Texas. These troops, about 2,500 in number, were commanded by Major-General D. E. Twiggs, with headquarters at San Antonio. He was a Georgian and his sympathies were with the South; and it may be said in partial extenuation of his later action, that since the middle of December he had been incessantly appealing to Washington to know what he should do in case Texas seceded, and had received no instruction in reply.[2]

---

[1] The delegates were Senators Louis T. Wigfall and John Hemphill, with John H. Reagan, John Gregg, W. S. Oldham, Wm. B. Ochiltree and T. N. Waul.

[2] *Official Records, War of the Rebellion*, Ser. I, vol. i, pp. 579-586.

The committee waited upon Governor Houston and secured his approval of their designs, and then opened negotiations with Twiggs on February 9th for a surrender of the federal stores on March 2d. The negotiations had not been concluded when on the 15th it was learned that General Twiggs had been relieved by Colonel Waite, who was not expected to be so compliant. Waite had not yet arrived, however, and during that night a large body of state troops under the command of Ben McCulloch were rushed into San Antonio and placed at points of vantage. Nothing but surrender of the stores would avoid a conflict now, and terms were agreed upon two days later. The troops were allowed to retain their arms, the light batteries and sufficient supplies and equipment for transportation to the coast, where they were to embark for the North. Waite arrived next day, too late for anything but acquiescence in the terms. Twiggs was dismissed from the United States Army for " treachery to the flag of his country," and was eulogized by resolution of the Texas legislature as a " pure patriot." [1] His surrender was undoubtedly " a military necessity " at the time it occurred, but he might have forestalled it had he chosen to act in time, concentrate his forces and retreat, if necessary, to New Mexico.

In the meantime other state troops under Colonel Henry McCulloch had received the surrender of the small federal posts north of San Antonio; and Colonel John S. Ford, with a third party, had done the same for the lower Rio Grande valley and the adjacent coast region.

While these events were taking place, the campaign for the ratification of the secession ordinance was closing. The authors of the measure were determined that it should not be defeated; the Unionists, unorganized, were making a last

[1] *Official Records,* Ser. I, vol. i, p. 597; Gammel, *Laws of Texas,* V, p. 396.

desperate stand. It was a time of wild excitement; intimidation and violence too often replaced argument. Charges of unfair tactics and of fraud came up from all parts of the state against the secessionists, who controlled for the most part the machinery of election. There are scores of persons living to-day who insist that the majority of the people were opposed to secession, but that enough were kept from the polls by intimidation to determine the result. That is hardly probable; but what the result would have been, if the election could have been carried through in a quiet spirit, cannot be said with absolute certainty. However, when the convention came together again on March 2d, the returns showed 44,317 for the ordinance to 13,020 against it.

Governor Houston regarded the work of the convention as finished; the people, he argued, should be allowed to call another convention if other important work was to be done. But the members had no intention of giving way, and regarded the vote for secession as a sufficient endorsement of their actions to warrant them in doing more. Accordingly the convention, when reassembled, formally approved the provisional constitution of the Ccnfederacy, gave official character to the delegates representing the interests of Texas at Montgomery, and urged them to secure the admission of Texas to the new Union. Houston had acquiesced in secession, but to this later action he was bitterly opposed, regarding it as wholly unauthorized by the people and an arrant usurpation of power. He refused to recognize the convention any longer. It replied by a declaration that it not only had power to pass and submit the ordinance of secession, but also possessed and would exercise the right to do whatever might be incidental to the same, and necessary for the protection of the people and the defense of the state.[1] In pursuance of the supreme powers thus

[1] *Comprehensive Hist.*, II, 120-121.

asserted, the convention next proceeded so to modify the
state constitution that it should conform to the constitution
of the Confederacy—for the Texas delegates had now been
admitted to the provisional Congress. Among other things
the convention prescribed an oath of office professing allegiance to the Confederacy, and ordered that all state officers must take this oath or vacate their offices. When
notified, all responded except Governor Houston and his
secretary of state, E. W. Cave, the former replying orally
that he did not recognize the existence of the convention.
It was known that the removal of the governor was imminent, and an indignation meeting of the numerous Unionists
in the vicinity of Austin was held at which Houston and
A. J. Hamilton, who had just returned from Congress,
made speeches denouncing the course of the convention.
On the same day, March 16th, the office of governor was
declared vacant and the lieutenant-governor, Edward Clark,
was instructed to take up its duties.   Upon retiring, the
venerable governor issued, as an address to the people, a
spirited but dignified protest against the " usurpations " of
the convention.   He made no further resistance and soon
retired from public life, to die two years later.[1]   An effort
of the Unionists in the legislature to repudiate the depo-
sition of the governor was defeated, and the members
themselves were required to take the oath.   On March 23d
the Constitution of the Confederacy was formally ratified
and its authority extended over Texas.   Three days later
the convention adjourned *sine die,* leaving the reorganized
state government to resume its wonted authority.

[1] It was suspected at this time that Houston and the Unionists were
planning to collect a force to sustain him as governor and hold Texas
neutral.   An agent was sent to Austin by Lincoln to confer with
Houston, but the latter refused to countenance the plan or to receive
assistance from the United States.—*Official Records,* Ser. I, vol. i,
550-551.

CHAPTER II

Texas during the War

Texas was formally admitted to the Confederacy by an act of Congress approved March 1, 1861. On the previous day, Jefferson Davis, in accordance with another act, had assumed control over all military operations in the various states having reference to other states or foreign powers; but not until Houston was removed was this authority fully recognized in Texas. When the attack on Fort Sumter and Lincoln's call for volunteers dissipated the hope that war could be avoided, Texas was called upon for 3000 troops and then for 5000 more. In addition to those raised through the agency of the state, a number of battalions and regiments were raised by individuals and mustered directly into the Confederate service. During the following winter the legislature provided for a mounted regiment of rangers for frontier service, and, to expedite and regulate enlistment in the Confederate army, divided the state into thirty-three " brigade districts " in each of which all able-bodied men between the ages of eighteen and fifty years, with necessary exceptions, were to be enrolled in companies subject to the call of the Confederate government. The Confederate " conscript law " of April 16, 1862, brought into active service immediately all men between the ages of eighteen and thirty-five, for three years or for the war. This age limit was extended again and again until the country was almost drained of its men. It is estimated that Texas furnished between 50,000 and 65,000 men for military service,[1] of whom about one-fourth were east of the Mississippi. The rest were scattered about in the Trans-Mississippi Department, in Louisiana, Arkansas, on the frontiers and coast of Texas, in garrisons or on special detail in the interior.

When once the war was fairly on, most of those who had opposed the measures which brought it about, yielded and gave their support to the state and the new government. In every Texas regiment, from Virginia to the Rio Grande, were to be found recent Unionists who gave to the Confederacy an allegiance as sincere and as strenuous as did the original secessionists. There were others who never parted with their Unionist belief but went into the army from necessity; for often it was safer to stand in line of battle than to remain at home as a known opponent of the Southern cause. Some escaped active service by securing appointment upon special details near home, some by election or appointment to political office. All of these things, however, required an oath of allegiance to the Confederacy, and there were many whose strength of conviction would not permit this. To avoid it some left the state immediately and made their way North; others lingered with their families, hiding at times in the woods and hills to escape conscript officers, provost-marshals, vigilance committees, and mobs, until compelled or enabled to slip out of the country and get into the Union lines for safety. This was held to be desertion to the enemy, and capture meant ignominious death. Many were murdered by mobs for the expression of unpopular opinions, and many more because of private grudges screened by charges of treasonable designs. The

---

[1] The lower figures are probably more nearly correct. The bewildering merging of battalions into regiments and the reduction of the latter to battalions again make any estimate uncertain.

story is a painful one, but it could hardly have been otherwise. When a desperate war is being waged, when the enemy is thundering at the gates, perfect tolerance can hardly be expected for expressions of sympathy with the invader. The North never suffered as did the fire-encircled South, but the experiences of the northern "copperhead" were often as harsh as those of the southern loyalist. In Texas this inevitable tendency to lawlessness was accelerated by the presence of so many turbulent characters in her frontier population.[1]

In general, Texas was fairly prosperous during the war —especially during the first two or three years. She lay well outside the circle of conflict; no hostile armies laid waste her towns and fields nor withdrew her slaves from the plantations. Good crops were raised every year, although nearly all the able-bodied men were away in the army. Slaves were in fact more plentiful than ever before, for great numbers of them had been run in from Louisiana, Arkansas, and states even further east, for safe-keeping. Texas was, therefore, in a position to perform a unique service to the rest of the Confederacy in furnishing supplies not only from her own fields and ranches but also, by way of Mexico, from Europe. The early blockade of all or nearly all southern ports and the uncertain dependence upon blockade runners rendered the Mexican trade of particular importance. It was, however, beset with many difficulties. A distance of nearly four hundred miles, through a region part desert, without railroads, infested with brigands, had to be traversed by wagon trains heavily guarded. Nor was this all. Hard cash was necessary for purchasing the goods needed, as the commercial world looked askance at

---

[1] For an account of the work of vigilance committees in the region about San Antonio, see Williams, *With the Border Ruffians*.

Confederate notes and bonds. In lieu of gold and silver, recourse was had to domestic articles—cotton, wool, and hides. Cotton, especially, was in demand abroad and found ready sale. The problem now was for the government to get the cotton and secure its transportation to some point of exchange.

The state first undertook the task, and in April, 1862, a military board was created to purchase arms and ammunition for the state. After disposing of a quantity of United States indemnity bonds, obtained in 1850, the board began purchasing cotton with eight-per-cent state bonds, and during the first year transported some five thousand bales to the Rio Grande. For several reasons, however, the board was never able to accomplish all that it had designed. Planters were loath to exchange their cotton for doubtful state bonds so long as there was a chance to get gold for it, and often refused to deliver cotton actually contracted for. Failure to get the cotton promptly to the Rio Grande damaged the board's credit with the importers of foreign wares. The peculation of officials engaged in the work created confusion; and rivalry with the cotton bureau that was established by the Confederate authorities in 1863, weakened the efforts of both the state and the general government. It is needless to go into the story of mismanagement, misfortune and peculation that characterized so much of this business; for a great deal of real benefit was derived from it notwithstanding. Important also is the fact that a great deal of private cotton found its way into Mexico and across the Gulf to Cuba and Europe, and that a slender but steady stream of hard cash flowed back into Texas; and although the greater part of the money went into the pockets of favored speculators, " exempts ", " details " and officers, the state at large profited somewhat. Texas came out of the war with plenty of food for her people and more hard money than all the rest of the South together.

The military operations in the state are worthy of but slight notice. They were never extensive and were confined to the border, and they therefore left no such reconstruction problems in their train as existed in the other states. In the summer of 1861 an expedition under General H. H. Sibley for the capture and occupation of New Mexico reached Santa Fe, but was driven back the following spring. In August, 1862, a band of some seventy German Unionist refugees were overtaken on the Nueces River by a superior force of " partisan rangers " and almost annihilated. Some prisoners were taken and afterwards killed—a dastardly outrage which the Germans of western Texas never forgave. A few minor engagements along the coast resulted in the better fortification of the ports. In October, 1862, a Federal squadron forced the evacuation of Galveston, which was occupied by United States troops just before Christmas. On New Year's eve the Confederate General Magruder, who had just assumed command of the District of Texas, moved troops over to the island and in the early morning light attacked the forces stationed there, while improvised gun-boats fortified with cotton bales assailed the fleet in the harbor. The attack resulted in a complete victory; the city was taken and the Federal ships captured, driven off, or destroyed. Galveston remained in the hands of the Confederates during the rest of the war and was valuable as a port of entry, though United States warships patrolled the Gulf. In September, 1863, an attempt was made by General Banks to invade Texas by way of Sabine Pass, Beaumont, and Houston; but the invading force with its convoy of gun-boats came to grief in its attack on the small fort at the Pass and got no further. The next attempt was by way of the Rio Grande. Brownsville was taken in November, 1863, and forces were pushed along the coast and up the river to cut off communication

with Mexico; for there was some fear of French intervention from that quarter. The next spring all these garrisons except those at Matagorda and Brownsville were withdrawn and Banks made a third attempt by way of the Red
River and Shreveport. He was defeated at Mansfield before reaching the Texas line. In March, 1864, Colonel E.
J. Davis, a Unionist refugee from Texas, with a force of
some two hundred Texan Unionists, was defeated in an
expedition against Laredo. In return, a force of Texans
under Colonel John S. Ford advanced against and recap-
tured Brownsville, July 30, 1864. Near here, at Palmito
Ranch, occurred the last battle of the war, May 13, 1865,
in which Ford defeated a body of eight hundred Federals.
From their prisoners the victors learned that their government had fallen and that the war was over.

CHAPTER III

THE BREAK-UP.

1. *Decline and Collapse of Confederate Military Power.*

WHEN General Lee surrendered, in early April, 1865, that part of the Confederacy east of the Mississippi was already overwhelmed and exhausted. In the Trans-Mississippi Department, however, a large area, comprising western Louisiana, parts of Arkansas and the whole of Texas, was still untouched by invasion. The Federal forces having been kept at bay here throughout the war, it seemed probable that a severe struggle would be necessary for the reduction of the Confederates in this region; yet, within six weeks from the surrender at Appomattox the Trans-Mississippi Department presented a scene of universal disorder and confusion nothing short of anarchy—and that, too, without the advance of a single Federal soldier. In reality the defences of this department, and particularly of Texas, formed simply a thin shell incapable of sustaining any heavy or prolonged attack.

The country had long been showing unmistakable signs of exhaustion. The cotton trade, upon which so much depended, had gradually succumbed under the weight which official mismanagement and corruption superadded to its inherent difficulties. Repeated issues of Confederate paper money had driven out all other currency and the paper itself steadily depreciated. By March, 1865, even this was cut off, as there was no ready or safe communication with the

Confederate seat of government. Taxes were extremely heavy; the tithe of the cotton taken by the Confederacy was increased to a fifth, then to a half; everything was levied upon. Military authorities impressed beef, corn and other supplies for the army, and having no money wherewith to pay, gave worthless certificates of indebtedness which the government would not even receive in payment of taxes.[1] Driven on by its dire necessities, the government adopted desperate and oppressive regulations that destroyed even its own credit and threatened the extinction of what little trade had survived in the state. During the spring of 1865 other troubles came. A threatened attack by the Federals on Brownsville, the chief cotton depot, had diverted the export trade to the less exposed but also less profitable and less satisfactory points on the upper Rio Grande. At the same time there was a serious drop in the price of cotton, a foreshadowing doubtless of the fall of the Confederacy. All trade was coming to a standstill. Although the crops had been good in 1864, they could not be marketed. There was plenty to eat, but there was very little else to be had.

The military outlook reflected the gloom of economic conditions. There were probably about fifty thousand men in the Trans-Mississippi Department when Lee surrendered. A large part of these were in Louisiana near the department headquarters at Shreveport. Several thousand were in Arkansas. Possibly fifteen thousand men were under arms in Texas. Of these last some three thousand were at Galveston, with others near by at Houston. Small forces were stationed at Brownsville, San Antonio, Hempstead, Sabine Pass, Marshall, and other points. All of these soldiers

[1] Gen. E. Kirby Smith to Gray, Seddon and Wigfall, *Official Records, War of Rebellion,* Ser. I, vol. xlviii, pt. i, 1381-84.

had for months been serving practically without pay, for they were paid in paper. They were poorly clad, and often had to furnish their own clothing and equipment. There was much discontent in the army because of alleged mismanagement and peculation in the commissary and supply departments. Swarms of deserters made their way to Matamoras in Mexico, or took refuge with a body of Federals on the island of Santiago de Brazos. The conscript laws had become more and more severe, and young boys and old men were forced into the ranks. The discontent increased. Certain regiments were wholly unmanageable.[1]

The people were plainly growing weary of the burdens of a hopeless war. Sherman's march through Georgia, despite the ingenious explanations of the press, had shown the utter impossibility of ultimate success. Even General E. Kirby Smith, commander of the department, sought timely provision for the future as early as February 1st, when he offered his military services to Maximilian in case of the overthrow of the Confederacy.[2] Nevertheless, when the news of Lee's surrender reached Texas in the latter part of April, it produced consternation. It was discredited and denied at first as a "Yankee rumor"; then, when too fully confirmed, hope was held out still that most of the army had escaped and were with Johnston. Anxiously tidings were awaited from this general. There was a widespread belief that he was about to cross the Mississippi and join with Kirby Smith; then came the crushing news of his surrender to Sherman. The next attack of the Federals would be upon Texas. All was gloom and anxiety.

A desperate effort was made to preserve a bold front. Governor Murrah and Generals Smith and Magruder made

[1] Magruder to Boggs, *Official Records,* vol. cit., pt. ii, 1271.
[2] *Ibid.,* pt. ii, 1359.

speeches and issued stirring addresses urging the soldiers to fight to the last. Patriotic editors demonstrated conclusively that it would be impossible for the Federals to invade Texas and maintain themselves in its vast stretches without a year's preparation; and that meanwhile help would be secured from abroad, or at least better terms would be offered than had been granted to Lee and Johnston. Everywhere public meetings were held and citizens pledged themselves never to submit to Northern tyranny or to abandon the cause of the South. Meetings of a similar nature were held in the army in the effort to revive the waning devotion of the discontented and the disheartened. Most of these army meetings were meagerly attended; many of the men held aloof, while others attended only in order to pass resolutions expressing contempt for the war meetings of " exempts and details," and bitter hatred of the cotton speculators, upon whom was placed the blame for the failure of the war.[1] But meetings and speeches and valiant " last ditch " resolutions were all in vain. The majority of the soldiers were convinced that the war was over, and the accumulated discontent of the past month expressed itself in desertion. Magruder declared as early as April 29th that the men at Galveston were deserting by tens and twenties every night.[2]

In the meantime by order of Grant, General Pope had despatched Colonel Sprague to Shreveport to demand of Kirby Smith the surrender of the Trans-Mississippi Department upon the same terms that were granted to Lee. Smith immediately, May 9th, rejected these, hoping to obtain more liberal terms. With a view to determining upon methods

[1] *The Tri-Weekly Telegraph* (Houston), April 26, and throughout May, 1865; *The Patriot* (La Grange), May 6 and 20, 1865.

[2] Magruder to Boggs, *Official Records*, vol. cit., pt. ii, 1291.

and means of resistance or suitable conditions of surrender, he had just before this summoned to meet him in conference at Marshall, Governors Allen of Louisiana, Murrah of Texas, Reynolds of Missouri, and Flanigan of Arkansas. All attended save Murrah, who was ill, but who sent Colonel Guy M. Bryan of his staff to represent him. It was determined to endeavor to secure more favorable terms, and meanwhile to concentrate the forces of the department at Houston to resist an expected attack upon Galveston. On May 13th, the members of the conference drew up a set of terms which they ventured to demand, hoping to preserve the political integrity of their states. In substance these demands were: that officers and soldiers were to be allowed to return directly to their homes; immunity was to be guaranteed against prosecution for offences committed against the United States during the war; officers, soldiers and citizens were to be able to retain their arms and to leave the country if they so desired; the existing state governmnts were to be recognized until conventions could be called " to settle all questions between the states ";[1] and after a certain date each state should be allowed full military authority within its own borders for the preservation of order. This conference at Marshall is notable more for what it hoped for than for what it accomplished. General Pope had already expressly disclaimed any authority to settle political questions.[2] Nevertheless, Sprague, who had been detained for this purpose, now returned to Pope, bearing these de-

[1] An expression which betrays the strong state-rights feeling of the conferees. Any suggestion of the authority of the national government over the states was carefully avoided. The chief " question " involved was, of course, the continuance of slavery.

[2] The members of the conference sought to send Governor Allen to Washington to urge the acceptance of the proposed terms, but he was not permitted to go.

mands and a letter from Smith urging reasons for their acceptance, which were chiefly the expense of prolonging the war and the possibility of " foreign complications." [1] The Confederate authorities had already spent much vain effort in endeavoring to entangle Maximilian and the French in Mexico in an imbroglio with the United States. On May 2d Smith had made a last attempt to arouse the anxiety of the Mexican emperor at the prospect of having the distinctly hostile power of the United States re-established on the Rio Grande.[2] But such hopes were futile, if indeed Smith expected any realization of them.

Hardly was the Marshall conference concluded and the counter-demand for terms despatched to Pope, when Magruder sent word from Houston that, on the night of the 14th of May, four hundred of the troops at Galveston had attempted to desert the post with arms in their hands, but had been persuaded by Colonel Ashbel Smith, aided by a couple of regiments, to remain a while longer. The troops were all becoming unmanageable, Magruder further reported; they had lost their fighting spirit and could not be depended upon. They insisted upon dividing the public property before leaving, and he thought it best to comply with this demand and to try to send them away to their homes as quietly as possible.[3] Almost immediately came similar reports from Brownsville. The commander at that place announced that at least one-half of his troops had deserted because they thought it was of no use to fight longer, and that war meetings and speeches had no effect upon them. The troops that remained could not be depended

[1] For the Marshall conference, see *Official Records*, vol. cit., pt. i, 186-194.

[2] Smith to Rose, *Official Records*, vol. cit., pt. ii, 1292.

[3] *Ibid.*, 1308.

upon.[1] Similar accounts came from other points. In many
places the soldiers had taken possession of the government
stores, sacked them, carried off what they could, and gone
home.

The situation was fast becoming desperate indeed. Without waiting for a response from Pope, Smith immediately
despatched General Buckner as commissioner to General
Canby, commanding the United States forces at New Orleans, to take up again the question of terms of surrender.
He then ordered the evacuation of Galveston and, preparing to concentrate the Texas troops at Houston, removed
his headquarters thither. Before he arrived, about May
29th, his army had disappeared. The long dreaded
break-up had come.

The order for the evacuation of Galveston had been received on Sunday, May 21st, and the movement began the
next day. The troops perceived that the end had come and
at once became unmanageable. Ranks were broken and
almost the whole force swarmed up to Houston. Here a
few men of De Bray's brigade maintained sufficient disci-
pline to patrol the streets and preserve order. The city
authorities were greatly alarmed, for wild rumors had flown
about that the troops had threatened to sack and burn the
town, and arrangements were hurriedly made by the mayor
and citizens to feed them until they could be passed on
through. Saloons were ordered closed, and the disobedient
suffered confiscation and destruction of all liquors. For
some reason the military patrol was suddenly withdrawn
early in the morning of Tuesday, the 23rd. By 8 o'clock a
crowd of some two thousand persons had collected before
the doors of the ordnance building. It was broken into

---

[1] Smith to Rose, *Official Records*, vol. cit., pt. ii, 1313.

and speedily sacked. The mob then proceeded to the clothing bureau. Everything portable was taken. " Blankets, made-up clothing, bolts of domestic, buttons, flannels, shoes, mosquito bars, gray cloth, sides of leather, mule whips, hammers, head stalls, *etc.*, all went into the division and were accepted as the new issue." Soldiers, citizens, women, negroes and children participated. Some of the soldiers held aloof. The crowd was surprisingly quiet, and by 12 o'clock all was over. The city authorities seemed paralyzed with fear. Later in the day other troops arrived from Galveston and, finding the booty gone, angrily threatened to pillage the town; but some of the citizens produced part of the stores and they were redistributed among the late comers. Hastily the mayor made provision for feeding them. Again a patrol, partly of soldiers, partly of citizens, was placed over the city, and within a few days quiet was thoroughly restored.[1]

As the disbanded soldiery swept on homeward up through the state similar scenes, on a lesser scale, occurred in many places. There had been no personal violence at Houston, nor was there elsewhere for a time. The soldiers simply took possession of Confederate and generally of state property wherever they could find it, alleging that as it had originally been collected for their use and as they had protected it, they were the nearest heirs of the defunct Confederacy and entitled to this much of the estate. Added to this was the irritating conviction that while they had suffered hardships in the army they had not been adequately supported by the mass of those who had been allowed to remain at home, and that the resources of the country had been speculated upon and wasted by the incompetent or un-

[1] *The Tri-Weekly Telegraph*, May 24 and 31, 1865.

principled men into whose hands they had fallen.[1] Nor did
public opinion often condemn the soldiers. It was greatly
felt that they had a better right to the Confederate property than any one else.[2] Private property was generally
respected, but that of the state frequently suffered. At La
Grange the soldiers of Fayette county held a meeting on
May 27th and appointed a committee to gather up all government property in the county and distribute it, looking
especially to the interest of indigent soldiers or their families. At Huntsville they levied upon penitentiary cloth,
and for a time a fixed amount was given to each applicant.
The towns through which they passed, usually in squads,
furnished them food: " they are masters of the situation,"
explained the Huntsville *Item* significantly. As they penetrated farther into the interior of the state they became more
reckless. At La Grange and San Antonio stores were
openly pillaged. Governor Murrah, in an effort to save the
state property, issued a proclamation on May 25th to all
sheriffs and other officers, enjoining them to gather up and
preserve for future and more equitable distribution all property of the state, and all that of the Confederacy in which
the state had an interest. It was impossible for this order
to be very generally carried out. The widespread feeling
of insecurity and the tendency to disorder were not lessened
by the presence of bodies of armed men marching towards
Mexico. General Joe Shelby, with a force estimated variously at from three thousand to twelve thousand men, was
on his way to join Maximilian,[3] and he levied upon the
country as he passed along. Numbers of smaller groups,
composed largely of late officials who had elected political

[1] *The Tri-Weekly Telegraph*, June 16, 1865.

[2] *The Patriot* (La Grange), June 2, 1865.

[3] *San Antonio News*, May 30, 1865.

exile, were bound for the same destination. Governor
Murrah, on May 27th, issued a call for a special session of
the legislature in July, and at the same time he proclaimed
an election for a general convention. The program was
" to adopt the speediest mode of harmonizing the state
government with the new condition of affairs, to repeal the
ordinance of secession, and to enact other legislation necessary to render Texas a faithful member of the Union."
Neither the legislature nor the convention ever met. It
was soon apparent that civil officials would not be recognized by the Federal government. Helpless in the midst
of the general disorder, from the highest to the lowest, they
gradually ceased to attempt to perform their functions. In
the absence of responsible authorities lawlessness increased.
Jayhawkers, guerillas and highwaymen appeared. An attempt was made to capture and rob the penitentiary at
Huntsville. The state treasury at Austin, left without
adequate protection, was looted. Bands of robbers and
jayhawkers infested all the roads between San Antonio and
the Rio Grande. One stage was said to have been held up
on an average once every five miles on the road from the
Rio Grande to San Antonio. Affairs were not much better
in other sections. Here and there the towns began to organize local police or " home guards " and to clear the
country round about. The newspapers besought the people
to restore order, as it was the only way by which to obviate
the establishment of a military government.[1]

Amid this general confusion Kirby Smith arrived in
Houston about May 29th. On the 30th he issued an address
to the soldiers in which he declared that it had been his intention to concentrate the army at Houston, await negotia-

[1] *Texas Republican* (Marshall), June, 1865; *Tri-Weekly Telegraph*,
June 16, 1865.

tions and carry on the struggle until favorable terms could be secured. He was now left a commander without an army; and, by destroying their organization, he declared, the men had thrown away their only chance of securing honorable terms.[1] On the same day he addressed a letter to Colonel Sprague of General Pope's staff, saying that the Trans-Mississippi Department was now open to occupation by United States troops, since the Confederate soldiers had disbanded. At the same time he declared his intention of leaving the country.[2] In the meantime his commissioner to New Orleans, General Buckner, had been discussing terms of surrender with General Canby. Buckner failed to secure the settlement of any political question, since Canby was not authorized to treat of those matters. However, a convention was finally agreed upon, May 26th, providing, in substance that the Confederate troops, officers and men, were to be paroled and to return home, transportation being furnished them where possible. All Confederate property was to be turned over to the proper officers of the government of the United States.[3]

Before General Smith arrived at Houston, General Magruder and Governor Murrah made an independent effort to secure favorable terms of peace for Texas. On May 24th, the next day after the sack of the military stores at Houston, they appointed Colonel Ashbel Smith and W. P. Ballinger as special commissioners to proceed to New Orleans and negotiate with General Canby or other proper authority of the United States for " the cessation of hostilities between the United States and Texas."

The commissioners arrived at New Orleans on May 29th

---

[1] *Tri-Weekly Telegraph*, June 2, 1865.

[2] *Official Records*, vol. cit., pt. i, 193.

[3] *Official Records*, vol. cit., pt. ii, 600.

and at once solicited a conference. They had seen in the newspapers a copy of the convention between Canby and Buckner, but hoped " to facilitate the prompt and satisfactory restoration of relations between Texas and the United States government." Canby granted the conference, but distinctly stated that he had no authority to entertain officially any questions of civil or political character. The Texas commissioners frankly stated at the outset the actual conditions in Texas—the mutiny and the break-up of the army, the seizure and distribution of Confederate property, the helplessness of the Confederate officials. The people, they said, were heartily tired of the war and ready in good faith to return to their allegiance to the government of the United States; but they were greatly concerned with respect to the course to be pursued by the national government. The commissioners suggested that, inasmuch as the machinery of the civil government of the state was still intact and the regular election of state officers under the constitution in force in 1860 was to fall due the next August, that citizens of proven loyalty to the Union be allowed to proceed with this election. It would be a good policy to recognize the existing state government as a government *de facto* in preference to establishing a military government. They also pointed out the great evils to be feared from the dislocation of the labor of the state. There was more cotton in Texas than elsewhere, the crop was far along toward maturity, and its production involved the interest of all, white and black. It was of the greatest importance, therefore, that the negroes should be kept on the farms, and it was suggested that they be paid wages under proper regulations until the whole subject of labor could be properly adjusted.[1]

[1] *Official Records*, vol. cit., pt. ii, 648, 675.

This conference was necessarily fruitless; for not only was Canby without authority to treat upon the subjects broached by the Texans, but the United States authorities were not likely to yield on a matter of such wide importance as even the partial recognition of the " rebel " state government. As the final effort of the state authorities to save something from the wreck, it is interesting; but it seems impossible that, knowing the outcome of the Sherman-Johnston agreement, they could have hoped for very much along this line.

On June 2d General Smith went on board a United States ship of war at Galveston and formally signed the Canby-Buckner convention. The last vestige of Confederate military authority now vanished. For three weeks, however, after the surrender, the Federals were not able to send an army to take possession of Texas because of the lack of transports.

Meanwhile conditions in the state grew worse. Wild rumors were afloat of dire punishments to be inflicted upon prominent rebels by the victorious Yankees. Trials for treason before military commissions and wholesale confiscation of property were fully expected; and a sort of panic seized upon many of those who had held office under the Confederacy. Some declared they could not live under the odious rule of their enemies and prepared to emigrate. A lively exodus to Mexico ensued. Among those to go were the highest officials in the state, Generals Smith and Magruder and Governors Clark and Murrah, whose flight was bitterly resented by those left behind.

On May 29th General Sheridan was assigned to the command of the Military Division of the Southwest, headquarters at New Orleans. On June 10th he ordered General Gordon Granger to proceed with eighteen hundred men to

Galveston.[1] Granger arrived at Galveston on June 19th
and immediately, in conformity to instructions, assumed
command of all forces in the state and issued orders declaring that by proclamation of the President all slaves were
free, that all acts of the governor and the legislature of
Texas since the ordinance of secession were illegal, that all
officers and men of the late Confederate army were to be
paroled, and that all persons " having in their possession
public property of any description, formerly belonging to
the late so-called Confederate States or the State of Texas,"
should turn it over to the proper United States officer at
the nearest of the previously designated stations.[2] As rapidly as possible troops were pushed into the interior of the
state and posted at the most important points. The military
was to serve the double purpose of carrying out the provisions of the surrender and of preserving order until a
civil government could be established. Most of the troops
sent to Texas were ordered to the Rio Grande as a sort of
demonstration against the French in Mexico. The rest
were wholly inadequate to the efficient policing of the state.
The posts established were widely separated and extensive
districts, comprising sometimes several counties, were without proper surveillance; and this, too, at a time when society
was convulsed with sudden and momentous changes and
lawlessness was everywhere. Even under these conditions

[1] Sheridan says in the dispatch: "There is not a very wholesome
state of affairs in Texas. The governor and all the soldiers and the
people generally are disposed to be ugly, and the sooner Galveston
can be occupied the better " (*Official Records*, vol. cit., pt. ii, 841). If
by this it was meant that further resistance to Federal authority was
contemplated, there seems to be absolutely nothing to support his
statement. It is true, that there was widespread disorder and lawlessness, but the reference could hardly have been to that.

[2] These were Houston, Galveston, Bonham, San Antonio, Marshall
and Brownsville.

General Sheridan, to provide against local resistance or guerrilla warfare, issued orders, June 30th, that no home guards or bands for self-protection should be allowed anywhere in the state, on the ground that the military were sufficient for all such purposes. By the same order, neighborhoods infested by guerrillas were to be held responsible for the deeds of the latter—an act indicative of the harsh suspicion with which Sheridan always regarded Texas.

The military authorities now proceeded to confiscate all public property that could be found. Such as had belonged to the Confederacy or had been used in the prosecution of the war became the property of the United States, while that belonging solely to the state was held until the proper time should arrive for turning it over to the state officials. But very little of the public property had been left by the soldiers during the riotous days of the "break-up," and the Federals charged that the Confederate officials had not observed the terms of the convention and their parole. These charges, later reiterated, were undoubtedly unjust; for the soldiers had seized most of the property before the surrender, and afterwards the officers were unable to restrain them. Many commands, in fact, never surrendered at all but simply disbanded, as has been shown, even before the convention had been agreed upon at New Orleans.

2. Confusion about Cotton

If most forms of Confederate property had disappeared or evaded Federal confiscation, it was otherwise with cotton. When the war closed there was scattered all over the country a considerable amount of unmarketed cotton, and as soon as hostilities ceased the holders were anxious to get it to market without delay in order to obtain the enormous prices then being paid for it. General Grant had given orders to the commanders in the Southwest not to interfere with its shipment, since it was to the business interests of the whole country that it be marketed, but to encourage shipment in every way. The military were instructed not to institute inquiries as to ownership, but to leave the treasury agents to seek out such property as belonged to the government.[1] Accordingly, General Granger, upon his arrival at Galveston, issued orders to the effect that until the arrival of treasury agents all cotton should be turned into the quartermaster's department for shipment to New Orleans or New York, there to be sold to United States purchasing agents. Bills of lading were to be given and the owners were to be allowed to accompany the cotton in order to effect the sale.[2] This order was in force for little more than a month. Treasury agents soon arrived and swarmed over the state, seeking out and taking possession of everything belonging to the late Confederacy, especially cotton. Some of this cotton had actually belonged to the Confederate government; some had been set aside to pay the tax but had never been delivered; some had been purchased by the state military board but had never been paid for nor delivered; some had gone to pay state taxes and was now state property; but a great part had never been anything but private property. The greatest possible confusion arose in regard to the ownership of these various classes of cotton. The planter who had produced it was unwilling to give up, as Confederate property, cotton that had never been paid for, and he still claimed it as his own; nor, it must be confessed, was he always active in turning over

[1] Instructions from Grant to Sheridan, *Official Records, War of Rebellion,* Ser. I, vol. xlviii, pt. ii, 639; Sheridan, General Orders, no. 3, *ibid.,* 713; Canby, General Orders, no. 65, *ibid.,* 694.

[2] Granger, General Orders, no. 5, *Flake's Bulletin* (Galveston), July 18, 1865.

that which had actually been paid for (in Confederate
paper), or which had been raised for the government under
the terms of an " exemption contract." [1]　On the other
hand, the claims of the treasury agents were sweeping. By
order of the general agent for Texas, H. C. Warmoth, all
personal property that was " actually or constructively in
the possession of the Confederate States at the time of the
surrender " was to be seized. [2]　In all cases persons who
wished to ship cotton from any point in Texas were required to give satisfactory evidence that the cotton for
shipment was not " surrendered " cotton. [3]　The burden of
proof, therefore, was on the owner of the cotton.

It is obvious that in the confusion involving the subject
and incident to public affairs generally, it must have been
no easy task even for the most upright and generous-minded
agent to keep clear of popular disfavor; but the almost un-
limited powers delegated to these agents and the constant
opportunities for fraud and peculation, with little danger of
punishment, were in themselves demoralizing.　There seems
to have been a large amount of truth in the charges of
fraud, robbery and extortion that were made against so
many of these officials.　A petition to President Johnson,
printed in the *Washington Republican* (Washington,
D. C.), and signed by merchants, business men and planters
of Louisiana and Texas, declared that great frauds and
acts of oppression were continually practiced by treasury
agents in the matter of cotton; that the planters west of the
Mississippi had rarely received anything in payment from
the Confederate government, and had been informed by

[1] An arrangement whereby a planter had been granted exemption
from military service upon condition of raising a certain amount of
cotton, corn or beef for the Confederate government.

[2] *Flake's Bulletin*, August 30, 1865.

[3] F. H. Coupland in *Flake's Bulletin*, July 31, 1865.

agents, military officials and by the Secretary of the Treasury himself, that cotton not thus paid for or delivered would pass like any other cotton. Yet when the cotton had been sold to the merchants the treasury agent stepped in and took possession of it. Trade was paralyzed, capital made timid, and the planters were unable to sell their cotton or to hire the labor they needed.[1] A correspondent of the *New Orleans Picayune,* writing from Eastern Texas, gives an account of similar difficulties, and declares that every agent under whose inspection the cotton passed required new proof, which was always inconvenient to obtain.[2] Several cases of fraud came to light at Jefferson, Texas, where a treasury agent was later indicted on three distinct charges of fraud and swindling. He was released by the military authorities. Usually there was no recourse whatever for the parties claiming to have been wronged. A favorite device of the dishonest treasury agent was to hold back a lot of cotton from shipment, under pretense of investigating the title, until the owner was willing to give a bribe for its release. Sometimes an agent took possession of the cotton outright and shipped it on his own account. At other times he ordered it shipped to certain points at high rates and received a rebate on the transportation charges.[3]

These troubles involved only the cotton left over from the crop of 1864; but so slowly was the crop marketed that they did not cease until the beginning of 1866.

3. *The Negro Question and Labor Conditions.*

The turmoil and confusion of the "break-up" and the general dread of all that a military occupation might entail

[1] See *Flake's Bulletin,* September 6, 1865.

[2] *Ibid.,* August 30, 1865.

[3] H. Ware to L. D. Evans, Jan. 30, 1866, MS. in *Executive Correspondence,* Texas State Archives.

had at first diverted public attention somewhat from the most serious problem that the close of the war had forced upon the people of the South. What was to be done with the negro? Was he to be set free, and if so, what measure of freedom should he have? How was his labor to be secured and so regulated that he should be an economically efficient member of society? What was to be his position in this society, in the broad domain of civil rights and privileges, and in political affairs? The magnitude of the problem was not at once appreciated; for the time being public attention was engaged solely with that part which was of most immediate concern, the measure of freedom to be accorded to the late slave and the best method of securing his labor. The other and more intricate phases of the question were of later development, and the contingencies which gave rise to them were at first but dimly apprehended.

It had been long foreseen that in the event of Federal victory a change in the status of the negro would be inevitable. Indeed, the certainty of his emancipation in case of the failure of the South had been wielded as a goad to a " last ditch " struggle. Yet the Confederacy itself, in final desperation, proposed to grant freedom to the slaves as a reward for military service The plan came to nothing, for the Confederate government was then on the point of collapse. Then, too, slavery as a system had already been shattered east of the Mississippi by the presence of the Federal armies. In Texas, undisturbed by invasions, the institution had remained essentially unimpaired; but with the break-up of the Confederate armies and the approach of the Federals the changed status of the negro was sharply emphasized. Long before Granger's proclamation at Galveston, June 19th, it was generally known that the slaves would be freed. In some cases the planters anticipated the emancipation by setting their negroes at liberty; sometimes the negroes themselves slipped away from their homes and began roaming about the country; but for the most part they were kept at home to await Federal action.

Even at this time, despite the attitude of the national authorities, there was considerable belief that slavery as an institution was not dead nor yet doomed to die. The *Texas Republican,* the most important weekly of eastern Texas, in its issue of June 16th, reviewed the situation, describing the demoralization of the negroes, who were lapsing into vagrancy and consequent " filth, disease and crime." The negroes would not work when once it was definitely known that slavery was to cease, and the crops could neither be cultivated nor gathered. The *Republican* affected to believe that

the ruinous effects of freeing four millions of ignorant and helpless blacks would not be confined to the South, but that the blight would be communicated to the North, and that the time would come when the people of that section would be glad to witness a return to a system attended with more philanthropy and happiness to the black race than the one they seem determined at present to establish; for they will find that compulsory labor affords larger crops and a richer market for Yankee manufacturers.

The masters were advised, therefore, not to turn their slaves loose to become demoralized, but to maintain a kind and protecting care over them.

The amendment to the Federal Constitution abolishing slavery has not been ratified by three-fourths of the states, nor is it likely to be in the ensuing ten years. When the state governments, therefore, are reorganized, it is more than probable that slavery will be perpetuated. We can tell better then than at present how long it is likely to endure and prepare for the change.

Emancipation, if adopted at all, should be gradual, but "there is but little reason to doubt that whether or not slavery is perpetuated in name, there will be a return to a character of compulsory labor which will make the negro useful to society and subordinate to the white race."

The *Houston Telegraph,* while conceding that emancipation was "certain to take place," was of the opinion that paid compulsory labor would replace unpaid. Since the negro was to be freed by the Federal government solely with a view to the safety of the nation, his condition would be modified only so far as to insure this, but not so far as materially to weaken the agricultural resources of the country. Therefore, the negroes would be compelled to work under police regulations of a stringent character. Under this happy system insolence was to be provided against on the one hand and injustice on the other.

Such seem to have been the hopes of the well informed. To men accustomed to dealing with the indolence of the negro in slavery, such a thing as successful free negro labor was absolutely unthinkable. No other than negro labor seemed available on the great bottom farms of the "black belt"; without this labor the planting interests were threatened with ruin; and, moreover, to leave the negro the prey of the vice and misery certain to result from idleness and vagrancy would be criminal. Compulsory negro labor, then, seemed the natural and necessary arrangement. It was clear enough, too, that slavery as an institution, recognized by the constitution, could not be abolished by proclamation; and that three-fourths of the states would adopt an amendment abolishing slavery, seemed preposterous. Thus the life-long beliefs and prejudices of the Southerner conspired with the exigencies of the situation to lead him into a policy which, certain to be distorted in reports given to the North, was in its reaction to force upon him the very things he would have feared most—his own disfranchisement and negro domination.

Serenely unconscious of negro incapacity and unembarrassed by constitutional guarantees, the Federal authorities proceeded to complete the work cut out for them. In his emancipation proclamation, issued at Galveston on the 19th of June, General Granger declared that in accordance with the Presidential proclamation all slaves were free, and that this involved an absolute equality of personal and property rights between former masters and slaves, the previous bond between them giving way to that between employer and free laborer. Mindful of the propensities of the freedmen, he advised them to remain at home and work for wages, and warned them that they would not be allowed to collect at military posts, nor would they be supported in idleness there or elsewhere.

As long as the regular army officials were in control, that is, until the officials of the Freedmen's Bureau arrived, efforts were made to keep the negroes under strict supervision. In the published general orders of post commanders at various points during June and July, Granger's proclamation is reflected: the freedmen are repeatedly urged to stay at home and go to work for their former masters for wages; they are assured of their freedom and of protection from injustice, but are warned against vagrancy under penalty of being put to hard labor without compensation; and in many cases they are not permitted to travel on the public thoroughfares without passes from employers.[1] That the army officials failed to keep the negroes from vagrancy is not surprising. The army posts were too far apart to keep all communities under surveillance, and the freedmen them-

[1] General Orders published in *Texas Republican*, June 23, 1865; *Tri-Weekly Telegraph*, June 30 and July 5; *Flake's Bulletin*, July 18.

selves were too ignorant to understand that their new freedom did not mean immunity from work, and that they could
not be fed and clothed forever by their liberators.

The military officials made no effort at first to superintend
the drawing-up of contracts between the freedman and his
employer, nor to act for the freedmen in stipulating wages
or other terms. The provost-marshal-general for Texas,
Lieutenant-Colonel Laughlin, issued a statement that negroes would be allowed to make contracts with whomsoever
they wished, and that both parties would be held to the
terms of the contracts; that unless other regulations should
be promulgated by the Freedmen's Bureau, the amount and
kind of consideration for labor should be *entirely* a matter
of contract between the employer and the employees.[1] Perhaps it would have been better if the rate of wages had been
fixed in some way, for some contracts were practically nullified later by the Bureau. It had frequently happened that
a planter, not feeling able to pay wages—for ready cash was
scarce, political conditions unsettled, and the outlook uncertain—had arranged for his freedman to work temporarily for food and clothing for himself and family. In
most cases the freedman was to receive a part of the crop
in the fall. To the child-like negro, concerned only with
the immediate present, there was no difference between this
and his old condition as a slave, and he soon wished to leave.

From a few sections the reports were favorable—the
blacks were making contracts and remaining at work;[2] but
as the summer wore on complaints came from all sides that
vagrancy, theft, vice and insolence were increasing, and that
where negroes had made contracts they broke them without
cause, often leaving their families for their employers to

[1] *Tri-Weekly Telegraph*, June 28, 1865.
[2] Communication to *Tri-Weekly Telegraph*, June 28, 1865.

feed.[1] The *Houston Telegraph* thought it necessary to warn the people not to allow themselves to develop a feeling of hostility and bitterness toward the blacks, who, although they were doing very many foolish and vexatious things, were " not responsible for their own emancipation." It would have been well if the whites generally could have shown this tolerant spirit; but for his former master to show indulgence to the freedman who broke his contract when it suited his whim, disobeyed orders just to see how it felt to be " free ", and spent most of his time " visiting around " when the crops were most in need of work, was more than could be confidently expected of the average employer. For the time being, fortunately, in the southern part of the state, where the demoralization was worst, the crops were already well advanced and would need but little attention until fall. In the north and northeast, where the Federal troops had not yet penetrated, the negroes had shown less inclination to wander about or else their former masters had taken steps to keep them at home. While in a few instances these planters endeavored to keep their negroes in ignorance of their freedom, in most cases their efforts took the form of combinations to control the labor of their former slaves; and usually each planter agreed to hire no negro without the consent of his former master. Sometimes freedmen who broke contracts and went away were brought back by force, and in some cases the planters were guilty of needless cruelty. The army officials generally endeavored to hold the negroes to their contracts, but at the same time they refused to allow coercion on the part of the employers. The discontent grew steadily worse and found expres-

[1] *Tri-Weekly Telegraph*, July 7, 1865; *San Antonio Herald*, July 9, *Jefferson Bulletin*, August —, *Caddo Gazette*, August —; *Texas Republican*, August 18; *Southern Intelligencer*, September 29.

sion in a more and more insistent demand, chiefly on the part of planters and newspapers in the interior, for state regulation of black labor. The *Telegraph* alone pointed out that the " North would not likely allow the South thus to enjoy the fruit of the contest over slavery after having lost the contest," and advocated securing the immigration of white labor.

Conditions in the black belt did not materially improve during the summer. There was much uneasiness because of persistent rumors that negro troops were to be sent to Texas for garrison duty; for it was generally felt that their presence could only aggravate the situation and might make it positively dangerous by inciting unruly negroes to lawlessness and precipitating racial disturbances. It was also known that the Freedmen's Bureau was to be established in Texas, and the anxiety and distrust that were felt as to its attitude on the labor question did not tend to alleviate the growing discontent. Public opinion had become skeptical of the ability of the army officials to provide the usual and necessary supply of black labor, and manifested a greater eagerness for the speedy restoration of the regular state government, which could be expected to deal with the problem in a manner agreeable with the customs and social ideas of the people. For this reason, largely, the arrival of the newly-appointed provisional governor, who was to restore civil authority and set in motion again the machinery of state government, was greeted with expectant interest.

PART I
PRESIDENTIAL RECONSTRUCTION

CHAPTER IV

THE STATE UNDER PROVISIONAL GOVERNMENT

1. *Inauguration of the New Régime*

ON June 17, 1865, soon after it became known that armed. resistance had ceased in the Trans-Mississippi Department and that troops had been despatched to occupy Galveston, President Johnson, in pursuance of the policy adopted in other southern states, appointed A. J. Hamilton provisional governor of Texas. Hamilton was a native of Alabama, who had come to Texas in 1847 and had become prominent in politics before the war. He had been attorney-general of the state and in 1859 had been elected to Congress. Along with Houston and others he had vigorously opposed secession and refused adhesion to the Confederacy, but had remained in Texas until 1862, when, threatened with military arrest, he escaped into Mexico and thence to New Orleans. Here he entered the Federal army as a brigadier-general of volunteers, and in 1863, when the Brownsville-Red-River expedition into Texas was projected, he received a commission as military governor of the state from President Lincoln. He was, therefore, regarded by President Johnson as logically the man for provisional governor after the surrender of the Confederate authorities. Hamilton was a man of energy and ability, of sturdy honesty, aggressive and uncompromising, and though prone, when excited, to violence and harshness of speech, restrained and governed in action by an unfailing generosity and abundant common sense. He was an orator of extraordinary power and had enjoyed the reputation of being one of the ablest lawyers in the South. The news of his appointment was received with general satisfaction by the Unionists and with some misgivings on the part of those who feared he was returning for purposes of vengeance.

The proclamation which contained his appointment declared it to be the duty of the United States to guarantee to each state a republican form of government, and that, inasmuch as the rebellion had deprived the people of Texas of all civil government, it was now the solemn duty of the President, imposed by the constitution, to enable the loyal people there to organize a state government. The provisional governor was directed to prescribe at the earliest practicable period rules and regulations for holding a convention of delegates for the purpose of altering or amending the constitution of the state; and he was given authority to exercise all necessary and proper powers to restore the state to its constitutional relations to the United States. The convention was to represent only that portion of the people who were loyal to the United States; and to this end the proclamation provided that in the election for delegates no person should be qualified either as an elector or as a member of the convention unless he had previously taken the oath of amnesty, as prescribed in the President's proclamation of May 29, 1865, and was a voter as prescribed by the constitution and laws of the state in force immediately before secession. The military commander of the department and all other military officers in the service of the United States were directed to aid and assist the provisional governor in carrying the proclamation into effect, and were enjoined to abstain from hindering or discouraging in any way the loyal people from organizing a state government. The Secretary of State was directed to put in force all the laws of the United States, the administration of which belonged to his department and which were applicable to the state of Texas; the Secretary of the Treasury was to proceed to nominate the officers necessary to put into operation the revenue laws, giving preference in each case to loyal persons residing within the district; the Postmaster-General was directed to re-establish the postal service; the United States district judge for the district of Texas was authorized to hold courts according to the acts of Congress; the Attorney-General was directed to instruct the proper officers to libel and bring to judgment, confiscation and sale such property as had become subject to confiscation; and the Secretaries of the Navy and the Interior were directed to put in force such laws as related to their respective departments.[1]

Governor Hamilton arrived in Galveston on July 21st, where he was welcomed by a delegation of Unionists. From there he sent a cheerful letter to the President, expressing the conviction that all classes, except certain of the ex-slaveholders, were friends of the government and were rapidly availing themselves of the President's amnesty proclamation. He deprecated a tendency on the part of the planters to keep the negro in some sort of bondage and to talk of " gradual emancipation," even after having subscribed to emancipation in their oath of amnesty.[2] On the 25th he issued from Galveston a proclamation " to the people of the state of Texas," reciting the manner and purpose of his appointment and indicating in a general way the course he expected to take with respect to the election of a convention and the appointment of civil officers. Suitable persons were to be appointed in each county to administer the oath of

[1] *Messages and Papers of the Presidents*, vol. vi, p. 321.

[2] MS. in *Johnson Papers*.

amnesty [1] and register the loyal voters. Civil officers for the state, districts and counties were to be appointed provisionally. The general laws and statutes in force in the state immediately prior to the ordinance of secession, except in so far as they had been modified by the emancipation of the slaves and by acts of Congress for the suppression of the rebellion, were declared in force for the direction of courts and civil officers; all pretended state laws passed since secession were inoperative, null, and void. There was to be " amnesty for the past, security for the future," but the people must accept the fact that slavery was dead and that the negroes would be protected in their freedom by the United States. Finally, loyal men from every part were invited to visit the capital and confer with the governor upon the condition of the state.

When the provisional governor arrived in Austin a few days later, he was received with enthusiastic ceremony by the Unionists, of whom there were a large number in the city. He found all affairs of state in confusion. There were no officials of a civil character, the treasury had been

[1] General pardon and amnesty had been proclaimed by President Johnson for all who had taken arms against the United States, except certain specified classes, provided they would first subscribe to the following oath: " I ...., do solemnly swear (or affirm), in the presence of Almighty God, that I will henceforth faithfully support, protect and defend the Constitution of the United States and the union of the states thereunder, and that I will in like manner abide by and faithfully support all laws and proclamations which have been made during the existing rebellion with reference to the emancipation of slaves. So help me God." The classes, fourteen in number, excepted from the privileges of the general amnesty were, chiefly, high officials under the Confederacy, or those who had left the service of the United States to take service with the Confederacy, or those who owned property to the value of over $20,000. It was necessary for these to secure special pardons from the President.—*Messages and Papers of the Presidents*, vol. vi, pp. 310-312.

looted, the various departments were untenanted, the records were precariously exposed, there was even no roof on the capitol building. Immediately a commission was appointed to look into the condition of the treasury and the comptroller's department and to audit their accounts; state agents were appointed to look after and take charge of state property of whatever description in the various districts; and other agents were empowered to locate and recover if possible bonds alleged to have been illegally disposed of during the war. Judge James H. Bell, associate justice of the supreme court of the state before and during the war, but always a Union man, was appointed secretary of state; Wm. Alexander, another Union man, who, it appears, had secretly opposed Hamilton's appointment, was made attorney-general. Taxes were assessed by proclamation and ordered collected. In response to the invitation above mentioned, within a short time deputations of loyalists from over eighty counties made their way to Austin to aid in reorganizing the government. These men furnished the governor with names of loyal citizens from their counties for appointments to office, and were generally relied upon by him for information concerning conditions in the various parts of the state.

As rapidly as possible officers of district, county, and justice courts, sheriffs, tax assessors and collectors, and county commissioners were appointed, and the machinery of the law set in motion. The courts were directed to proceed with the trial of all civil and criminal cases in conformity with existing laws of the state passed prior to 1861, and of the United States.[1] The time of holding district

---

[1] In one important particular a limitation was placed upon the jurisdiction of the courts. Suits for the collection of debts and for the determination of rights of every kind could be instituted, and in those

courts and the boundaries of the districts were to conform to acts passed since secession, " out of considerations of public policy and convenience." Negroes were to be tried and punished in the same manner as whites, but the governor left the question of their admission as witnesses to be determined by the courts themselves, on the ground that it was a judicial and not a political question, and that an executive decision might be overruled by some subsequent supreme court, or that the principle might fail to be embodied in the constitution by the future convention.[1]   Attorneys-at-law not in the classes excepted from the general amnesty were,

involving titles to land, damages, *etc.*, the courts could proceed to final judgment and execution; but in suits for the collection of debts where the plaintiff was entitled to a writ of injunction, sequestration, or attachment, the court could not proceed to final judgment and execution. —See proclamation of September 8, *Executive Records, Register Book*, 281.—The reason for this was that, in the prevalent condition of disorder and financial depression, property disposed of by forced sale would bring little or nothing and an injustice would be worked upon the debtor. Later, by proclamation of December 5, the courts were empowered to proceed in such cases to final judgment, but execution was stayed.

[1] A. J. Hamilton to I. R. Burns, *Executive Records, Register Book*, 281. The courts, thus left to themselves, varied greatly in their rulings. Judge C. Caldwell, in his charge to the grand jury of Harris county, instructed it that the abolition of slavery "has swept away those distinctions both as to protection and liability to punishment which have hitherto existed between whites and blacks." These distinctions and the exclusion of negroes as witnesses had been necessary to the secure tenure of the slaves; but "when the reason of the law fails, the law likewise fails," therefore "the late slaves, now freedmen, stand upon terms of perfect equality with all other persons in the penal code." Hence all persons were alike subject to the penal law, and it necessarily followed "that persons of African descent" were "competent witnesses where any of their race were parties."—*Tri-Weekly Telegraph*, November 29, 1865. This was the view that Hamilton himself held. In most cases, however, the courts considered themselves bound by the state laws of 1860 which prohibited negro testimony in any form.

upon taking the amnesty oath in open court, to be allowed
to practice.[1] In all appointments, subscription to the amnesty oath was required, but preference was given to men
of undoubted loyalty in so far as such matters could be determined. In many counties fit " union " applicants were
so scarce that it was necessary to appoint secessionists. A
notable case of this sort was the selection of Richard Coke,
later governor and United States senator, as judge of the
nineteenth judicial district. Though there were frequent
complaints from disgruntled " loyalist " office-seekers, the
appointments seem to have given general satisfaction.

The chief duty of the provisional governor, as set forth
in the proclamation containing his appointment, was to provide for the assembling of a constitutional convention
elected by the loyal people of the state. The test of loyalty
was simply the taking of the oath of amnesty—a policy sufficiently generous, and based, no doubt, upon the idea that
the majority of the people had entered the war reluctantly
and were at heart well-disposed toward the Federal government. In accordance with instructions, Governor Hamilton, on August 19th, issued a proclamation providing for
the registration of voters. In each county the chief justice,
the district clerk, and the county clerk were to act as a board
of registration and sit at least one day in each week at the
county seat. The oath of amnesty was to be administered
to all who applied, both to those who sought registration
as voters, and to those who, being within the exceptions to
the general amnesty, took it as a preliminary step toward
special pardon. Separate rolls were to be kept of these two

---

[1] This rule was later so far modified as to allow attorneys and other
persons in the excepted classes, when they had been recommended by
the governor to the President for special pardon, to follow their professions pending the decision of the President.

classes. Meanwhile, the order for an election of delegates was withheld until the results of the registration should become known. This work, however, proceeded very slowly. Since there were no mails, it was many weeks before the proclamation reached some of the counties, and for those who lived far from the county seat where the board held its meetings, registration was usually a process involving considerable inconvenience. But even when this was not the case the people responded to the invitation without enthusiasm. The newspapers throughout the state united in urging them to register in order to hurry along the restoration to normal conditions. At the same time they urged the governor to order an election and to assemble the convention as early as possible, for in all the other states the conventions had completed their labors by the end of October.

2. *Loyalty and Disloyalty in the State.*

The governor and his friends were of the opinion that Texas was not yet in proper condition for the çalling of the convention. It seemed to them that the people were not yet free from their ante-bellum delusions and did not yet clearly understand the problems they faced and the proper way in which to solve them. A lingering belief was manifest, for example, that compensation might yet be secured for the loss of slaves, and hence a reluctance to take the amnesty oath lest it should in some way estop claims for the compensation. There was still talk, here and there, of gradual emancipation; there was a disposition in some of the remote districts to keep the negroes in bondage and to treat with cruelty those who endeavored to exercise their freedom. A large part of the press and most of the secessionist politicians were prejudiced against the governor and secretly or openly hostile to the plans of the government.

Because of this Hamilton and his advisers considered it necessary, first to establish order and civil authority through the power of the provisional government and to enable the United States courts to repress treasonable action, and then allow time for the public mind to become tranquillized and to be directed fairly toward the changes that would be necessary in the constitution. Because of the vast extent of the state and the impracticability of distributing sufficient troops everywhere to secure a speedy restoration of order, and owing to the utter absence of mail facilities for informing the people of the intentions of the government, it seemed best to make haste slowly.[1] Accordingly, with the view of making clear the work that must be done in the convention, if the state was to enjoy a speedy restoration to its normal place in the Union, the governor issued, on September 11th, a lengthy address to the people of the state. After reviewing historically the whole question of slavery and secession, which he regarded as a long-continued and elaborate conspiracy against the Union, and warning the people against the press and the politicians "who were still trying to mislead them by the same deadly doctrines," he explained the necessity for his actions as governor, and then proceeded to state his views on that problem which he thought the people were least ready to solve in a manner satisfactory to the Federal government. Slavery, he declared, was already wholly dead and could not be revived in any form. Compulsory labor laws would be regarded by the people of the North as a mere subterfuge and would not be tolerated; for the people of that section were united upon this one thing as they had never before been united upon anything—" that slavery must cease for-

[1] Letter of James H. Bell, E. M. Pease and others, also of A. J. Hamilton, MSS.. *Johnson Papers.*

ever." Now that the negro was to remain free, he must
be given equal civil rights with the white man, and should
have his testimony admitted in the courts in all cases, subject only to the rules which applied to the testimony of
whites. The governor warned the people that without some
such action it would be useless to expect that senators and
representatives from Texas would be allowed to take their
seats in Congress.[1] In conclusion, he promised that the
convention should be called as soon as the people should
have qualified by taking the oath of amnesty and should
have had an opportunity to discuss and consider well the
momentous questions upon which their delegates would be
required to take action; for it was essential to the speedy
restoration of the state that no mistake be made.

But whatever of wartime prejudice they may have har-
bored against Governor Hamilton, and whatever they may
have thought of his attitude upon the negro question, the
people gave abundant evidence of good-will toward the provisional government itself. So weary had they become of
disorder and lawlessness and so fearful of a purely military
government, that any civil authority, even though one not
of their own choosing, was welcome. As soon as the new
state government had been set up, public meetings, usually
without regard to political affiliation, were called in many
counties, and resolutions were passed tendering the provisional governor the support of the citizens in the maintenance of law and order and in the restoration of the civil
government on the basis of the President's policy. In addition, just and liberal treatment of the freedmen was
usually advocated, and sometimes the people were urged

[1] The *Tri-Weekly Telegraph* had long before, July 18, expressed
identical views. In commenting on the governor's address it emphati-
cally endorsed his recommendations and urged the people to " support
them promptly and in good faith."

to qualify as voters. In some instances where the secession element was preponderant, the resolutions simply " accepted the situation " and pledged support to the authorities.[1] Party lines had by no means vanished, though they were at times ignored. The secessionist leaders were, of course, generally quiet; but the approach of Federal troops and the return of numbers of refugees emboldened the Unionists in many localities to form Union associations that did not hesitate to take up a partisan attitude. " The Loyal Union Association " of Galveston, for example, organized the same day that Hamilton arrived from New Orleans, pledged itself " to vote for no man for office who had ever by free acts of his own tried to overthrow the government, but to support Union men always." [2] The " Union Association of Bexar County " in November declared that it was necessary for Union men to be on their guard lest the element which had endeavored to destroy the Union get into power; for the struggle, " not of arms but of principles," was to be fought over again.[3]

A cardinal doctrine of these Union associations was that a large portion of the people of the state ought not to be reinvested with political power, because of their continued disloyalty to the Federal government. Assertions to this effect were constantly reiterated and found prominent place in Northern journals, almost to the exclusion of reports of any other kind from Texas. As to the real strength of either the loyal or the disloyal sentiment in Texas at that time no accurate statement is possible. Beyond doubt, most people were not enthusiastic in their loyalty, and it

[1] For these meetings see the *Tri-Weekly Telegraph, Texas Republican, State Gazette, San Antonio Herald*, and other papers throughout July and August, 1865.

[2] *Flake's Bulletin*, July 22, 1865.

[3] *Tri-Weekly Telegraph*, November 29, 1865.

was but natural that after four years of war such should have been the case. On the other hand, there was less bitterness than was manifested under the harsh Congressional policy a few years later. Few had enjoyed the arbitrary regulations and exactions which the Confederacy had been obliged to impose, and there was little regret for the passing of that government. Perhaps the chief resentment against the conqueror grew out of the loss of property in slaves; and it seems certain that tardiness in taking the oath of amnesty, set down by some as a proof of disloyalty, was largely due to a fear that the oath might be a bar to any future compensation. The charge that the element that had been in power during the war hoped to get control of the state government again was beyond question true; but as they had not been disfranchised, there was no sensible reason why they should not have expected that. That they would have used the power thus recovered " to renew the rebellion ", is in every way inconceivable; but that they would have turned it against the radicals of the North is certain, though to condemn that as treason seems a curious perversion of the term.

Most of the charges of disloyalty in Texas were based upon alleged persecution and maltreatment of Union men and freedmen. It must be admitted that violence of this sort constantly occurred, but it appears to have been due far less to actual hostility to the Federal government than to the wide-spread disorder and lawlessness attending the break-up and the interregnum following it. The absence during that time of the ordinary peace officers had given free sway to turbulent characters of all sorts, encouraged pillage and robbery, permitted neighborhood feuds, jayhawking and guerrilla marauding; and it is notable that violence was not directed against Unionists and freedmen alone. The fact that Union men had not always fully recovered their popularity among their neighbors, was not evidence in itself of actual disloyalty on the part of the latter; and that advantage was taken of such unpopularity by the rowdies who bullied, threatened, and sometimes robbed or murdered Unionists, is proof of the weakness of the arm of the law rather than of anything else. The violence toward freedmen was due partly to that tendency of rowdyism to attack the weak and unprotected, and partly to resentment at the new insolence and the irrepressible bumptiousness of the freedman himself.

In many counties the outlaws were so numerous and so well organized that they could defy arrest, and in others so few of the citizens had taken the amnesty oath that the courts were hampered and delayed by the difficulty of procuring jurors.[1] The number and character of the general petitions to the governor from various parts of the state asking for troops or the organization of county police, is sufficient proof of the nature of the disorders. For example, one from Bell County, October 9th, recites that "the civil authorities are helpless because the county is full of ruffians and lawless men," and demands troops. Another from Grayson County, November 10th, declares that "laws can not be enforced without the aid of the military."[2] In a letter to General Wright, September 27th, the governor said that crime was everywhere rampant, that the civil authorities alone could not be depended upon for some time, and that in many counties civil process could not be executed. He requested that military forces pass through the counties where none were stationed.[3] But there were large districts

---

[1] Jno. A. Buckholts to Governor Hamilton, MS. in *Executive Correspondence.*

[2] MSS. in *Executive Correspondence.*

[3] *Executive Records, Register Book,* 281.

comprising several counties that contained not a single soldier, and the troops were not sufficient to police thoroughly the vast territory over which they exercised authority. Therefore, in response to petitions [1] from various quarters where outrages were occurring, and from others where fears of a negro uprising existed, the governor issued a proclamation, November 18th, authorizing the organization of a police force in each county, to be subject to the civil authorities and to act with the military. This police force was actually organized in several counties and seems to have been very effective in checking disorders.

Under conditions of such universal violence and confusion, it would have been strange indeed if Union men had not been subject to insult and outrage. Undoubtedly there were cases of unprovoked violence against them, and there were cases in which mobs were guilty of intensely disloyal conduct, as when a crowd tore to pieces a United States flag on the court house at Weatherford,[2] or when another mob at Bonham beat and shot at a number of negroes and destroyed a flag.[3] But such occurrences were few and the preponderance of evidence goes to show that most of these outrages were committed in the northern part of the state and were the work of outlaws who had their headquarters in the Indian Territory and plundered and murdered without distinction of party.[4]

---

[1] Various MSS. in *Executive Correspondence.*

[2] B. F. Barkley to Governor Hamilton, MS. in *Executive Correspondence.*

[3] R. B. Sanders to Anthony Bryant, endorsed by Col. M. M. Brown, U. S. A., MS. in *Executive Correspondence.*

[4] Judge Robert Wilson to Governor Throckmorton, MS. in *Executive Correspondence;* testimony of Ben C. Truman before Reconstruction Committee, *House Reports,* 1st sess., 39th Cong., vol. 2, pt. iv, p. 137; Kendall to Schuyler Colfax, in *San Antonio Herald,* April 20, 1866.

Whether intended for that purpose or not, the reports that went from Texas of the mistreatment of Unionists made excellent political capital for the radical extremists in Congress, who had already begun their attacks on the President's policy of restoration. Many of these stories were of the most extraordinary sort—such, for example, as those in the anonymous letters which Mr. Sumner was so fond of reading in the Senate [1]—and are unworthy of serious attention. Perhaps the statements that gained most credence at the North were those of Federal officers who had been stationed in Texas. One of these, General Wm. E. Strong, inspector general on the staff of General O. O. Howard, is quoted in the *New York Herald,* in January, 1866, as saying that Texas was in the worst condition of any state that he had visited; that almost the whole population was hostile in feeling and action to the United States; that there was a mere semblance of government; and that the whites and negroes were everywhere ignorant, lawless, and starving.[2] When before the Reconstruction Committee in March he reiterated the statements, adding that " one campaign of the United States army through eastern Texas, such as Sherman's through South Carolina, would greatly improve the temper and generosity of the people." General David S. Stanley, who had been stationed at San Antonio after the " break-up ", stated before the same committee that " Texas was worse than any other state because she had never been whipped," that the women were universally rebels, and that in case of a foreign war almost the entire population, with the exception of the Germans, who were very loyal, would

[1] See *Congressional Globe,* 1st sess., 39th Cong., pp. 91-95.

[2] *Flake's Bulletin,* though a staunch Unionist paper, declared this interview "a mere reporter's yarn" because it contained so many false statements.

go ever to the enemy.[1] It was also commonly asserted that many rebels who had been quiet and submissive at the close of the war, were now, at the prospect of recovering control of the state, growing insolent and defiant.

3. *The Freedmen and the Freedmen's Bureau.*

There was no subject connected with the restoration of the state government to the control of its people that the general public in the North watched with greater solicitude than the adjustment of the new relations with the freedmen. It had been announced that the treatment accorded these wards of the nation could be taken as a sure index of the loyalty of the Southern people. It was unfortunate that this mistaken idea should have been so generally accepted, and unfortunate, again, that the people of the South could not at once appreciate its power and the necessity of being guided by it. To the North, as the rebellion had been in behalf of slavery, the complete destruction of that institution was the surest guarantee of the preservation of the Union, and any attempt to evade it seemed to be an expression of rebellious sentiments. To the Southerner, emancipation had presented itself chiefly as a confiscation of his property, as an unwise and arbitrary upsetting of the industrial system to which the negro belonged, and as an injustice to the negro himself. The most immediate and pressing problem, it seemed, was to preserve the normal balance of society, and to provide for the freedman an industrial position in that society such that agricultural interests would suffer the least possible additional shock; for it was generally believed that free negro labor would be a failure and that a labor famine was imminent.[2]

[1] See *House Reports*, 1st sess., 39th Cong., vol. 2, part iv, pp. 37 and 39-40.

[2] It was because of this that throughout 1865 and 1866 a constant

In fact, the experiences of the summer of 1865 in Texas
had been such as to warrant no other opinion. In the south-
central and south-eastern counties in particular, where the
actual presence of the military made it difficult for the whites
to apply coercion, the blacks had, with some exceptions,
either preferred not to enter into contracts to labor or had
not kept them when made. How could they be free, the
negroes reasoned, if they still had to work in the fields?
Throughout the summer months they had slipped away
from the plantations as opportunity offered or whim suggested, and despite the military regulations to the contrary,
large numbers collected around the towns where, luxuria-
ting in idleness and heedless of the next winter, they eked
out a meagre subsistence by petty thieving, begging, or
doing occasional odd jobs. Crowded together indiscrimi-
nately in small huts, they rapidly fell victims to disease and
vices of all sorts.[1]

Meanwhile the harvest time approached and despite the
fact that the acreage was not large, there were not enough
laborers to gather the crops. The freedmen had become
possessed of the singular delusion that on the following
Christmas the government would divide among them the
lands of their former masters. The government had given
them their freedom without their asking for it; they had
heard rumors from various quarters that they would be
given property—why should it not be true? There was no
use in working if they were to be made rich in a little while;
so they met all propositions to work with the response:

agitation was going on for promoting the immigration of white labor.
One meets it everywhere, in the press, in public speeches, in resolutions
of public meetings, in the deliberations of the constitutional convention
and of the legislature.

[1] See *The Southern Intelligencer* (Austin), September 29. All newspapers of the late summer bear evidence to this effect.

" We'll wait 'til Christmas." [1] It is small wonder that the planter who saw his old field hands idling their time away in town, improvident as children, making no preparations for the rigors of winter, sinking into demoralization and crime, while his crop went to waste for the lack of their labor, should have looked forward to some remedy, some law that would bring back these victims of a mistaken philanthropy to the work which their own welfare as well as that of the general public seemed to demand. None but a system of coercion, he thought, offered any promise of the necessary relief.

The Freedmen's Bureau, created by act of Congress, March 3, 1865, to take control of all subjects relating to freedmen, refugees, and abandoned lands in the conquered states, did not begin operations in Texas until much later than elsewhere. The assistant commissioner appointed for Texas, General E. M. Gregory, arrived at Galveston late in September, and, although he seems to have been actively at work, it was not until December that he so far perfected an organization as to appoint a dozen local agents, of whom five were civilians, at the most important points in the in-

---

[1] *Weekly State Gazette* (Austin), November 25, 1865. It is impossible to fix the whole responsibility for this belief. The Federal officers said that it should fall upon those citizens and public speakers who during the war declared that if the "Yankees" won, the negroes would be freed, property confiscated and given to them, and the whites enslaved. The negroes believed and remembered. Strong, *House Exec. Docs.*, no. 70, p. 308, 1st sess., 39th Cong. The citizens, on the other hand, asserted that the Northern radicals who talked of "forty acres and a mule" had started it; and that many of the Federal soldiers, in order to wheedle money from the negroes, fraternized with them, told them there would be a division of land at Christmas, and that the soldiers who had won them their freedom would help them and stand by them.—C. B. Stuart to Governor Hamilton, MS. in *Executive Correspondence*. Probably both accusations were true.

terior.[1] In the meantime, the local work had been carried
on by the various post commanders. From the beginning
General Gregory addressed himself assiduously to amelior-
ating the labor situation. In his first circular order, October 12th, after emphasizing the freedom of the blacks and
making clear that the Bureau was authorized not only to act
for them and to adjudicate all cases in which they were concerned if the civil courts had failed them, but also to give
them substantial protection, he urged upon the freedmen
the necessity for their going to work under contracts carefully drawn up and approved and registered by the Bureau.
All officers and good citizens were enjoined to disabuse the
minds of the freedmen of any idea of a Christmas division
of property. In November, General Gregory, in company
with Inspector-General Strong, made a tour through the
eastern counties for the purpose of acquainting himself with
conditions there. During the trip he endeavored to give
the blacks a knowledge of their real situation, especially
with reference to the necessity for and the manner of making contracts for the next year. He returned exceedingly
optimistic with regard to the character and promise of the
sable populace.[2]

In the meantime, so many petitions had poured in upon

---

[1] See his Circular Order no. 2, *House Exec. Docs.*, no. 70, p. 147,
1st sess., 39th Cong.

[2] In the light of over forty years of subsequent history, the following
statement, made soon afterwards, is highly diverting: " The freedmen
are, as a general thing, strongly impressed with religious sentiments,
and their morals are equal if not superior to those of a majority of the
better informed and educated. We find them not only willing but
anxious to improve every opportunity offered for their moral and intellectual advancement," *etc.* It is also an example of the pathetic ignorance which some of these high officials had of their wards. Report to
General O. O. Howard, *House Exec. Docs.*, no. 70, p. 375, 1st sess.,
39th Cong.

the governor to forestall a threatened uprising of the blacks at Christmas that he authorized the organization of county police.[1] Furthermore, on November 17th, he issued an address to the negroes which he caused the chief justice of each county to read to them. He told them in the plainest terms that they must go to work, that they could not remain idle without becoming criminal, that they would get nothing more from the government either at Christmas or at any other time, and that if they disturbed the property of others they would be severely punished. Reinforced by the efforts of General Gregory and the army officials, the address seems to have had a very good effect, but many of the negroes still cherished a lingering hope until it was dispelled at Christmas.

General Gregory exerted himself during December and January to put labor upon a firm basis for the next year; and, though his lack of intimate understanding of the negro character and his failure to appreciate and to take into account the common notions of social precedence often gave offense to the whites and retarded somewhat the success of his plans, his energy and perseverance did much to bring about a more hopeful situation. Planters were urged to settle with the laborers for the past season and to make contracts with them at once for the ensuing year on fair and liberal terms.[2] In order to promote the contract system he made a trip through the lower river-bottom counties

---

[1] *Supra*, p. 64.

[2] There was considerable complaint on the part of the blacks that they were not promptly paid for the season past. The delay was sometimes due to the scarcity of specie, sometimes to disputes over alleged violations of contracts by negroes, sometimes to the employer's dishonest endeavor to take advantage of the freedman's ignorance. Frequently the contracts made in the early summer had provided that the negroes work for board, clothing, and medical attendance, and these also were prolific sources of trouble. *Supra*, p. 45.

where the black population was densest. General conditions came to his aid. Cotton planting was immensely profitable because of the high prices then being paid for the staple, and planters who were sceptical of free negro labor grew willing to give it a trial. With the calling of the constitutional convention, political affairs began to assume a more stable aspect, so that people were no longer apprehensive of confiscation. Many of the blacks who had been brought into Texas during the war were now making their way back into the other states.[1] The demand for labor grew keener. On the other hand, the negroes, having been disappointed in their Christmas expectations, were more ready to work. In many instances, too, where they were out of reach of the Bureau's commissary stores, their previous improvidence now forced them to work to secure food. A report from Washington County in the black belt, January 24th, stated that in that county two-thirds of the freed population were then at work at good wages, that seven thousand contracts had been filed already, and that unemployed freedmen were becoming scarce.[2] Similar reports came from other communities and the situation gradually grew more promising throughout the state.

It may not be inappropriate at this point to indicate briefly the general character of the work the Bureau had to do in Texas. There were no abandoned lands in the state and the Union refugees usually depended upon the military for such protection as they needed; consequently the activities of the Bureau were confined to looking after the interests of the negro. These activities may be classified roughly as relief work, educational work, labor supervision, and

---

[1] Report of General Strong, *House Exec. Docs.*, no. 70, p. 312, 1st sess., 39th Cong.

[2] *Flake's Bulletin*, January 24, 1866.

judicial protection. Its supervision of labor interests, that is, oversight of contracts and wages, has already been considered, and for the others brief statements will suffice. The actual relief work done was comparatively slight. Rations were issued somewhat extensively by the military authorities in the early summer, but since there was plenty of food to be had for work, this practice was gradually checked. During the winter the number fed increased, but by the end of January only sixty-seven were receiving government support.[1] One hospital had been established, but ceased to be used after the close of winter.[2] The educational work was under the charge of Lieutenant E. M. Wheelock, who, by the end of January had in operation twenty-six day and night schools with an enrollment of about sixteen hundred pupils.[3] These schools were supported partly by voluntary contributions, partly by a small tuition fee. But that function of the Bureau which, from the manner in which it was exercised, caused more irritation to the whites than any other, was the extension of protection over the negro in the state courts. In localities where such courts, by reason of the old code, refused to allow the negro to give testimony or otherwise denied him justice, it was made the duty of all Bureau officials to withdraw from the courts and themselves adjudicate cases in which a freedman was concerned.[4] Unfortunately, the wide powers here implied were not always used with honesty or discretion; and too often, by arbitrary or needless interference with the regular courts, the Bureau forfeited public

[1] Gregory to Howard, *House Exec. Docs.*, no. 70, p. 305, 1st sess., 39th Cong. Sick and aged negroes were required to be supported by their former masters.

[2] Peirce, *The Freedmen's Bureau*, p. 90.

[3] Gregory to Howard, *House Exec. Docs., loc. çit.*, p. 307.

[4] O. O. Howard, Circular Order, *Ibid.*, p. 146.

confidence and weakened its efforts along other lines. However, the worst abuses developed only after the suffrage had given political power into the hands of the negro and had made it profitable for the ambitious Bureau agent to court his favor. For the time the zealous activity of the assistant commissioner in clearing the towns of idle negroes won the good will of the press and the public.[1]

4. *Relations of the Civil and the Military Authorities*

The proclamation appointing Governor Hamilton had neither clearly defined the powers of the provisional governor, nor explained his proper relations with the military authorities further than to order that they should aid him in the performance of his duties and not interfere with him. It was evident, however, that while each within a certain sphere enjoyed exclusive authority, there was a region over which they exercised concurrent or rival jurisdiction; and it early became clear that conflicts were likely to arise in matters pertaining to the maintenance of public order, especially in criminal cases. Prior to the establishment of the provisional civil courts, all criminal cases had been disposed of through military courts; and, while it was generally expected that the latter would now abandon a large class of cases to the civil authorities, the military jurisdiction over such matters had not been expressly abrogated or curtailed. The establishment of the Freedmen's Bureau courts increased the opportunities for conflicts. There were, therefore, three classes of courts in the state, all claiming criminal jurisdiction. The army claimed control of all matters in which soldiers or employees of the government were involved, and was responsible for the maintenance of order

[1] *Flake's Bulletin,* January 24; *San Antonio Herald,* March 5; *Galveston News,* March 6, 1866.

where the civil courts were not organized; the Freedmen's Bureau exercised jurisdiction over matters relating to freedmen, especially where it was believed that the civil authorities would not do them justice; the civil courts claimed jurisdiction in all criminal cases, though in the face of the military power, these claims were not always strenuously asserted.

Governor Hamilton and General Wright, the department commander,[1] preserved amicable relations throughout, and endeavored in every way to prevent a conflict. On August 17th the governor wrote to General C. C. Andrews, one of the district commanders, requesting that a white man, whom the military had arrested for the murder of a freedman, be turned over to the civil court for trial.[2] The governor was evidently not sure of his ground, for he asked what course the military authorities proposed to take in criminal cases. He expressed the opinion that it would be entirely safe to remit all offenders to the civil courts for trial and that it would be good policy to do so, since the people felt much anxiety in the matter. Soon afterwards he changed his mind. On September 27th he wrote to General Wright, asking that the military branch of the government execute vigorous punishment upon criminals, and confessing that the civil authorities could not be depended upon for some time. With respect to the relations between the two, he did not regard the provisional government of the state as having superseded the military authority. His view of the political condition of Texas was this:

There is no *constitutional* state government. The provisional

[1] General H. G. Wright relieved General Granger of command of the Department of Texas on August 6, 1865.

[2] *Executive Records, Register Book,* 281.

government of Texas is created by and exists at the will of the President. My authority as provisional governor is limited to such measures as may be necessary to prepare the people of the state and provide means for a convention to organize a new constitutional state government, which, when adopted and recognized by the general government, will supersede, within the limits of its jurisdiction, the military power in all things not properly pertaining to the military authority of the United States in time of peace. For the present, the action of the civil authorities created by me is allowed only as a means—to the extent that they can be made available—of aiding the authorities of the general government in preserving public peace and order, and in protecting individual rights and property. I have felt sure the general government would not object to such quasi-civil government as I have temporarily effected, but it would be in conflict with the views of the government to claim for the provisional government any power except such as emanates directly from the President. In this view I not only see no objection to the trial of offenders before military tribunals, but believe it a necessity unavoidable without great detriment to the highest interests of the people.[1]

In reply to this, General Wright disclaimed any wish to interfere with civil processes when it could be avoided. He said:

It was understood when I assumed command that, 1st, all matters between white citizens of the state were to be acted on by the civil authorities constituted by you, as far as practicable. 2d. That matters in which freedmen were concerned were to be left to the action of the Freedmen's Bureau, which was to act through specially appointed agents, of which your officers might form a part. 3rd. That the military authority should confine itself to matters pertaining to the military, and

[1] MS. in *Executive Correspondence.*

should give necessary aid either to the civil authority or to the Freedmen's Bureau.

Since it seemed that this program, though highly desirable, could not be carried out, he agreed

to issue an order directing military commanders to turn over to civil tribunals all criminal cases, wherein soldiers are not concerned, where the civil authority is in condition to act, and where justice to all concerned can be looked for—the colored man being put upon perfect equality with the white before the courts—and where such justice can not be expected, to bring the cases for trial before a military commission or a Freedman's Bureau court.[1]

An understanding was thus effected defining more clearly the limitations within which each class of officials was to exercise jurisdiction; but it necessarily left unsettled the questions as to when the civil authority was strong enough to deal with public disorders without the interference of the military, and whether the civil court was granting the freedman the privileges to which he was entitled. The effectiveness of such an agreement would depend chiefly upon the mutual forbearance of those entrusted with carrying it out in detail, and it was too much to expect a great measure of that quality from the average post commander, ignorant of the civil law and impatient of a less direct method than that to which the camp had accustomed him, or from the judge who sought to uphold the dignity of the civil authority and felt constrained to base his acts upon what remained of the old code.

The first serious trouble was at Victoria, where Colonel I. T. Rose, of the 77th Pennsylvania, was stationed. Eight

[1] MS. in *Executive Correspondence.*

distinct charges of outrageous conduct on the part of Rose were laid before the governor.[1] Finally, a white man, M. M. Gwinn, who had killed a negro and had been acquitted in a preliminary trial in open court, in which the testimony of negroes was freely admitted, was, after being released, rearrested by Rose and confined in jail. A certified copy of the proceedings of the court was put in the hands of the governor, who sent a peppery letter to the Colonel, demanded the release of Gwinn, and laid the matter before General Wright. Wright ordered the release of Gwinn and soon afterwards Rose was transferred to duty elsewhere.

A more serious affair occurred at Jefferson. R. L. Robertson, acting as treasury agent, was indicted by a grand jury on three distinct charges, two of swindling and one of theft. He was released by the interference of Captain Jones, the post commander. He was again arrested and his release was ordered of District Judge Gray by Major Clingman, at Marshall. After the judge had twice refused, Captain Jones with a body of soldiers forcibly took Robertson from jail. The civil authorities appealed to the governor; the military appealed to their superiors. General Canby issued the following: " State courts have no jurisdiction over their [treasury agents'] official conduct, nor can they, without usurpation, investigate the title of prop-

---

[1] Among these charges were the following: (1) Robert Tibbett was confined in jail for nine days on no charge whatever. He employed counsel, who was threatened with imprisonment if he pressed matters. (2) A negro, arrested and jailed for horse-stealing, was released by Rose. (3) Another negro, committed on two distinct charges, was likewise released by soldiers. (4) Judge L. A. White, who had gone to Rose to complain of depredations of soldiers, was cursed, abused, shot at, and jailed by the drunken colonel. He was released only when he agreed to drop the matter.—C. Carsner and others to Governor Hamilton, MSS. in *Executive Correspondence*.

erty held by the United States as captured and abandoned."
Concerning this Judge Gray wrote to Hamilton: " The district court of Marion County has never claimed jurisdiction
over the official acts of agents of the government, but when
an agent violates the penal code, the district court has
claimed and exercised jurisdiction over him. As well had
the agent claimed freedom from arrest for murder as for
any other crime." The judge then said that if he could
not punish cotton thieves he would not punish any, and
declined to hold other courts. In the meantime, his arrest
was threatened if the indictments were not withdrawn.
The matter dragged along in this fashion until all attempts
to bring Robertson to justice had to be abandoned.[1]

Aside from the disputes over the respective jurisdictions
of the civil and military, in some localities the conduct of
the troops was a source of irritation and complaint. In the
summer of 1865 *Flake's Bulletin,* of Galveston, was full of
references to outrages perpetrated by the Federal soldiers
stationed in that city. Open robbery, insults to women, and
disorderly conduct were matters of daily comment. The
troubles at Victoria have already been indicated. The troops
here were white. By far the greatest complaint was against
the colored troops that were brought into the state in the late
summer and fall to replace the white volunteer regiments
that were being discharged. In November a petition was
sent Governor Hamilton from Jackson County for relief
from a body of three hundred negro troops that had been
detailed there to cut ties for the Lavaca and San Antonio
Railroad. These negroes were heavily armed and parties
of them roamed about the country robbing plantations, in
sulting and sometimes outraging women, inciting the resi-

[1] See various letters, MSS., in *Executive Correspondence.* Also *The
Southern Intelligencer*, December 21, 1865.

dent negroes to like conduct, and keeping the whole country in constant terror.[1] Negro troops were quartered at Galveston in the winter, and were constantly giving trouble. In the latter part of February they broke loose from all restraint and spread terror over the city. A young lady, a member of one of the most respectable families, was assaulted and horribly treated, and several persons were attacked and shot at. The *Bulletin* of February 28, 1866, says: " On Saturday these outrages reached their climax, stimulated, no doubt, by the terrible homicide of the day. During Saturday and Sunday a reign of terror, which has not yet wholly subsided, held sway over the city." After recounting a number of unprovoked attacks upon the citizens, it goes on to say: " The peace of the city must be preserved. If the police force can not do it, then let the military officials take entire control; and if they can not, then the citizens must do it for themselves." There were numbers of other collisions less conspicuous. Ben C. Truman, the able correspondent of the *New York Times,* in a communication published March 5th, says that large numbers of deserters from the volunteer regiments in the western part of the state were committing all sorts of murders and outrages in the country, most of which were charged against the people of that section.

One of the most troublesome problems that the state had to face at this time was the condition of its frontier. This region had been subject to Indian attacks throughout the war, but some attempt at organized protection had been made by the state and Confederate authorities. After the withdrawal of the Confederate troops from the west, the Indians, the Comanches in particular, began raiding and

[1] Petition and letters to Governor Hamilton, MSS. in *Executive Correspondence.*

murdering in the exposed settlements. The people were unable to defend themselves from the sudden attacks, and the depredations became more frequent and of greater magnitude. Throughout 1865 and 1866 the whole extent of the frontier from north to south was in constant terror and became almost depopulated. The governor was besieged with petitions for troops and made repeated requests to General Wright for cavalry. Wright disclaimed any authority over the cavalry and referred the matter to Sheridan. Sheridan refused the troops on the ground that they were needed at interior garrisons for the protection of freedmen. Hamilton, too, believed that there were not enough troops in the interior to maintain order, and thereafter contented himself with appealing to Washington for more soldiers for Texas. Almost two years elapsed, however, before frontier posts were finally established and some measure of protection afforded.

CHAPTER V

THE CONSTITUTIONAL CONVENTION OF 1866

IT was not until November 15th, nearly three months from the beginning of registration, that, a majority of the voters having qualified, a proclamation was issued fixing the date of the election for January 8, 1866. The convention was to meet at Austin on February 7th and was to consist of delegates equal in number to the members of the lower house of the state legislature and distributed among the counties in like manner. Delegates were not required to be residents of the districts selecting them, and no person within the classes excepted from the general amnesty was eligible as a delegate unless pardoned by the President. This last provision was criticised as exceeding the governor's instructions, for the only restriction imposed by the President's proclamation was that each delegate should have taken the amnesty oath.

Now that the election and the assembling of the convention were definitely provided for, candidates appeared and a livelier interest was shown in the questions that must come up for settlement. By this time the example of the other states and the known attitude of the President had wrought practical unanimity on the points that seemed most important: that slavery was a thing of the past and that the fact should be recognized in an amendment to the constitution; that the war debt should be annulled or repudiated; and that the act of secession should be nullified. But as to the manner in which these things should be done, and as to the settlement of certain related problems, there was wide divergence of opinion. Should the secession ordinance be repealed simply, or declared null by reason of the failure of the war, or null and void from its inception? The war debt must be nullified; but what of a certain portion of the civil debt that had been used indirectly in prosecution of the war, and another portion that had been contracted in a manner prohibited by the constitution of 1845? It was agreed that slavery must be abolished; but what of the status of the freedman? To what extent would it be safe and expedient to invest him with those civil rights that had long been the very foundations of liberty for the dominant race?

All of these were matters of the highest importance, but perhaps the last received the greatest attention. With respect to it most of the candidates showed varying degrees of conservatism. W. C. Dalrymple, who proved the successful candidate in Williamson and Travis counties, said in a published letter:

My opponents, . . . each and all, concede something to the negroes; some more, some less, approximating to equality with the white race. I concede them nothing but the station of " hewers of wood and drawers of water ". . . . If a republican form of government is to be sustained, the white race must do it without any negro alloy. A mongrel Mexico affords no fit example for imitation. I desire the perpetuation of a white man's government. . . . The negro is and must remain free. This is one of the results of the late conflict. He must be protected in person and property; this is due to justice and humanity, but I hope and believe that legislative wisdom can devise some mode of securing fully those rights without an equality in the courts of the country. Of course I am opposed to negro suffrage in whatever form or with whatever limitations it may be proposed.[1]

This was the ultra-conservative view. Another candidate,

[1] *State Gazette*, January 6, 1866.

also successful, Colonel M. T. Johnson, of Tarrant county, a moderate Unionits, declared in a published circular his opposition to granting the negro any political rights whatever, and insisted that he should be made to work by uniform laws regulating pauperism, labor, and apprenticeship; but at the same time asserted the necessity of treating him with justice and kindness in his helpless condition.[1] A large number favored allowing the freedman a right to testify in cases in which a negro was concerned. A few, the most advanced, would have extended this right to all cases. There seems to have been only one candidate, E. Degener, a prominent German of San Antonio, who openly advocated negro suffrage.

The most notable contribution to the public discussion was a long and earnest letter to the people of Texas from John H. Reagan, then a prisoner of war at Fort Warren, Boston, where he had been confined since his capture in May. This letter was truly remarkable for the clearness with which it grasped the real facts of the situation and predicted the results that must inevitably flow from a failure to apprehend the spirit prevailing among the people of the North. It was written on August 11, 1865, and was published in the Texas papers about the first of October. The state, Reagan thought, occupied the position of a conquered nation. The state government would not be restored until a policy should be adopted acceptable to the will of the conquerors. " A refusal to accede to these conditions would only result in a prolongation of the time during which you will be deprived of the civil government of your own choice, and will continue subject to military rule." In order to avoid this danger it was necessary to recognize the supreme authority of the United States government and its right

[1] *San Antonio Daily Herald*, January 3, 1866.

to protect itself against secession, and to recognize the abolition of slavery and the right of freedmen to the privileges and protection of the law. It seemed probable, however, that this alone would not satisfy the people of the North; it was very probable, in fact, that they would demand nothing less than suffrage for the freedmen. Reagan thought the South in no position to resist such a demand, although bitter opposition was to be expected on the part of Southern men. The demand could be satisfied by: *First,* admitting the testimony of negroes in the courts, subject only to the same rules as applied to whites; *second,* fixing an intellectual, moral, and if necessary, a property test for the admission of all persons to the elective franchise, regardless of race or color, provided that no person previously entitled to vote should be deprived of the right by any new test. The results of such a policy would be to remove the grounds of hostility between the races and put an end to sectional and interstate agitation.[1]

Whatever the inherent soundness of these views, they failed to find much support in Texas. The public was far from ready for a strategic move involving so many concessions, and a perfect storm of disapproval arose. Reagan was compelled to suffer for a time the opprobrium so often the lot of those who can see further into the future than their fellows.[2]

[1] This letter is reprinted in Reagan's *Memoirs,* pp. 286-295. The original MS. is in the *Executive Correspondence, Executive Archives.*

[2] His course, however, won him a measure of executive clemency. Hamilton warmly approved the letter, and both he and ex-Governor Pease wrote to President Johnson to secure a parole for Reagan in order that he might return to Texas, where it was hoped his great influence and integrity of character would be useful in securing the best interest of the state. (See MS. in *Johnson Papers.*) He was immediately released, but found his opinions in such disfavor that he retired to the privacy of his farm without taking any further part in the discussion of public matters.

The elections passed off quietly, only a small vote being cast because of the inclemency of the weather. Until the delegates assembled at Austin, as appointed, February 7th, there was considerable doubt as to what element would be in control. It was soon apparent that a strong minority were " unionists ". Of these the more prominent were I. A. Paschal and E. Degener, of San Antonio; John Hancock, of Austin, always a staunch opponent of secession, but now inclined to a moderate policy; J. W. Throckmorton, later " conservative " governor; E. J. Davis, later " radical " governor; Shields, X. B. Saunders, Latimer, R. H. Taylor, Ledbetter, and J. W. Flanagan. A number of equally aggressive " secessionists " were present; some of whom were in the classes excepted from the general amnesty and had so far failed to secure Presidential pardon. The most conspicuous was O. M. Roberts, who had been president of the secession convention in 1861 and whose presence was therefore especially resented by those who regarded secession as treason. Of the same class were ex-Governor H. R. Runnels, John Ireland, C. A. Frazier, D. C. Giddings, R. A. Reeves, ex-Governor Henderson, J. W. Whitfield, and T. N. Waul. A considerable element in the convention, the group which really held the balance of power, should be classed as merely conservative. They were likely to vote against the unionists out of opposition to radicalism rather than because of hostility to the United States government.

The convention took up its work in the most leisurely manner. The greater part of the first three days was consumed in the mere preliminaries of organization. J. W. Throckmorton was elected president on the second ballot. His election was regarded with satisfaction on all sides. He was an original unionist, one of the seven who had voted against the ordinance of secession in 1861, but he had entered the Confederate service as commissioner to the Indians and had risen to the rank of brigadier-general. As president of the convention he was drawn more and more to the side of the majority and became the chief defender in Texas of President Johnson's policy.

The first skirmish between the opposing factions came on the third day, when Paschal introduced a resolution to appoint a committee to notify the governor that the convention was organized and " ready to take the constitutional oath," and to receive any communication he thought proper to make.[1] The secessionists were up in arms immediately against taking the constitutional oath. Roberts, Reeves, and Frazier hotly insisted that the delegates had met only in " a primitive capacity " to make a constitution and to organize a government; that they had no status as officers of the United States, and therefore it was not incumbent upon them to take an oath of such character. Paschal and Saunders defended the resolution by pointing out that as the convention had been called by the authority of the United States to frame a state government in accordance with the laws of the United States, it was just as necessary for the members to take the regular oath as it was for any other officials acting under that government to take it. At this juncture, Hancock, reputed a " soft unionist," offered as a compromise an amendment under which those members who had not already done so should take the amnesty oath, while no oath at all should be required of the other members.[2] This was by no means satisfactory to the unionists and in an effort to strike out the amendment they were defeated by the narrow margin of thirty-nine to forty-one. Han-

---

[1] See *Convention Journal*, p. 11.

[2] *Convention Journal*, p. 12. For report of debate, see *Flake's Daily Bulletin*, February 15, 1866, or Ben C. Truman in *New York Times*, March 5, 1866.

cock's amendment was adopted and the resolution passed.
It was the first alignment of forces and it is worth noting
that the president, Throckmorton, supported Paschal's resolution. Before the next day the victorious reactionaries re-
pented of their action. It would not do for the news to go
abroad that the first act of the convention had been an expression of hostility, or at least of disrespect, toward the
national constitution. After a hurried consultation they decided to retrace their steps. Immediately after convening
next morning, Hancock moved a reconsideration of his resolution, and it was carried by an overwhelming majority,
only eleven irreconcilables, among whom were Giddings,
Ireland, and Runnels, opposing. Paschal then offered the
resolution for taking the regular constitutional oath, and it
passed this time without a division.

On the same day the message of Governor Hamilton was
received. He recapitulated the instructions contained in his
appointment, explained the necessity for his going beyond
the letter of them in placing on the registration boards persons not designated by the President, and called attention
to the fact that, contrary to the provisions of his proclamation governing the election, several persons who had been
excepted from the amnesty and had not received the special
pardon, were now occupying seats in the convention. After
defending his course in not calling the convention earlier,
and expressing concern at the apathy of the people in the
elections, he pointed out that the other states had by too
hasty action passed measures that debarred them from securing representation in Congress, and suggested that Texas
might, by observing the developments elsewhere, profit by
this delay. It was expected by the President, by Congress,
and by the people of the United States that such changes
would be made in the organic law of the state as would make
it conform in spirit and principle to the actual changes

wrought by the war. In the first place it would be expected that the convention express a clear and explicit denial, in such form as seemed proper, of the right to secede from the Union. In the second place it would be expected to manifest " a cheerful acquiescence " in the abolition of slavery by a proper amendment to the constitution. Both of these questions had already been definitely settled on the field of battle and the sole function of the delegates was to recognize fittingly an accomplished fact. The next duty of the convention would be to repudiate the debt incurred by the state in support of the war; for to provide for its payment would be to justify its purposes. What portion of the total public debt incurred since the beginning of the war was of this character it would be difficult to ascertain; but it seemed that it would probably amount to three-fourths, and the report of ex-Governor Pease and Swante Palm was furnished to facilitate an investigation. Finally, and most important of all, was the determination of the civil and political status of the freedmen. Here the governor expressed an apprehension that his views would not be acceptable to the majority of the convention, but he repeated his previous warning that if any legislation tending to re-establish slavery or to nullify any of the proper effects of emancipation were indulged in, or anything less than the full civil rights of free citizens were granted the blacks, it would delay indefinitely the return of the state to its normal place in the Union. In addition to full rights in the courts and in the holding of property, he earnestly advised the convention to make it possible in the future for the negro to attain to political suffrage.

I do not believe [he said] that the great mass of the freedmen in our midst are qualified by their intelligence to exercise the right of suffrage, and I do not desire to see this privilege conferred upon them; [but] if we fail to make political privileges depend upon rules of universal application, we will inevitably be betrayed into legislation under the influence of ancient prejudices and with a view only to the present. I think that human wisdom can not discern what is to be the future of the African race in this country. . . . I would not be willing to deprive any man, who is qualified under existing laws to vote, of the exercise of that privilege in the future; but I believe it would be wise to regulate the qualifications of those who are to become voters hereafter by rules of universal application.[1]

On the next day the governor's complaint about the presence of unpardoned rebels in the convention bore fruit in a resolution by E. J. Davis to the effect that no person excepted from the amnesty should be entitled to a seat until pardoned. Ex-Governor Henderson offered a substitute referring all credentials to the committee on privileges and elections, and the matter was finally referred to that committee. On the next day the committee called before it the delegates whose seats were thus in question, Runnels, Waul, Whitfield, and Ireland, and after consideration reported that these had all made application for special pardon and that the applications had been endorsed by the governor. A resolution was finally passed allowing them to retain their seats pending the action of the President.[2]

The convention got down to work very slowly. It had been in session a full week before any move at all was made with respect to the secession ordinance. It was still four days later before the abolition of slavery was brought up for discussion. In fact as much time was taken up with the mere preliminaries of organization as had been required for

[1] See *Convention Journal*, pp. 16-27.

[2] *Ibid.*, pp. 29, 32, 42, 48.

the complete work of any of the state conventions of the previous summer.[1]

On February 13th Latimer, of Red River County, introduced an ordinance on the first serious question with which the delegates were called upon to deal, the disposition of the ordinance of secession. There proved to be a great variety of opinions as to its character, and upon the subject party lines came to be closely drawn. The chief point at issue was whether the secession ordinance was null and void from the beginning, or became null and void as a result of the war. The first view was based upon the principle that there never was such a thing as a " right of secession "; the second view implied that the right of secession had been at least an open legal question until the war had settled it. Latimer's ordinance simply declared null and void and of no effect from the beginning the ordinance of secession and all

---

[1] Mr. Ben C. Truman, who as correspondent of the *New York Times* and confidential agent of President Johnson toured the South and attended all the conventions, and who was certainly one of the keenest and sanest observers of conditions everywhere, seems for a time to have lost all patience with the dilatory progress of the Texans. In the *Times* of March 11 he said: " The convention spends all its time electioneering for the United States Senate. It is a weak set." And he appended this sarcastic summary of its work up to that time:

" 1st day. Convention met and adjourned without doing a thing.

2nd day. Met and elected president and clerk. Adjourned.

3rd day. Met and elected more officers. Adjourned.

4th day. Met and refused to take the oath. Adjourned.

5th day. Met and reconsidered their refusal to take the oath and took it. Adjourned.

7th day. Met and argued whether the convention should do something or nothing. Adjourned.

8th day. Ditto.

9th day. Ditto.

10th day. Ditto.

11th day. Agreed to do something. Adjourned.

12th day. Did nothing. Adjourned."

the other acts of the convention of 1861. Hancock proposed a substitute to the effect that the ordinance had been " in legal contemplation void, being a revolutionary measure, and subject to the general principles of revolutions." [1] This was a clever compromise, but suited neither side. On the next day Henderson offered an ordinance declaring that, inasmuch as the government of the United States " by the exercise of its power " had determined that no state had the constitutional right to secede, the said ordinance was repealed. [2] Later, Reeves wished simply to accept the decision of the war and, in order to restore the state to its former relations to the Federal government, merely to renounce the doctrine as asserted in the aforesaid ordinance of secession. [3] Judge Frazier was able to evolve another interpretation: that the inhabitants of Texas were a conquered people, governed by the laws of war and of nations, by which alone the United States government was restrained, and that these laws required no more of the people than that they should accept the will of the conqueror; and hence it was " not necessary to repeal, annul, or declare null and void that ordinance, since the surrender of the South had settled the question." [4] X. B. Saunders introduced an ordinance to the same effect as Latimer's, declaring the ordinance of secession and all other acts of the secession convention null and void *ab initio*. This was the position of the staunch unionists. When the committee on the condition of the state reported, its ordinance was one that simply acknowledged the supremacy of the Constitution of the United States and declared the troublesome act " annulled and of no further effect." [5] The minority report of this

[1] *Convention Journal*, p. 35.   [2] *Ibid.*, p. 38.
[3] *Ibid.*, p. 44.   [4] *Ibid.*, pp. 47-48.
[5] *Ibid.*, p. 62.

committee asserted that, as no warrant for the act of secession could be found in the constitution, which was the
supreme law of the land, it must have been a nullity from
the beginning; and even viewing it as a revolutionary measure, the result of the struggle forced the same conclusion,
for "abortive attempts at revolution never impress any
changes upon the fundamental laws of the government."
Moreover, the minority argued, the report of the majority
virtually asserted that the secession ordinance had a legal
existence up to the present time and was in actual force—
a theory in every way untenable. The minority therefore
reported an *ab initio* ordinance.[1]

The real fight over this question began on March 9th and
extended over three days. The *ab initio* men, or "radicals,"
as they were beginning to be called, struggled hard to substitute some form of the minority report for that of the
majority. Not quite equal in numbers to their opponents,
they failed in this, and then resorted to obstructive tactics.
Finally, the conservatives by sheer strength pushed through
to engrossment, on the afternoon of the 12th of March, by
a vote of 43 to 37, the ordinance finally adopted—acknowl-
edging the supremacy of the Federal Constitution, declaring the act of secession null and void without direct reference to its initial status, and distinctly renouncing the right
previously claimed by Texas to secede from the Union.[2]

The radicals were not at first disposed to accept their
defeat gracefully. At a caucus of the minority held that
night in the office of the secretary of state, Hancock strongly
urged the withdrawal of the *ab initio* men, for the purpose
of breaking the quorum and dissolving the convention in

[1] *Convention Journal*, pp. 79-81.
[2] *Ibid.*, pp. 146-165; Gammel, *Laws of Texas*, V, p. 887.

order that a new one might be called. However, Governor
Hamilton would not promise to call another one at once,
and there was nothing for the minority to do but to return
to their seats.[1] *Flake's Bulletin,* a radical weekly paper of
Galveston, declared as late as March 21st that the convention had " shown its hand by passing an emasculated ordinance known to be unsatisfactory to Union men everywhere "; that the majority had proved itself disloyal; that
" the sole intent and meaning of this ordinance was to gain
a rapid entrance into the national councils in order to renew
the struggle and fight the rebellion over again "; and it
suggested that as the majority was " still wedded, like
Ephraim, to its idols," it might yet " become the duty of the
loyal minority to withdraw from the convention."

It had been widely asserted by the radicals that nothing
less than a distinct admission of the original illegality of the
attempted secession would satisfy President Johnson and
the North, and that without such an admission the new
state government would not be recognized; and indeed the
Houston Tri-Weekly Telegraph, the ablest of the conservative papers, had pointed out in November that the result
of the fall elections in the North meant that the issues of
the war had not been abandoned by the South in terms
sufficiently decisive, and that to *repeal* the ordinance would
not be enough: " if it was ever valid it still is; . . . the
whole idea of reserved state sovereignty and of partnership
in the government must be expelled from the system forever." On the other hand it could hardly have been expected that the secession leaders would be willing to violate

---

[1] See letter of H. Ledbetter in *Flake's Weekly Bulletin,* May 23,
1866. The names of those at the caucus and absent from the convention are given in the *Convention Journal,* p. 165.

their records of " political consistency ";[1] while there were
many others who refused to " brand as traitors their fathers,
brothers, and sons who had died in battle for the South." [2]
In commenting on the action of the convention, the *Tele-graph* of March 17th said:

They [the radicals] desired the convention should say that
secession or revolution was a crime in itself, and consequently
void. It was understood that this significance should attach
to the words " null and void, *ab initio.*" The idea attached to
the ordinance passed is that *the war has decided* that it was
null and void *ab initio.* On this difference the issue is raised.
It is whether the people in their sovereign capacity shall de-clare that they did wrong knowingly and willingly in 1861 in
attempting secession.

Flake's Bulletin, in commenting on the foregoing, said:

The difference in position is defined with unusual clearness
and great candor. . . . We do certainly desire that the ordi-nance of secession be declared a wrong knowingly forced upon
the people of Texas by their political leaders. We contend
that rebellion was wrong, that it was, in the theological lan-guage, original sin, that it was *malum in se,* and that the next
rebellion will be just like it, wrong from the beginning.

The most important subject that engaged the attention of

[1] Governor Hamilton is quoted as saying about this time: "After all,
our people are doing about as well as a reasonable man ought to ex-pect. Politicians must have their 'explanations' and their 'records';
they must be allowed to retreat gracefully and to fall gently; but the
vast majority of them are all right at heart. They must have time."
Truman to Johnson, MS. in *Johnson Papers;* see also in *Senate Exec.
Docs.,* vol. ii, no. 43, 1st. sess., 39th Cong.

[2] See speech of John Ireland in *Tri-Weekly State Gazette,* March 20,
1866.

the convention was the status to be given the negro. There was practical unanimity of opinion in regard to the abolition of slavery. All were now agreed that the institution had ceased to exist, for the Thirteenth Amendment had been ratified and declared in force in December; neither was there any division of opinion concerning the right of the freedmen to be secure in person and property. There was considerable debate upon the question of admitting negro testimony in the courts. The majority of the members were willing to admit such testimony in any case, civil or criminal, involving a right of, or injury to, any negro in person or property; but there was a large and active minority, chiefly the political friends of Hamilton, that strongly urged the admission of negro testimony in all cases under the same rules that governed the testimony of the whites.[1] The latter proposition was repugnant to popular sensibilities because it was regarded as the first step toward social equality, and this was the chief argument against it; though it was also strongly urged that if the negro were allowed to testify only in cases affecting the negro, he was legally placed upon a better foundation than the white man, since he would be able to subpoena witnesses from both whites and blacks, while the white man, where no negro was involved, could summon only those of his own color.[2] The radicals answered that a liberal policy was expected, nay, demanded both by the government at Washington and by Northern sentiment, and would be prerequisite to readmission to the national councils; and furthermore, it was pointed out that as long as the freedmen labored under any disabilities in the

[1] Strangely enough, Frazier, "the bitter rebel," as Truman calls him, was among the advocates of this measure. See the *Journal*, p. 97.

[2] Truman to Johnson, MS. in *Johnson Papers;* also in *Sen. Exec. Docs.*, vol. ii, no. 43, 1st sess., 39th Cong.

civil courts there was no prospect of a release from the annoyance of the Freedmen's Bureau.

The article first reported by Hancock from the committee on general provisions, February 17th, provided that slavery should not exist in the state and that freedmen should be secure in all rights of person and property, and should not be prohibited from testifying in any case affecting one of their own color. A number of amendments were offered to this section defining the rights of freedmen in the courts; but despite the efforts of a few to restrict these rights more narrowly, and of a strong minority to extend them, the provision went through essentially unchanged. As finally adopted, the ordinance, which became Article VIII of the Constitution, declared that, African slavery having been terminated by the United States government by force of arms and its re-establishment prohibited by an amendment to the Constitution of the United States, neither slavery nor involuntary servitude, except as a punishment for crime, whereof the party should have been duly convicted, should exist within the state. Negroes were to be protected in their rights of person and property; to have the right to sue and be sued, to contract and be contracted with, to acquire and transmit property; and all criminal prosecutions against them were to be conducted in the same manner and with the same penalties as in the case of whites. They were allowed to testify orally in any case, civil or criminal, involving the right of, injury to, or crime against, any of their own race in person or property, under the same rules of evidence that were applicable to the white race; and the legislature was empowered to authorize them to testify as witnesses in all other cases, under such regulations as should be prescribed, " as to facts hereafter occurring." [1]

[1] See Gammel, *Laws of Texas*, vol. v, p. 881.

This last clause, if not distinctly a concession to the minority, at least wisely left the matter open for determination according to future developments. Whether the Texans were more liberal in this respect than the delegates to the other state conventions or whether they felt themselves driven to this position by the Civil Rights Bill then under consideration in Congress, is not easily apparent. Truman thought them freely inclined to favor the negro;[1] and it was evident that few of them believed that the bill could pass over the President's veto. Moreover, the most of them, including many that had favored the most liberal policy toward the negro, were very hostile to that bill because it invaded a field which they regarded as being exclusively under the jurisdiction of the states.

The idea of negro suffrage found little favor on any side. Degener offered a long minority report from the committee on legislative department in advocacy of unrestricted suffrage, but he stood practically alone. Few, even of those who did not oppose it, would openly advocate it.[2] On the whole, Texas had granted the freedmen more civil rights than had any other southern state, though she had not gone as far as it was understood that President Johnson desired. Still, it was asserted by the radicals, now becoming identified with the anti-Johnson party, that it was the President's veto of the Freedmen's Bureau Bill during this time that

[1] Truman to Johnson in *Sen. Exec. Docs.*, vol. ii, no. 43, 1st sess., 39th Cong.; also his testimony before the Reconstruction Committee in *House Com. Reports*, vol. ii, part iv, p. 137, 1st sess., 39th Cong.

[2] Ben C. Truman testified before the Reconstruction Committee that there were seven men in the convention who favored negro suffrage and that four voted for it. See *House Com. Reports*, vol. ii, part iv, pp. 136, 137, 1st sess., 39th Cong.

had encouraged the majority to refuse the negro wider privileges.[1]

The question of the public debt presented a peculiar difficulty. There was no hesitation in repudiating the war debt, but the third section of the ordinance reported by the committee on finance repudiated the entire civil debt incurred between January 28, 1861, and August 5, 1865.[2] On this point there was a sharp debate, but the majority in its favor, comprising men of both parties, was so strong that obstructive tactics availed little; and with slight modifications the ordinance was passed on March 15th. The reasons advanced for repudiating the civil debt were: (1) that the treasury warrants, comprising the greater part of it, had been issued in plain violation of the constitution of 1845, which must be regarded as still in force;[3] (2) the state authorities had recklessly piled up a debt of nearly eight and a half millions of dollars, and to impose upon the state the obligation to carry so heavy a burden would not only drive away immigration but would bankrupt the state; (3) that nearly all of these warrants had found their way into the hands of the " gang of heartless stay-at-home speculators "[4] who had shirked their duty during the war, and it would be unfair to tax for their benefit the poverty-stricken soldiers in the ranks; (4) that a large amount of the debt had been issued to " regulators " for hunting down and executing without trial loyal citizens of the United States then resi-

[1] Wm. Alexander to Alonzo Sherwood, MS. in *Johnson Papers*.

[2] *Convention Journal*, p. 117.

[3] Article VII, Section 8, of that constitution provided that "in no case shall the legislature have the power to issue treasury warrants, treasury notes, or paper of any description intended to circulate as money."

[4] J. K. Bumpass in *State Gazette*, quoted in *San Antonio Daily Herald*, April 3, 1866.

dent in Texas.[1] How much support each one of these arguments contributed to the measure it would be difficult to
determine; but, combining strong legal and partisan reasons,
they presented an array that was overwhelming. This act
was attacked by the press, however, with perhaps more
bitterness than all the other measures together. Certain of
the conservative journals in particular exhibited a resentment that was most acrid.[2] The *San Antonio Herald,* which
had shown some anxiety on this point previous to the convention, asserted that the warrants of the state had nothing on their face to show that they were in any way connected with the rebellion; that most of the debt was for
purely civil services and that the rest was for the defense of
the frontier against the Indians. The *State Gazette* declared the repudiation an act of bad faith, one that had not
been required by the Federal government, and had not been
adopted in the other states of the South that had suffered far
worse during the war than had Texas.

Although these important measures concerning secession,
the freedmen, and the war debt were the only ones that the
convention had been specifically required to take up, there
were other matters that naturally came up for consideration.
An ordinance of great importance was one recognizing certain acts of the government *de facto* as it existed during the
war. When the Federals first took control of the state all
the acts of the state government subsequent to the ordinance
of secession were declared invalid. This, however, was
felt to work an unnecessary hardship in many cases, and

---

[1] For the arguments here presented in favor of this ordinance I am
indebted to the Hon. X. B. Saunders of Belton, Texas, who was a
member of the convention.

[2] It was asserted at the time that several held in their possession
large amounts of the now worthless state warrants.

Governor Hamilton had gradually adopted the policy of recognizing as valid such acts and laws as were not in conflict with the laws of the United States. It was generally felt to be absolutely necessary for the peace and well being of society that the private-law ctatus of citizens sholud not be disturbed by reason of the war. Under the authority of the state government during the war property had been transferred; estates administered; contracts entered into; business relations formed; courts held, judgments rendered, and decrees executed; marriage relations entered into and children born. To have disturbed or destroyed the legitimacy of all these acts would have been to undermine and destroy the very foundations upon which depended the stability of society. Such a course could have subserved no useful purpose in state policy, for these acts would not be construed as having been " in aid of the rebellion." Consequently, long before the convention was called, the provisional authorities had made and recognized a distinction between acts in aid and support of the rebellion and those which had been primarily for the purpose of regulating the private relations of the people and without any direct relation to the war. But though this distinction was already recognized and acted upon, it was necessary for the convention to embody it in the organic law of the land in order to insure the permanence of the principle. The ordinance passed on the subject was a sort of omnibus bill, covering a wide range of related subjects. All laws and parts of laws enacted by the legislature subsequent to the 1st of February, 1861, and not in conflict with the constitution and laws of the United States, nor with the constitution of Texas as it was prior to that date, nor in conflict with the proclamations of the provisional governor, were declared to be in full force as laws of the state; and all acts of the different officers of the state, executive, legislative, and judicial, done in compliance with the laws not in conflict as above stated, were declared in force, unless annulled by act of the convention. All acts of the secession convention were annulled. The acts of the provisional government and its officers were declared valid. Furthermore, it was provided that no suit or prosecution should be maintained or recovery had against any agent, bailee, executor, administrator, or trustee, who had been compelled to deliver up property or money held by them to Confederate States' receivers. No person was to be sued or prosecuted for any action done in compliance with superior orders under Confederate authority.[1] Persons absent from Texas during the war, against whom any judgment was rendered in a civil suit during such absence, were allowed two years from April 1, 1866, in which to reopen and set aside such judgment, with the effect to set aside any sale or disposition of any property affected.[2]

A number of minor matters are worthy of passing notice.

[1] This part of the ordinance was attacked by Governor Hamilton in a violent and angry speech before the convention on March 31. He said: "The convention have passed a measure legislating wholesale robbery and murder throughout the land. A measure of peace! Does it bring peace to the bereaved hearts made desolate by such deeds? . . . I imagine the friends of this resolution had in their minds certain gentlemen here and there who were receivers under the Confederate States' laws. . . . The loyal citizens were robbed, and now because these receivers acted under authority, they must be protected and you imagine this convention is powerful enough to protect them. They will and shall be called to account. There is but one cure. They must leave this country or account for it just as sure as the sun is shining in Heaven above us. . . . You [the members] have an account to settle before the people yet. You have not done with this. You shall confront them, and shall answer to them, and if God spares my life, I pledge myself to go before the people of the state and draw these men up and make them answer." See *Southern Intelligencer,* May 24, 1866.

[2] See Gammel, *Laws of Texas,* V, pp. 895-898.

Certain amendments were added to the constitution—that of 1845—lengthening the terms of most state officers to four years and increasing the salaries. Some changes were made in the form and jurisdiction of the courts with a view to greater efficiency. The governor was requested to peti·tion the President for more adequate frontier protection. An ordinance was passed on the last day providing for a possible division of the state, the vote standing 31 to 17.[1] One of the last acts of the convention was the appointment of four delegates who were to proceed to Washington and lay before the President the result of their deliberations and to " endeavor to imprèss upon the national authorities the loyal and pacific disposition of the people of Texas." On several occasions the majority had attempted to get through resolutions endorsing President Johnson's policy, but action was delayed until the last minute, when the measure failed for want of a quorum.

The action of the convention in passing the ordinances concerning secession, the freedmen, and the debt was to be regarded as final, but the amendments to the constitution were to be voted upon at the first general election for state, district, and county officers, which was fixed for June. The new state government was to be inaugurated in August.

The convention adjourned April 2d, after a session of eight weeks. By this time the two parties, radical and conservative, which had been in evidence almost from the first, had become something more nearly approaching definite organizations. The acts of the convention were looked upon as being chiefly the work of the conservatives, and were in consequence bitterly attacked by the radical news-

---

[1] The demand for separation was especially strong in the western part of the state where the Union sentiment had been very strong and where there were a great many Germans.

papers, especially by the *Southern Intelligencer,* which had become the recognized organ of the radicals. The *Intelligencer* declared that the convention had done things it ought not to have done and had left undone the things that it ought to have done. It had failed to declare secession null and void from the beginning; only a portion of the civil rights had been conceded to the freedmen; and it had failed to submit all its ordinances to the people for ratification. Nor were the conservative papers altogether pleased with the last days of the session, and at first they did not attempt to conceal their dissatisfaction. Each party in the convention had begun manœuvering in anticipation of the June elections, and, in haste to get an early start in the canvass and unwilling to wait for a state nominating convention, each had resorted to the old expedient of a caucus nomination. The San Antonio *Herald,* the Austin *State Gazette,* and the Houston *Telegraph* joined in denouncing this caucus nomination, which, taken with the refusal to submit certain of the ordinances to the people, they regarded as proof that the delegates cared only to grab all the offices and considered this as more important than the welfare of the state. Some of these papers, too, were still smarting over the repudiation of the civil debt. But this did not last long; the conservatives were soon forced by the pressure of party strife to accept and defend the work of the convention and to support the caucus-made nominees of their faction.

CHAPTER VI

THE RESTORATION OF STATE GOVERNMENT

1. *The State Elections of 1866*

THE last day of the constitutional convention had been given over largely to preparations for the approaching elections. About two weeks before adjournment a caucus of the radicals had tendered to Hamilton the nomination for the governorship, which he declined. Thereupon a new ticket, headed by ex-Governor E. M. Pease and B. H. Epperson, was made out and published with a declaration of the principles for which this party had contended in the convention. Their opponents, after some hesitation on the part of the ultra-secessionists, centered upon Throckmorton, president of the convention, and Geo. W. Jones, delegate from Bastrop in the same body. In a public letter, April 2d, announcing their candidates, the conservatives endorsed the President's policy for the restoration of the state governments, asserted their opposition to the negro-political-equality policy of the radicals in Congress, and declared that the Texas radicals were preparing "to aid and abet Stevens, Sumner, and Phillips . . . in the establishment of a consolidated, despotic government." [1] The tickets thus put out did not, however, remain intact. Epperson, although always a strong Union man, refused to align himself with the radicals and was finally replaced by Lindsay; while several of the conservative nominees either withdrew

[1] *Southern Intelligencer*, April 19, 1866.

or declined to run.   Changes continued to be made in both
tickets up to the eve of the election.

From the outset the canvass was bitter.   The radicals,
their defeats in the convention still rankling, charged that
their opponents were unwilling to abide by the true results
of the war; that they refused even to accept the President's
policy which they professed to endorse and support—in
proof of which it was pointed out that the convention had
fallen short of the President's recommendations; in fact,
that they were as rebellious as in 1861; and that their real
object was to get possession of the state offices and once
more work into control of the national government in order
to establish there the principles overthrown in the "rebellion," or failing in that, to reopen the "rebellion" at a convenient opportunity, and meanwhile to drive all Union men
out of the state and nullify the emancipation of the negroes.[1]
On the other hand, it was charged upon the radicals that,
being disappointed, first in the hope of prolonging the provisional government indefinitely, and next in securing control
of the convention, and having little chance of securing a
new lease of power at the coming election, they were preparing to desert President Johnson whom they still professed
to admire and endorse, and to align themselves with the
ultra-radical element in Congress in its evident intention of
re-establishing military rule over the South and enforcing
political equality between whites and negroes.   While the
conservatives were stigmatized as "disloyal" and "rebellious" because of their hostility to the Civil Rights and
Freedmen's Bureau Acts, they accused their antagonists of
being the real disunionists because they supported the "de-
structive, unconstitutional legislation" of Congress and

[1] See files of *Flake's Bulletin, San Antonio Express,* and *Southern
Intelligencer* (radical papers) for April, May, and June, 1866.

favored delay in the restoration of the state to its normal place in the Union.

Probably there was as much truth in these charges as in those of the average heated political campaign. It is certainly true that the conservatives were unwilling to concede more changes in the characters and relations of the state and Federal governments than they would be obliged to, and it seems true that their admiration of the President at this time was closely related to, and in direct proportion to, their fears of the Congressional radicals; but to confuse their hatred of the latter with their attitude toward the government, or to assert that desire for political power and influence was tantamount to rebellion, or that they were preparing a crusade against Union men and a renewal of rebellion, was the sheerest nonsense, and beyond the threats of a few braggarts and ruffians there seems to have been no foundation for the charge. Surely nothing disloyal could be found in the utterances of their candidate, Throckmorton. In the course of one of his speeches, while discussing the relations of the people to the government, he said:

The President may be defeated in his policy; other laws equally as objectionable as the civil rights statute may be enacted; the Northern people may refuse to believe in our sincerity and loyalty; we may be kept out of the halls of legislation and yet be required to meet our portion of the public burdens; . . . We may continue to be misrepresented and traduced; troops may be quartered among us where there is profound peace and the frontier remain unprotected. . . . But if these things happen it is our duty to bear them patiently. Whatever law is passed, however odious it may be, it should be obeyed by us as long as it the law of the land. Let us by our conduct and example sustain the majesty and supremacy of the law.[1]

[1] Clipping from *Houston Telegraph*, found in *Johnson Papers*.

Nor is it entirely true that the radicals had as yet embraced all of the doctrines of Thaddeus Stevens or of Wendell Phillips. Pease declared that he was opposed to complete negro suffrage because the blacks were not intelligent enough to vote; but, if the United States government should require it, he would be willing to concede the suffrage to such negroes as could read and write understandingly rather than have Texas remain under provisional government, and he claimed that this was the view of the majority of his party.[1] Nevertheless, it soon became apparent that that party was really in alliance with the enemies of the President. As the conservatives had found a natural ally in Mr. Johnson, their opponents had been brought more and more into dependence upon the Congressional radicals; and, as every day it became more evident that the conservatives would carry the state, while in the North the ultimate decision in the great problem before the nation was to be with Congress rather than the President, an alliance with Congress offered the radicals advantages of an exceedingly seductive character. Long before the date of the election the alliance was made known. Governor Hamilton's attorney-general, Alexander, had written to the leaders in Washington beseeching them to delay restoration as long as possible, and the correspondence found its way into the papers.[2] Hamilton himself, after a brief but stormy campaign tour, turned over the duties of his office to Bell, the secretary of state, and hurried north to enlist in the campaign against the President, where his violent denunciations of both Johnson and the people of Texas won him fame in the North and increased hatred in his own state. Pease had been personally popular and he conducted his campaign in the state with

[1] *San Antonio Express*, May 24, 1866.
[2] *Weekly State Gazette*, May 12, 1866.

characteristic moderation; but the anti-radical feeling was too strong, and the conservatives were overwhelmingly victorious in the elections. The Throckmorton ticket was elected by an immense majority, 49,277 to 12,168 votes. At the same time the amendments to the constitution were ratified by 28,119 to 23,400 votes. This comparatively small majority may have been due to the fact that the general increase provided for in the salaries of state officials was very unpopular.

2. *Inauguration of the New Government*

As soon as it was positively known that the conservative ticket was elected, the secretary of state, Judge Bell, telegraphed President Johnson for instructions, expressing the opinion that the provisional officers should retain control until the President should consent to the installation of those newly elected. His course received the approval of Mr. Johnson, who, however, gave no immediate indication of the action he expected to take. In the meantime it was rumored that the conservatives would not be allowed to take possession of the state offices, and that the provisional government would be continued. A number of the radicals had gone North and it was feared that their representations as to the disloyalty of the victorious party might have a disquieting effect upon the government at Washington. Pease denied that there was any truth in the rumor, but a number of anxious dispatches were sent by Throckmorton and his friends to assure Mr. Johnson that the newly-elected officials were " alike the friends of the President's policy and lovers of the Union of the states." [1]

---

[1] Throckmorton, John Hancock, Burford, Buckley to Johnson, MSS. in *Johnson Papers.* See also *Tri-Weekly Telegraph,* July 12, 1866; *Southern Intelligencer,* July 19, 1866.

The Eleventh Legislature assembled at Austin on August 6th. The votes for governor were counted and Throckmorton was declared duly elected; and, although no word had come from Washington, arrangements were made for the inauguration. On the morning of August 9th, the governor and lieutenant-governor were inaugurated in the presence of the two houses of the legislature, the officers of the provisional government, several officers of the United States army, and a large concourse of citizens. Four days later a telegram was received from the President by the provisional secretary of state, ordering that the care and conduct of affairs in Texas be turned over to the constituted authorities chosen by the people. Governor Throckmorton and his subordinates at once took possession unopposed and entered upon the discharge of their duties. The military authorities in the state received orders to render the same support to the newly-organized authorities as had been afforded to the provisional government. On August 20th President Johnson issued a proclamation declaring that the insurrection in Texas was at an end, and that peace, order, tranquillity, and civil authority existed throughout the whole of the United States.[1]

Nevertheless, the outlook for the new state government was not auspicious. In his inaugural address the governor described the situation in graphic language:

At a time like the present, when we have just emerged from the most terrible conflict known to modern times, with homes made dreary and desolate by the heavy hand of war; the people impoverished, and groaning under public and private debts; the great industrial energies of our country sadly depressed; occupying in some respects the position of a state of the Federal Union, and in others the condition of a con-

[1] *Messages and Papers of the Presidents*, VI, 434-438.

quered province exercising only such privileges as the conqueror in his wisdom and mercy may allow; the loyalty of the people to the general government doubted; their integrity questioned; their holiest aspirations for peace and restoration disbelieved, maligned and traduced; with a constant misapprehension of their most innocent actions and intentions; with a frontier many hundreds of miles in extent being desolated by a murderous and powerful enemy, our devoted frontiersmen filling bloody graves, their property given to the flames or carried off as booty, their little ones murdered, their wives and daughters carried into a captivity more terrible than death, and reserved for tortures such as savage cruelty and lust alone can inflict; unprotected by the government we support, with troops quartered in the interior where there is peace and quiet; unwilling to send armed citizens to defend the suffering border, for fear of arousing unjust suspicions as to the motive; with a heavy debt created before the late war, and an empty treasury; with an absolute necessity for a change in the laws to adapt ourselves to the new order of things, and embarrassments in every part of our internal affairs, . . . the surroundings are uninviting, the future appears inauspicious.[1]

3. *The Eleventh Legislature*

Comparatively few members of the convention returned to the legislature. Many of the conservatives from the earlier body had been elected to various state offices, while the radicals had been retired to private life. Only a few of the latter, chiefly from the German counties in the southwest, were successful in the elections, and the membership of the legislature, therefore, was overwhelmingly conservative. But now that the power of the radicals was removed, the discord in the conservative ranks at once became apparent. The recent alliance between the " conservative

[1] *House Journal, Eleventh Legislature*, 19.

Unionists," headed by the governor, and the secessionists
had never been more than a *mariage de convenance,* and
neither party was willing to yield to the other the control
of the state. In the organization of the House the secessionists were defeated in the selection of the Speaker, Nat
M. Burford, of Dallas county, being elected over Ashbel
Smith, of Harris county, by 39 to 30 votes.

Of the many tasks which confronted the legislature, the
one which demanded the most careful handling was the
selection of two United States senators, and it was precisely
in this that the conservative party laid itself open to the
attack of its enemies. Of the eight or ten candidates whose
names were submitted, four were clearly in the lead. These
were O. M. Roberts, David G. Burnet, B. H. Epperson,
and John Hancock. According to agreement one was to be
chosen from eastern Texas, the other from the western part
of the state. Hancock and Epperson had both been Union
men throughout the war,[1] but since the adjournment of the
convention they had acted with the conservatives. Roberts
had been one of the most prominent secession leaders in the
state and was universally regarded as the candidate of that
element. Judge Burnet, formerly president of the Republic
of Texas, had also been a secessionist, but because of his
advanced age had for many years taken no active part in
political affairs. The two houses met in joint session on
August 21st for the election of senators. There had been
some rumors of an alliance between the forces of John Hancock and Roberts, but if such an arrangement was ever
made it had broken down.[2] The candidates from the west-

---

[1] Epperson, however, had served in the Confederate Congress, while
Hancock had remained in retirement.

[2] D. M. Short to O. M. Roberts, August 24, 1866, MS. in *Roberts
Papers.*

ern district were Judge Burnet, John Hancock, and ex-Governor Pease, lately defeated for the governorship. Burnet was elected on the first ballot, the vote standing 65 for Burnet, 43 for Hancock, and 7 for Pease.[1]

Angered at the attitude of the secessionists, Hancock's followers went in a body to the support of Epperson against Roberts. The next ballot stood, Roberts 30, Epperson 43, with 41 more votes scattered among five other candidates. It was not until the thirteenth ballot two days later that Roberts received a majority, 61 to 49, and was declared elected.[2] The contest was not fought out entirely upon factional lines, but sufficiently so as to emphasize the strained relations between the " Union conservatives " and the original secessionists.[3] Thanks, however, to the common fear of the Northern radicals, they never came to the breaking-point.

As might have been expected, the election of two uncompromising secessionists, neither of whom was able to take the test oath,[4] only confirmed the Northern mind in its sus-

---

[1] *House Journal, Eleventh Legislature*, 119.

[2] *Ibid.*, 119-139.

[3] Short to Roberts, *Roberts Papers*.

[4] The " test oath " or " iron-clad oath " was required of all officials of the United States according to Act of Congress, July 2, 1862. It was as follows:

" I, (A. B.), do solemnly swear (or affirm) that I have never voluntarily borne arms against the United States since I have been a citizen thereof; that I have voluntarily given no aid, countenance, counsel, or encouragement to persons engaged in armed hostility thereto; that I have neither sought nor accepted nor attempted to exercise the functions of any office whatever, under any authority or pretended authority in hostility to the United States; that I have not yielded a voluntary support to any pretended government, authority, power, or constitution within the United States, hostile or inimical thereto. And I do further swear (or affirm) that, to the best of my

picions of Texas " loyalty ". *Flake's Bulletin* expressed the opinion that Hancock's defeat was due to " his *ability* to take the test oath," and added: " It is clear that the legislature does not want its senators admitted. . . . It has closed the doors of Congress against the representatives of Texas." The Houston *Telegraph* confessed that " this election will be a tremendous weapon in the hands of A. J. Hamilton and the radicals in the coming fall elections. It is an awkward response to the utterances and actions of the Philadelphia convention." [1] However, the *Houston Journal* boldly declared that it was " a simple indication that for the restoration of the Union the test oath must be repealed. The South loves its soldiers and will not forget them or admit that the ' lost cause ' had in it any element of treason."

The senators-elect proceeded to Washington, where they were joined later by three of the four representatives elected in the fall, Geo. W. Chilton, B. H. Epperson, and A. M. Branch.[2] Not only were their seats refused to them, but their credentials were ignored and they were not welcome even in the lobbies. Thus the " accredited representatives of a sovereign state " were reduced to watch the doings of Con-

knowledge and ability, I will support and defend the Constitution of the United States against all enemies, foreign and domestic; that I will bear true faith and allegiance to the same; that I take this obligation freely, without any mental reservation or purpose of evasion, and that I will well and faithfully discharge the duties of the office on which I am about to enter, so help me God." *U. S. Statutes at Large,* XII, p. 502.

[1] The National Union Convention, composed of supporters of President Johnson's reconstruction policy, had demanded the admission of the Southern representatives to Congress and had indignantly denied that the South was still disloyal.

[2] C. C. Herbert, from the Fourth Congressional District, remained in Texas.

gress from the galleries.[1] They found that they had been preceded at Washington by Hamilton, Pease, and other Texas radicals, who, in close alliance with the opponents of the President, were doing all in their power to defeat the recognition of the new state government and to substitute some form of Congressional control.[2] After attending to such business for their state as was possible in the executive departments, and after futile efforts to come to a definite understanding with the President and his supporters upon a program to be pursued, the Texan delegation issued an address " to the Congress and People of the United States," setting forth their view of the rights of Texas in the Union and the condition of affairs in the state,[3] and then, with the exception of Epperson, returned home.

In his first message to the legislature the governor submitted the joint resolutions of Congress proposing a thirteenth and a fourteenth amendment to the Constitution of the United States. In regard to the first he offered no recommendation, on the ground that it had already been adopted by the requisite number of states and had been embodied in the constitution of Texas by the convention. With respect to the second, he expressed " unqualified disapproval " of it as " impolitic, unwise, and unjust," and recommended its rejection. The two resolutions were referred to the committee on federal relations, but no action was taken until two months later. The House committee in reporting on the Thirteenth Amendment stated that, inasmuch as the people of Texas through their convention

[1] Roberts to Throckmorton, MS. in *Executive Correspondence.* See also " The Experiences of an Unrecognized Senator " in *The Texas Historical Association Quarterly,* XII, 145.

[2] " The Experiences of an Unrecognized Senator," *op. cit.,* XII, 100, 102-103.

[3] *Ibid.,* 106-119.

had already acknowledged the supremacy of the Constitution of the United States, of which the said amendment was an integral part, the legislature had no authority in the matter and any action on its part " would be surplusage if not intrusive." The committee asked and was allowed to be relieved of any further consideration of the measure.[1] The Senate committee seems to have made no report on this subject.

The report made on Article XIV by the House committee through its chairman, Ashbel Smith, was an able and interesting document. It expressed very clearly the fears aroused by the program of the radicals, and stated succinctly the practical and constitutional grounds of Southern opposition. In the first place, so the committee declared, the submission of the article was in itself a nullity, because, contrary to the plain intent of the constitution, the representatives of the states most concerned were denied participation in the Congress proposing it. Moreover, the article as submitted was clearly intended to deprive the states of certain rights and powers over their citizens that they had held without question since 1776, and to give to the Federal government authority that would be dangerous alike to the constitutional autonomy of the states and to the liberties of the people. Furthermore, it would degrade the governments and social institutions of the Southern states by enforcing wholesale negro suffrage along with a practical disfranchisement of the whites. It was dictated not by statesmanship, but by " passion and malignancy," and it required that the members of the legislature be the instruments of their own and of their people's degradation. The committee admitted that it was thoroughly aware of the dangers involved in rejecting the amendment:

---

[1] *House Journal, Eleventh Legislature,* 219, 493.

for the radical leaders had threatened the complete prostration of the state through the abrogation of its government, the establishment of martial law with a military governor, the confiscation of property and the granting of negro freehold homesteads therefrom, the abrogation of Presidential pardons to be followed by trials before military commissions, the impeachment of the President and the establishment of a negro government for bringing Texas back into the Union. Yet refusing to yield to mere expediency when it meant the abandonment of principle, the committee would recommend the rejection of the article proposed. The recommendation was sustained by a vote of 70 to 5.[1] The Senate committee made a similarly adverse report and was also sustained.[2]

The most interesting and important of the purely legislative work of the session was that dealing with the freedmen and labor. Reagan, from his home near Palestine, again issued a public letter, to the governor this time,[3] calling attention to the prospective fulfilment of his prophecies in the Fort Warren letter,[4] and again urging a qualified suffrage and wider privileges in the courts for the freedmen, in order to ward off the attacks and forestall the plans of the Northern radicals. For the present, however, he had no following in his own party, and this letter only increased the irritation produced by the former one. Laws were passed on the subjects of apprenticeship, vagrancy, labor contracts, and the enticing away of laborers; and although

[1] For full report of the committee and the vote, see *House Journal, Eleventh Legislature*, 577-583.

[2] *Senate Journal, Eleventh Legislature*, 417.

[3] Reagan's *Memoirs*, 301. The original is in *Executive Correspondence*.

[4] *Supra*, p. 83.

no apparent distinction was made in their application as to whites and blacks, it is clear enough that they were intended solely for the regulation of negroes and negro labor. The labor situation had not cleared entirely, despite the energetic work of the Freedmen's Bureau during the winter and spring and the efforts of its officials to keep the freedmen at work during the crop-growing season. When paid a monthly cash wage, the negro usually preferred to spend it before going back to work; and, when offered better wages elsewhere, he had no hesitation in breaking a contract in order to accept. On May 15th, General Kiddoo, who had just succeeded General Gregory as assistant commissioner for Texas, found it necessary to issue a circular order forbidding the enticing of contract laborers from one employer to another. The person thus inducing a freedman to leave his contract was to be fined from $100 to $500 and the laborer from $5 to $25. A fine of $50, moreover, could be assessed against a freedman for voluntarily leaving his employer without just cause before the expiration of the contract.[1] General Kiddoo seems to have appreciated the needs of the planters better than did his predecessor, and he enjoyed a corresponding share of their confidence. In June, when the crops had got into a "precarious condition by reason of the excessive rains and grass," all Bureau agents were instructed to advise the negroes to work early and late and to stand by their contracts in order to save the crops, because they had therein a common interest with the planters.[2]

The *Texas Republican,* August 11th, published an order from the Bureau agent at Marshall containing a list of

[1] Circular Order no. 14, from file in *Executive Correspondence.*
[2] Circular Order no. 17, *ibid.*

twelve freedmen who had left their employers, also named, and notifying other employers not to hire them. Notice was given that a weekly list of delinquent laborers would be published. These lists appeared in the paper from time to time. Evidently the Bureau officials were being driven to the adoption of measures they had formerly condemned. Again, it was found necessary, when the cotton picking season came on, to instruct agents everywhere to see to it that the negroes employed the utmost diligence in gathering the crop, which was short on account of excessive rains, grass, and the ravages of the army worm.[1]

When it was possible for an arm of the national government itself, organized and operated in the interest of the freedman and enjoying his full confidence, to keep him at work and out of mischief only by constant watchfulness and semi-coercion, it must have seemed urgently necessary that the state adopt a system of regulation more permanent than that of the Bureau professed to be. The legislature had before it, as a warning, evidences of the deep resentment of the North at the "black codes" enacted by the states reorganized during the previous year, and was able therefore so to frame its laws as to offend in a less degree the watchful prejudices of Northern voters.

The general apprenticeship law did not differ materially from those in force elsewhere. It provided that any minor, with the consent of parent or guardian, could be bound out by the county judge until twenty-one years of age unless sooner married. The master, or mistress, was to enter into bond to treat him humanely, teach him a trade, furnish medical attendance and schooling, and was allowed to inflict moderate corporal punishment. A runaway could be recovered and brought before a justice and punished, or

[1] Circular Order no. 21, in *Executive Correspondence.*

freed if he could prove he had good cause to run away.
The apprentice could not be removed from the county without an order from the county judge. Any one enticing
away an apprentice was subject to fine and suit for damages.[1] The vagrancy law defined a vagrant as " any idle
person living without any means of support and making no
exertion to earn a livelihood by any honest employment,"
and comprehended the usual assorted list of undesirables.[2]
Neither of these acts made any mention of race or color
and neither seems to have given enough offense to call for
annulment by the Bureau.

It was otherwise, however, with the labor law. The
original Senate bill provided that every laborer should enter
into a written contract for the whole year on or before the
10th day of January. Its authors undoubtedly had in mind
negro labor only, and intended to provide against a repetition of the troubles of the previous winter. Nevertheless,
a severer blow to the best interests of the state could hardly
be imagined, especially since no distinction was made between white and black laborers and efforts were being made
at the time to induce white immigration. In effect the bill
prescribed that any laborer who failed to make a contract by
January 10th, no matter what wages were offered, should be
liable to punishment under the vagrancy law. The *Southern
Intelligencer* furiously attacked the bill, denominating it " a
legislative monster," and declaring " its practical effect
would be to make labor synonymous with crime and to degrade the free laborer to the condition of a slave." The
House, however, so amended the bill as to allow contracts
to be made at any time for any length of time. The Senate
rejected the amendments and a joint conference committee

---

[1] Gammel, *Laws of Texas*, V, 979.
[2] *Ibid.*, V, 1020.

was appointed. The committee extended the time limit to January 20th, "or as soon as practicable thereafter," and made the law applicable only to "common laborers."[1] In this form the bill passed both House and Senate, but was later reconsidered in the House and cast into a more liberal form. As finally passed and approved, the act provided that all contracts for labor for periods longer than one month should be made in writing before a magistrate or two disinterested witnesses, signed in triplicate, and recorded. Laborers had full liberty to choose employers, but could not leave them afterwards, except for just cause or by permission, on pain of forfeiture of all wages earned. Employers had the right to make deductions from wages for time lost, bad work, or for any injury done to tools or stock, but the laborer had a right of appeal to a magistrate. Laborers were not allowed to leave home without permission or to have visitors during working hours, and were required to be obedient and respectful. They were given a lien on one-half the crop as security for their wages; the employer was subject to a fine for cruelty or non-fulfilment of contract, and the fine was to be paid to the laborer.[2] The supporters of the measure held that something of the kind was necessary for the proper regulation of the labor of an ignorant, improvident, and irresponsible people, still under the influence and traditions of recent slavery. Their opponents very sensibly urged that the act was ruinous to white labor and would keep it out of the state. But the law was not long in force; for at the beginning of the next year General Kiddoo issued an order to the effect that it would

[1] *House Journal Eleventh Legislature*, 442, 446, 456, 515, 562, 718. Also *Southern Intelligencer*, October 4 and 11, 1866.

[2] Gammel, *Laws of Texas*, V, 994.

be disregarded, and that the contracts made in accordance with its provisions would not be approved.[1]

Minor measures were passed, one to punish persons enticing away contracted laborers, another explicitly granting to freedmen all rights not prohibited by the constitution, except intermarriage with whites, voting, holding public office, serving on juries, and testifying in cases in which negroes were not concerned. The governor was directed to examine into the affairs of the late military board and to take measures to recover for the state the United States bonds alleged to have been fraudulently paid out during the war; state troops were provided for the protection of the frontier, and President Johnson was petitioned to have the interior garrisons also removed thither. In the last days of the session the governor informed the President of the chief results accomplished and asked for suggestions. Mr. Johnson's only reply was to urge that the legislature " make all laws involving civil rights as complete as possible, so as to extend equal and exact justice to all persons without regard to color," if it had not already been done; and to express a firm confidence in the ultimate complete restoration of the Union.[2]

The legislature adjourned November 13th. All in all, its members had taken the course they might most reasonably have been expected to take. If their selection of United States Senators was an unnecessary act of defiance, the rejection of the Fourteenth Amendment may be ascribed to a higher motive, the desire to maintain at any cost the fundamentals of their political philosophy, the cherished institutions which alone in their eyes made for free government. Even the labor law, harsh and stringent as it seems, was

---

[1] General Orders no. 2, January 3, 1867, in *Executive Correspondence.*

[2] *Annual Cyclopædia,* 1866, p. 743.

almost universally regarded as necessary both for the good conduct and for the protection of the negroes for whom alone it was intended. Keenly conscious only of local needs, the lawmakers had neglected to take sufficiently into account the forces preparing for their destruction in the North.

4. *Problems and Policies of Throckmorton's Administration*

Governor Throckmorton regarded Mr. Johnson's peace proclamation of August 20, 1866, as legally and definitely terminating the war and clearly establishing the supremacy of the civil over the military authority.[1] To secure the recognition of this supremacy as an accomplished fact became the chief aim of his administration. It was a course which, because of the hostility of a powerful party to the restoration policy of the President and because of the jealous suspicion of the local radicals and many of the military officials with whom he had to deal, was beset with many obstacles. But a definite and clear-cut plan is discernible throughout his term of office and one who follows its history closely must be impressed with the unfailing honesty and the strong common sense of the governor.

His purpose was, first, by the vigilance of peace officers and the regular and unhampered operation of the courts to secure the restoration of order and a just and more complete enforcement of the laws; second, in this way to eliminate the necessity of military courts, particularly those of the Freedmen's Bureau, and to induce them to yield to the state courts full jurisdiction of cases properly belonging to the latter; and, third, to secure the removal of the military garrisons from the interior to the unprotected frontier now devastated by the Indians.

[1] Throckmorton to Shropshire, *Executive Correspondence.*

During the spring and summer of 1866 the violence and
lawlessness which had characterized the previous year had
been steadily decreasing; yet conditions were still unsettled
and only relatively quiet. To travelers from the older states
there doubtless seemed to be very little of personal security
still, for bloody encounters were common, and in some
localities the offenders were unpunished. It should be remembered, however, that not only in Texas but in the
Southwest generally sharp disagreements between man and
man were settled as often by personal conflict as by legal
adjustment, and where it had been " a fair fight " peace
officers were likely to be negligent and juries lenient. It
was the rough way of the frontier, and Texas was pre-emi-
nently a frontier state. But so long as frontier methods
should prevail to the neglect of the duly organized judiciary,
it would be useless to expect that the military officials would
report Texas as peaceful, or the freedmen and " loyalists "
as safe; and, therefore, the governor exerted his influence
to the utmost to secure energetic action from the sheriffs
and promptness and impartial justice on the part of the
courts. To this end he was in constant correspondence with
influential citizens in all parts of the state and systematically
urged upon the military confidence in the civil authorities.

Had the governor and the army been in complete accord
in regard to their respective jurisdictions, clashes between
citizens and soldiers would nevertheless have been unavoidable, for there was no way of foreseeing and preventing private quarrels. Far more serious than these, however, were
several outbreaks which assumed a dangerous character
because of reckless official participation in them. Of these
the most notorious was the burning of Brenham, where a
battalion of the 17th Infantry was stationed under the command of Major G. W. Smith. On the night of September
7, 1866, a crowd of drunken soldiers forced their way into

and broke up a negro ball. Then, pursuing some negroes who fled for protection to a social gathering of some of the white people, they made their way thither and attempted to break up that. They were resisted, a fight ensued, and two soldiers were shot, but not seriously hurt. They went back to their camp and the whole force turned out and went to town, their commander with them. He arrested two citizens and threatened the town if others did not surrender themselves. Then, by his orders, two stores were broken into under pretense of searching for the citizens wanted, and were rifled of their contents. Shortly afterwards soldiers were discovered setting one of these stores on fire. An entire block of buildings was destroyed with a loss of over $130,000. The citizens appealed to the governor, and at his request an investigation of the affair was made by the regimental commander, Colonel Mason, then on duty at Galveston. Mason's report disclosed practically nothing and was a palpable " white-wash ". [1] A special committee of the legislature, after an extensive investigation, made a report identifying certain soldiers as guilty and implicating Major Smith, who had allowed the accused soldiers to desert and had refused to assist the committee. [2] A grand jury indicted Smith on a charge of burglary and arson; but although Throckmorton appealed to the President on behalf of the civil courts, [3] it proved impossible to bring the officer to trial in defiance of his military superiors. [4] A judgment

---

[1] It is given in *The Southern Intelligencer*, September 27, 1866

[2] The report of the committee, with the testimony of all witnesses examined by it, is given in the appendix to *House Journal, Eleventh Legislature*.

[3] Throckmorton to Stanbery, October 12, 1866, copy in *Executive Records, Register Book*, no. 84, p. 120.

[4] Sheridan accepted unquestioningly the statements made by Mason

for damages was rendered against him in favor of a firm whose store had been burned; but in July, 1867, when martial law was again supreme, General Griffin issued a special order reversing this judgment and dismissing all proceedings against the officer, because " the acts [of Smith] were committed in discharge of his duty as an officer, and the action of the court was dictated by a spirit of malicious persecution, fostered by vindictive and disloyal sentiments." [1]

In Bosque County occurred an incident that does much to explain the bitter hostility frequently shown to the Freed-men's Bureau agents. A negro, charged with the rape of a young white woman, had been arrested, jailed, and duly indicted, when a Bureau agent, living twenty miles away, came in and demanded the negro of the sheriff, threatening that officer with arrest and trial before a military commission at Houston if he refused to surrender the prisoner, and showing an order from his superior officer in justification of his action. The negro was turned over to him, only to be released shortly afterward.[2] A negro cook on a vessel entering Galveston was, at the request of the captain, arrested by the civil authorities on a charge of mutinous and disobedient conduct, but was released by order of General Kiddoo.[3]

In Matagorda County a freedman indicted for murderous assault was forcibly taken from the custody of the sheriff

and Smith, and in his report to Washington, said: "At Brenham two unarmed soldiers were shot. The grand jury found no bill against the would-be assassins, but indicted Major Smith for burglary because he broke into the house of some citizen in order to arrest these men." *Official Records, War of Rebellion,* Ser. I, vol. xlviii, part i, 301.

[1] Special Order no. 133, July 10, 1867.

[2] J. K. Helton to Throckmorton, August 21, 1866, in *Executive Correspondence.*

[3] Alvan Reed to Throckmorton, *ibid.*

by the local Bureau agent. The governor, seeing that his belief in the supremacy of the civil authority was not shared by the Bureau officials, endeavored to come to some understanding with them. He wrote to General Kiddoo concerning the affair at Matagorda:

I desire to know if the action of the agent of the Bureau in thus interfering with the enforcement of the law is by your order and if he is sustained by you in so doing. I would respectfully desire of you, at your earliest convenience, information of the extent of your power and authority, and how far you expect to exercise it to interfere with the civil authorities in the exercise of their duty in bringing freedmen to trial for offenses committed against the laws of the state. . . . I would also inquire if you recognize the President's peace proclamation as making the military subordinate to the civil authority.[1]

On the same date Throckmorton wrote Judge Shropshire at Matagorda that he had received information from General Heintzelman, commanding the forces in western Texas, that General Grant had issued an order declaring the President's peace proclamation had superseded military orders previously issued requiring the military to interfere with the civil authority in certain cases. " In other words," added the governor with evident satisfaction, " the proclamation restores the supremacy of civil over military authority."[2]

A serious situation existed at Victoria. The negro troops stationed there under the lax command of a Captain Spaulding had taken control of the county jail and rendered it

[1] Throckmorton to Kiddoo, November 7, 1866; copy in *Executive Records, Register Book*, no. 84, p. 125.

[2] Copy, *ibid.*, p. 152.

impossible for the civil authorities to keep a negro or Northern man confined there, no matter what his offense had been. It was alleged by the county judge that these soldiers had forcibly released two negroes convicted of horse-theft and an ex-federal soldier convicted of robbery. On the other hand, they had taken out and hanged a white man who was awaiting trial for the murder of a negro, and had arbitrarily imprisoned various citizens until the latter were willing to bribe their tormentors for their release.[1] The town was terrorized. No writ could be executed against any negro or friend of the soldiers. Throckmorton protested vigorously to General Heintzelman and insisted that Spaulding be court-martialed and that the troops be removed from Victoria altogether. When the case finally came before General Sheridan, three months later, he ordered that one of the soldiers be turned over to the civil authorities for trial, a concession that the governor found "very gratifying," in that "the military were disposed to recognize the civil authority of the state."[2]

A peculiar and yet in some ways a characteristic case came to notice in Bell County. In Collin County before the war a man named Lindley, who was a violent secessionist, was found to be connected with a gang of horse-thieves and was driven out. After the close of the war he turned up in Lampasas County engaged in the same business.[3] Threatened with arrest and fearing the testimony of two citizens of Bell County named Daws and Duncan, he pro-

---

[1] C. Carson and others to Throckmorton, MSS. in *Executive Correspondence*. Also Throckmorton to Heintzelman, September 25, 1866; copy in *Executive Correspondence*.

[2] Throckmorton to Shropshire, copy, *ibid.*

[3] Throckmorton to Sheridan, *Executive Records, Register Book*, no. 84, p. 246; also Throckmorton to Stanbery, *ibid.*, p. 122.

cured their arrest by the military authorities on the plea that he was a " Union " man and that his son had been hanged during the war by the said Daws and Duncan because of his Union sentiments. While these men were in charge of a military escort they were shot down by Lindley in cold blood, with no effort at interference by the officers in charge, who even attempted to protect Lindley from punishment. Both Lindley and the officer were indicted by the grand jury of Bell County, but the military authorities insisted that they be tried before a military commission and refused to allow any attorney to represent the state or even to submit written questions to the witnesses.[1] Whatever the reason for so doing, the military court acquitted both the accused; but later Lindley was arrested by the civil authorities and jailed at Belton. He loudly demanded a guard of troops; but, backed by the promises of the citizens, the governor assured the military that the prisoner was safe. Nevertheless, a mob broke into the jail and hanged him. Heralded to the world as the martyrdom of a " Union man ", his death furnished political capital to the radicals, while the failure of the citizens of Bell County to merit theconfidence and to sustain the promises of the governor seriously weakened his efforts to get rid of the military and caused him both anxiety and chagrin.

Numbers of instances could be cited wherein military officials over-rode the civil authority in true cavalier fashion. At Lockhart and at Seguin court records and papers were seized and destroyed or mutilated. In Houston a negro indicted and confined for an attempted murder escaped, and the Bureau agent resisted his rearrest by the sheriff. The county judge of Grimes County was placed under military

---

[1] Throckmorton to Heintzelman, September 24, 1886, MS. copy in *Executive Correspondence.*

arrest. At Brenham the Bureau agent seized and made use of the jail and imprisoned the editor of a local paper for publicly criticising the conduct of certain teachers of freedmen. The editor was released after three weeks through the intervention of the governor, who sent a protest to General Kiddoo. In Grayson County a government agent who had been arrested for offenses committed before entering upon his office was forcibly released by the military. To lay all the blame for these troubles upon the military would manifestly be unjust; in many cases they were provoked by the dilatoriness of the civil courts or by the prejudices occasionally manifested against those new rights claimed for the negro but not clearly granted him by the state code. Moreover, as the peace proclamation of the President could not abolish a jurisdiction established by Congress, the officers of the Freedmen's Bureau were still in duty bound to interfere in behalf of the negro whenever they believed he was being unjustly treated.

It was in obedience to this obligation that General Griffin, the new assistant commissioner for Texas, in a circular order issued January 26, 1867, directed his subordinates to " enforce the rights of freedmen according to the laws of Congress whenever injustice is done them or whenever the civil authorities neglect to render them justice." [1] A week later, however, relations with the civil authority were more carefully defined and the force of the above order somewhat modified by instructions that all criminal cases in which freedmen were concerned should be left to the civil authorities; but that unpunished or unnoticed outrages upon freedmen and all cases arising under the Civil Rights Act should be reported to military headquarters; that in civil suits the agents were merely to act as the advisers of the freedmen

[1] See *Flake's Weekly Bulletin*, February 6, 1867.

before the courts and to report the action of the courts to headquarters; and that the enforcement of the state vagrancy and apprenticeship laws should not be interfered with it fairly administered.[1] Though inclined at times to allow the civil authorities opportunity to prove their desire to administer real justice, it is, nevertheless, pretty clear that the man of arms was too often skeptical of their justice, too frequently disposed to bully, to resort to force when his jurisdiction was questioned, and to protect one of his own faith and party against the law of the "rebel" without inquiring very carefully into the merits of the case or into the right of the civil authorities to be respected.

More harmful, however, to the new state government than the troubles indicated above were the statements sent to Washington by high federal officials. In his final report of inspection of Bureau affairs in Texas, made in June, 1866, General Gregory had stated that Union men and freedmen were "trembling for their lives and preparing to leave the state," that murders and outrages upon freedmen had been on the increase since March (i. e., since the adjournment of the convention) and that the criminals were always acquitted in the civil courts.[2] In his zeal to aid his radical friends the commissioner had forgotten that the civil officials of whom he complained were those appointed by Hamilton, since the recently elected conservatives were not installed until August. Sheridan, in his official report, declared that conditions in Texas were such that the trial of a white man for killing a negro would be a farce,[3] and in a letter to Throckmorton, January 16, 1867, asserted

[1] See *Southern Intelligencer*, February 2, 1867.

[2] Gregory to Howard, printed in *Flake's Weekly Bulletin*, August 1, 1866.

[3] See *Official Records, War of Rebellion*, Ser. I, vol. xlviii, pt. i, p. 301.

that "there are more casualties occurring from outrages perpetrated upon Union men and freedmen in the interior of the state than occur from Indian depredations on the frontier. The former greatly exceed the latter and are induced by the old rebellious sentiment." [1] To this Throckmorton entered a prompt and vigorous denial. He told Sheridan that the latter and his officers had for the most part been imposed upon by men who proclaimed themselves "outraged Union men," but who had really never been Union men at all; more often they were rogues and horsethieves who set up that cry in order to get protection of the military. He himself had been a Union man before the war, had had extensive correspondence with Union men all over the state, and knew that some of these men who were now being outraged "for their Union sentiment" had formerly been "brawling, blatant secessionists" and notorious for their bad character.[2] Not content with this, the governor, on February 9th, sent out circular inquiries to the civil officers throughout the state, chiefly to the justices of the county courts, regarding the treatment of Union men and freedmen in the courts and at the hands of the people in general, and making specific inquiries concerning such cases as had been brought to his attention. In the answers to this circular it was claimed without exception that the law was impartially enforced upon all classes without distinction of color or politics. Some writers complained of the Bureau officials, some of the soldiers, while some were on the best of terms with the military, to whom they referred for endorsement of their statements. Although one is tempted to suspect that many of the civil officials en-

[1] MS. in *Executive Correspondence.*

[2] Throckmorton to Sheridan, *Executive Records, Register Books,* no. 84, p. 246.

deavored to make out as cheerful a picture of conditions as possible, a careful examination of the records of the executive office goes far to bear out their statements so far as the courts were concerned. In trials of homicide of freedmen the defendants were often acquitted, but numerous cases are found in which white men were convicted on this charge. On the other hand, numbers of negroes convicted of petty crimes, such as theft, were pardoned by the governor upon petition of judge and jurors. The longest and most interesting of the reports above mentioned is from Robert Wilson, county judge of Grayson County, who confessed that many foul murders had been committed in his county, but insisted that they were the work of a band of outlaws from across Red River in the Indian Territory. The freedmen, he said, suffered from no injustice in the courts, and the instances of their mistreatment by the people were rare. Union men were not persecuted: he himself had always been a Union man and had been elected over a secessionist of unimpeachable character. A " refugee " had recently gained a law suit, though several times beaten before the war. The cry of persecution had always come from some person who, having transgressed the law, wished to enlist for his defense the sympathies of the military and of the general government.[1]

On the whole, Throckmorton's confidence in the ability of the state and local officials to maintain justice and order seems to have justified itself, though a few localities still retained an undesirable reputation for violence and outrage.[2] The governor, however, had not been content to wait for conditions in the interior to become thoroughly

[1] For this and other reports see *Executive Correspondence.*

[2] For alleged outrages upon freedmen at Prairie Lea, see W. C Philips to Throckmorton, MS., *ibid.*

settled before trying to relieve the situation on the frontier. It will be remembered that Hamilton had spent some effort in that direction but had finally acquiesced in Sheridan's claim that the troops were needed more in the interior. Perhaps Throckmorton's previous experience on the frontier and as commissioner to the Indians under the Confederacy made him peculiarly alive to the situation in that region. Certain it is that the harrowing tales of cruelty and suffering and the constant appeals for protection that came to him weighed heavily upon his mind. Hardly was he seated in the governor's chair when he urgently requested General Wright to send troops to the desolated border,[1] and he gave the subject of frontier relief a prominent place in his message to the legislature.[2] Wright, keeping in line with Sheridan's former attitude, replied that he had no authority to establish new posts; that it was wholly within the power of General Sheridan; and that, besides, there was not sufficient force in Texas for the work without breaking up the interior posts. Seeing that it was useless to wait upon the military commander, the governor wrote on August 25th to President Johnson, as commander-in-chief, describing the conditions on the frontier and urgently repeating his request that troops from the interior go to its protection since they were not needed for the enforcement of the law.[3] Mr. Johnson referred the matter to Stanton, Secretary of War, who referred it to Grant and told Throckmorton to confer with Sheridan.[4] Thrown back upon the mercies of Sheridan, he next appealed to General Heintzel-

[1] See *Executive Records, Register Book*, no. 84, p. 37.

[2] *House Journal, Eleventh Legislature*, 80.

[3] Copy in *Executive Records, Register Book*, no. 84, p. 60; also MS. in *Johnson Papers*.

[4] MS. in *Johnson Papers*.

man, in command of the western division of Texas, and succeeded in persuading him to send two regiments of cavalry to the lower frontier.[1] The legislature authorized the raising of one thousand state troops,[2] which were tendered Sheridan, but were refused by him on the ground that the United States could furnish all the soldiers necessary.[3] In his annual report to the war department, Sheridan declared that justice was not done freedmen, Union men, and soldiers in the interior, and that troops were still needed there; and expressed the belief that the reports of Indian depredations on the frontier were " probably exaggerated " and that conditions were " not alarming." However, he stated that frontier posts would be established in the spring.[4] When a measure of protection was finally afforded, Texas had passed again into a " provisional organization."

5. *The Work of the Freedmen's Bureau*

The chief activities of the Bureau from the spring of 1866 to March, 1867, may be indicated in brief space. The measure of relief work carried on in Texas had never been very great.[5] Such indigent negroes as were not cared for by their former masters were transferred to the charge of the counties on the ground that they were citizens and entitled to poor relief, as clearly as were indigent whites.[6] During the fifteen months ending September 1, 1866, the

[1] Throckmorton to Heintzelman, and Heintzelman to Throckmorton, MS. in *Executive Correspondence.*

[2] Gammel, *Laws of Texas*, V, 928, 942, 1035.

[3] See MS. in *Executive Correspondence.*

[4] *Official Records, War of Rebellion*, Ser. I, vol. xlviii, pt. i, p. 301. Sheridan seemed to believe that the whole affair was a mere ruse to get the military out of the way in order that the freedmen and unionists might be left defenceless against "rebel" hostility.

[5] *Supra*, p. 71 *et seq.*

[6] Kiddoo, *Circular Order*, no. 16, June 18, 1866.

average number of rations issued daily in the whole state was only twenty-nine.[1] The number of pupils enrolled in the schools for freedmen was over four thousand five hundred, with forty-three teachers.[2]

The most constant watchfulness had not been sufficient to hold the negro to his contract, and, in his own interest as well as that of the planter, appropriate measures had been taken from time to time to keep him in the fields until the crop was gathered. On this account Kiddoo became convinced that contracts for labor should be made for the entire year instead of by months, especially in the cotton-growing districts.[3] In order to protect those who were employed by the month he ordered that all unpaid wages were to be held as a first lien on the crop, regardless of sales, rents, or other claims whatsoever; and that, where so specified in the contract, payments should be made in specie or its equivalent in currency at the time the contract was made.[4] Later, in the cotton-picking season, the officials of the Bureau were instructed to see that the freedmen who had worked on shares got their just portion of the crop and the market price for it. When necessary the agents were to arbitrate differences arising out of claims for supplies furnished the freedmen during the summer; but, except in extreme cases, this was to be avoided, and the agents were to confine themselves to the arbitration of differences arising out of written contracts for labor.[5] By a later order, he

---

[1] Howard, *Annual Report, House Exec. Docs.*, 39th Cong., 2 sess., I, 745.

[2] *Ibid.*

[3] Kiddoo to Howard, in *Flake's Weekly Bulletin*, August 22, 1866.

[4] *Circular Order*, no. 19, August 20, 1866, in *Executive Correspondence.* Paper money was at a discount at this time.

[5] *Circular Order*, no. 21, October 1, 1866, in *Executive Correspondence.*

insisted that no contract for labor to which a freedman was a party could be regarded as finally settled until arbitrated and fulfilment certified to by an officer of the Bureau.[1] In order to avoid misunderstanding growing out of indefinite terms in the contracts, all agents were instructed to take care that in the contracts for the next year every detail of the agreement should be specified and that nothing be left to be " understood "; and they were also required to urge the freedmen to take a portion of the crop rather than monthly wages.[2] The labor law devised by the legislature was repudiated by Kiddoo and contracts made in accordance therewith were disapproved; but General Griffin, who succeeded Kiddoo on January 24, 1867, uniting the military command of the state with the control of the Bureau, adopted some of its provisions. Contracts for labor could be drawn up before and ratified by a civil magistrate or any two disinterested witnesses, provided that a copy was sent to Bureau headquarters; a copy was also to be filed with the county clerk.[3] Within a few weeks Texas was again under military rule, when there was no question of the relative status of the civil and the military authority; but the Bureau had never been in doubt of its own authority and the protests of the state officials had made little impression upon its policies.

Hampered as he was on all sides by the open hostility of the radicals, the suspicion of the military officials, and the thinly veiled antagonism of the old secession wing of his own party, Throckmorton had maintained his difficult posi-

[1] *Circular Order*, no. 23, November 1, 1866, in *Executive Correspondence;* also in *Southern Intelligencer,* November 15, 1866.

[2] *Circular Order*, no. 21, December 25, 1866, in *Southern Intelligencer,* January 3, 1867.

[3] See *Flake's Weekly Bulletin*, February 6, 1867; also *Southern Intelligencer,* February 14, 1867.

tion with dignity and a large measure of success. Although prevented from affording relief to the suffering frontier, and unable to eliminate entirely the jurisdiction of the Bureau, he was, nevertheless, making steady progress in restoring the state to order and in inculcating a respect for legal processes. Much still remained to be done; but as lawlessness and violence gradually became less prevalent, the military had shown a tendency to acquiesce more and more in the extension of civil jurisdiction, and one can not escape the conclusion that, had Congress kept hands off, Texas would have been fully restored in a short while to that condition of real peace which it was the professed aim of the Reconstruction Acts to bring about.

PART II

CONGRESSIONAL RECONSTRUCTION

CHAPTER VII

THE UNDOING OF CIVIL GOVERNMENT

1. *The Reconstruction Acts*

ALTHOUGH neither in its form nor in its content could it have been accurately anticipated, the Reconstruction Act that became law March 2, 1867, was not wholly unexpected by well-informed people in any part of the South. The increasing strength and activity of the Radicals during the previous year, the general resentment of the North at the rejection of the Fourteenth Amendment by the southern legislatures, the widening breach between the moderate Republicans and the President, and the overwhelming support given to his opponents in the fall elections, had made it plain enough that Mr. Johnson's plan for the restoration of the southern states was already defeated when the Thirty-ninth Congress met for its last session. The question now was as to the plan that would be substituted for his.[1]

Although they had been slow to formulate any program of their own, the majority in Congress felt that something must be done towards settling affairs in the South before the close of the session on March 4th. Thaddeus Stevens had endeavored to force through a purely military bill, destroying the existing state governments, establishing martial law, and leaving the whole matter of re-admission to be arranged by the incoming and more radical Fortieth Congress; but the moderates were unwilling to become respon-

[1] See *Texas Republican*, January 5 and 12, 1867; *San Antonio Daily Herald*, Jan. 9, 10, and 14, 1867; other papers, *passim*.

sible for a scheme so drastic and so fraught with perilous precedents, and they succeeded in engrafting upon the bill a plan for the resuscitation of civil government.

In brief, the first Reconstruction Act [1] declared that no legal state governments or adequate protection for life or property existed in the " rebel " states; that they should be divided into military districts, of which Louisiana and Texas should constitute the fifth; that to the command of each district the President should appoint a general officer of the army, whose duty it should be to protect all persons in their rights of person and property, to suppress insurrection, disorder, and violence, and to punish disturbers of the peace and criminals. At the discretion of the commander, local civil tribunals could be allowed to try offenders or they could be tried before military commissions; and there should be no interference, under color of state law, with the exercise of military authority. However, no sentence of a military commission, affecting the life or liberty of any person, should be executed until approved by the district commander. It was further provided that whenever the people of any state, through a convention chosen by universal manhood suffrage (excluding such persons as were disfranchised for participation in the rebellion or for felony, or were debarred from holding office by the Fourteenth Amendment), had framed a constitution in conformity to that of the United States, and when such constitution had been ratified by a majority of the persons voting thereon and had been approved by Congress, and when the state legislature had adopted the Fourteenth Amendment, the state should be readmitted to the Union and its senators and representatives to Congress. Finally, it was declared that the existing state (Johnson) governments should be deemed

[1] *Acts and Resolutions*, 39 C., 2 s., p. 608. Also in Fleming, *Documentary History of Reconstruction*, I, 401.

provisional only, " and in all respects subject to the paramount authority of the United States at any time to abolish, modify or control, or supersede "; and that in elections held under them the same rules as to suffrage should apply as in voting for the constitutional convention, and the same disqualifications for holding office as were provided by the Fourteenth Amendment.

This act, however, failed to provide the initiative machinery for calling the constitutional conventions; and one of the first measures of the Fortieth Congress was the Supplementary Reconstruction Act of March 23rd,[1] designed to remedy this defect. It provided that the commanding general in each district should, before September 1st, cause a registration to be made of all qualified citizens in each county, and that each citizen so registering should take an oath that he was not disqualified by law; that, at an election subsequently to be held at a time designated by the district commander, the voters should vote for or against a convention and choose delegates to the same; but no convention should be held unless a majority of the registered voters should have participated in the election and a majority of those actually voting should have favored the convention. If declared for by a majority of voters, the convention should be called at a time and place designated by the military commander; and the constitution framed by it should be submitted to the qualified voters for ratification; and, if ratified by one-half of those actually voting—provided that the total number of actual voters equaled half of the registered voters—and approved by Congress, the state should be declared entitled to representation in Congress.

The purpose and effect of these two acts was to paralyze the state governments that had been restored since the war,

---

[1] *Acts and Resolutions*, 40 C., 1 s., p. 260. Also in Fleming, *op. cit.*, I, p. 407.

to place the whole South under potential martial law, to disfranchise the leading whites, and to enfranchise the blacks. It was expected by the framers and advocates of these measures that the negroes and their white radical friends would control the states, thereby insuring " loyal " governments. The authors of these acts had insisted that the South was in a condition bordering upon anarchy and that this was due to the rebellious and disloyal disposition of its people, that everywhere unionists and loyal freedmen were unsafe, were being outraged and murdered. Never, perhaps, was punitive legislation founded upon a more distorted array of evidence, upon a worse misrepresentation as to facts. Some few select witnesses had been examined, a great number of anonymous complaints of persecuted loyalists had been aired, but in the case of no state had there been an honest effort to gain an impartial knowledge of the whole truth, certainly not in Texas. It should be remembered that the accused were given no opportunity to state their own case, or to answer the allegations against them; at best, their protests were simply ignored. The only statements that gained credence were those of military officials, usually not unprejudiced and frequently imposed upon by designing persons, and of local radical politicians who were laboriously striving to excite feeling against the state government in order to serve their own ambitious purposes. It will be remembered that a number of Texas radicals spent the winter of 1866-67 in Washington in close attendance upon the radical leaders in Congress.

The people of Texas were not wholly surprised at the sentence pronounced upon their government by Congress, but they were not prepared to receive it with perfect equanimity. However, after the first bitterness had spent itself somewhat, the press, influenced perhaps by the governor, began to advise quiet submission to the will of Congress as the less of two evils—since delay would bring only harsher conditions—and to urge all who could to register as voters.[1] But neither press nor people were at heart reconciled to their political degradation, and while the latter for the most part relapsed into sullen despair, the former could not refrain from indignant and bitter comment.

2. *The Provisional State Government and the Military Commanders*

On March 19th, General Sheridan, who was already stationed at New Orleans as commander of the Department of the Gulf, was made commander of the new Fifth Military District, consisting of Louisiana and Texas. General Charles Griffin, already at Galveston, remained as commander of the District of Texas. As a soldier Sheridan had shown abilities that approximated to genius and he was justly popular in the North; but he was now called upon to perform duties and to carry out a task that demanded other qualities than those requisite for a military campaign, and his arbitrary methods as well as the harshness and suspicion which he had always manifested towards the people of the South, particularly of Texas, were not reassuring to those who had to live under his heavy hand.

Throckmorton, however, firm in the belief that every law should be honestly obeyed as long as it was the law of the land, and desirous of maintaining the most friendly relations with the military commanders, in order that some degree of civil government might be preserved in Texas, on March 27th telegraphed Sheridan requesting an opportunity to confer with him in order that the civil authorities of the state might co-operate to the best advantage with the military in executing the recent legislation of Congress.[2] He

---

[1] *San Antonio Daily Herald*, March 13, 17, 21, 26, 1867; *Texas Republican*, June 29, 1867.

[2] See Throckmorton, *Address to the People of Texas,* pamphlet in Texas State Library; also printed in the *Dallas Herald*, September, 1867.

received the curt reply that the civil authorities of Texas could assist in the reorganization of the state only by strongly supporting the military commander and by advising the people to participate with good feeling in the reorganization under the law; and that the details of the work in Texas had been entrusted to General Griffin.[1] To this the governor replied that the people of Texas would co-operate in carrying out the congressional plan, though they regarded the terms as onerous and oppressive.[2]

Despite the ungracious attitude of Sheridan, due perhaps to their earlier controversies, Throckmorton was hopeful of maintaining cordial relations with Griffin. But though he seemed to succeed for a time, he never really enjoyed the confidence of this officer, who was unable to comprehend his real unionism, but, like Sheridan, lumped all ex-Confederates together and hastily identified anti-radicalism with disloyalty. The governor's moderation, his efforts to follow a middle policy removed from the radicals on the one hand and from the secession leaders on the other, was lost upon the general as it was upon the secessionist extremists, who never had forgiven and never afterward forgave Throckmorton for his stand against them in 1861. On March 28th, Griffin had written to Sheridan that none of the civil officers of Texas could be trusted; for, though they would submit to the laws because they could not do otherwise, they nevertheless thought them unjust and oppressive; and " the laws ought to be executed in *spirit* ". He charged that the governor had allowed outrages upon loyal whites and blacks to go unpunished, and advised his removal as " absolutely necessary ", together with that of the lieutenant-governor, G. W. Jones. Judge C. Caldwell, an ultra-

---

[1] Telegram from Sheridan, in *Executive Correspondence*.

[2] Copy in *Executive Records, Register Book 84;* also in Throckmorton's *Address*.

radical, was recommended in the place of Throckmorton. Sheridan sent the letter with a favorable endorsement to Grant, who advised against the removals until it should become clear that the authority for such action belonged to the military.[1]

The acts of Congress had left the civil government of the state " provisional only, and in all respects subject to the paramount authority of the United States to abolish, modify or control, or supersede "; but the extent to which interference should be undertaken was apparently left to the discretion of the military commander of the district, subject, of course, to the approval of the President as commander-in-chief. Because, therefore, so much depended upon the course the commander would take, Throckmorton endeavored, as soon as possible, to come to a general understanding with him. On April 3rd, he wrote to General Griffin, asking how vacancies in state and county offices should be filled—whether by the governor's appointment, or by elections ordered by him, the persons so appointed or elected not being disqualified by the third section of the proposed Fourteenth Amendment. With reference to the disqualification of persons who, after taking an oath to support the Constitution of the United States, had taken part in in-

---

[1] Sen. Ex. Docs., 40 C., 1 s., no. 14, pp. 194-195. It may be that the governor had given Griffin some offense just before this by refusing to comply with the remarkable request that he pardon the two hundred and twenty-seven negro convicts then in the Huntsville penitentiary. A Bureau inspector, W. H. Sinclair, later to become a prominent radical politician under the carpet-bag regime, had interested himself in their behalf, and had readily accepted the statements of the negroes themselves that their offenses were wholly trivial. The governor easily disproved this, and went into a patient argument to show the fairness of the trial of freedmen, their frequent pardons at his hands, and the danger to society and to the freedmen themselves of granting the request for such a wholesale pardon. *Executive Records, Register Book 84*, p. 284.

surrection or rebellion, he also requested that the general give his construction of the term " executive or judicial officer of a state ", as to whether it should be extended to include clerks of courts, sheriffs, constables, coroners, notaries public, and so on. The governor, naturally, inclined to a narrower construction.[1] Griffin, not inclined to pass on the troublesome point himself, referred the query to Sheridan, who, on April 13th, answered Throckmorton as follows:

You can appoint to all vacancies which occur among your own appointees. You cannot appoint to any elective position. You are not authorized to call elections; and no elections will be permitted in your state until they are ordered, under the law, by the military commander. Any vacancies which occur by elections being forbidden will be filled by the military commander. The other questions in your letter will be settled authoritatively before the elections are ordered.[2]

In conformity with instructions sent at the same time to Griffin, the latter embodied the above pronouncement in a special order, which further required the governor to report to military headquarters all appointments made by him.[3] Throckmorton, thereupon, sent to Griffin a list of all officers that were appointed under the state law. The whole subject, then, of appointments to office in the civil government, with trifling exceptions, was summarily taken out of the hands of the governor, and he was given no satisfaction as to the last part of his question. Beyond doubt, Sheridan, in this extensive assertion of authority, was taking the course that the majority in Congress desired; but he seems

---

[1] *Executive Records, loc. cit.,* p. 296; also in Throckmorton's *Address.*
[2] MS., in *Exec. Corres.;* copy in Throckmorton's *Address.*
[3] Special Orders, no. 66, copy in *Exec. Corres.*

to have been actuated as much by his old suspicions of the people and authorities of Texas, as by his regard for the wishes of Congress.

On April 4th, Griffin wrote to Throckmorton, soliciting his aid in registering the qualified voters of the state—asking for the probable white and black vote of each county, and for the names of persons, irrespective of color, who could act as registrars and take the test oath, *i. e.,* the " ironclad oath ". The governor immediately issued a circular address to all county judges requesting them to forward the required information without delay. He concluded by urging upon them and the people of their respective counties " the propriety and absolute necessity, at this juncture of our affairs, of contributing to the fullest extent every aid possible in order that the military authorities may be enabled to execute the acts of Congress properly and fairly ".[1] The replies came in promptly and rapidly, and were forwarded to General Griffin with the assurance that the state officials were anxious to observe the law and aid in its execution.[2]

Although he knew nothing of Griffin's request for his removal, the governor soon found himself deprived of the hope of maintaining amicable relations with the military. The fact that each approached the delicate problems involved in the situation from a different point of view would alone have made a working agreement difficult enough to keep; but there was added the other factor of radical political opposition to the governor. Hardly had Congress pronounced its anathema against the state government, when the radical papers began a systematic attack upon the whole force of state officials, and radical politicians and office-seekers began to file complaints against " rebels in author-

[1] *Executive Records, loc. cit.,* p. 302. Published in *Southern Intelligencer,* April 11, 1867.

[2] *Executive Records, loc. cit.,* p. 307.

ity " with both Griffin and Sheridan.[1] On April 15th,
Throckmorton had complained to Griffin of the " lying and
slanderous attacks " of certain newspapers, and insisted that
he was exceedingly desirous to have the laws executed and
peace and good feeling restored; that he advocated compliance with the law, not because he approved it, but because
it was better to act under it than longer delay restoration.[2]
Griffin replied politely, expressing his gratification at these
assurances and adding that when such a favorable disposition should become " both sincere and prevalent in Texas "
the work of reconstruction would present no difficulties.[3]
The retort courteous was, on the occasion of transmitting
the lists from the county judges of persons qualified as registrars, that these promptly furnished lists were the evidence
of a desire, " both sincere and prevalent ", to aid in executing the law of Congress.

There seems no room to doubt that Throckmorton was
acting entirely in good faith. When a complaint came from
a group of unionists at Prairie Lee that freedmen and Union
men were being outraged and murdered by " reconstructed
rebels ", he immediately had a military force sent to maintain order. By his request soldiers were sent also to Lampasas County to assist the courts and the peace officers.
About the last of April he received notice from Griffin that
the latter was in receipt of a petition from sixty citizens of
Parker and Jack counties charging that in that district
Union men were being robbed and murdered with impunity,
that the guilty were never punished in the courts, that certain Union men acquitted of charges in Hamilton's administration were about to be tried again, and that the judges
of the courts were inciting rebellious sentiments. At once,

[1] See *Reconstruction Correspondence of General Grffin, MSS.*, filed
with *Exec. Corres.*

[2] *Executive Records, loc. cit.*, p. 300.

[3] MS. in *Exec. Corres.*; quoted in Throckmorton's *Address.*

April 29th, he wrote to County Judge Hunter of Parker County and Judges Good and Weaver of the fifth and seventh judicial districts, reciting in each case the substance of the complaints and asking for statements and sworn evidence as to the facts alleged. Urging upon them that the laws must be impartially enforced and every person protected in life and property, particularly that Union men should be protected and all excitement and prejudice allayed, he informed them that troops would have to be sent there, and that he intended to request that a discreet officer of the army be detailed to examine into the procedure of their courts. Writing the next day to General Griffin, he assured the commander from his personal knowledge of that region that both sides had been guilty of outrages, but that if it could be shown that any civil officer was guilty as charged he should be removed and punished. " I shall by no act of mine seek to smother investigation, screen guilt, or avert the blow when justice demands that it fall." In conclusion, he defended the character of the judges in question, but requested that troops under discreet officers be sent to the seat of trouble and that another discreet officer be detailed to watch the work of the courts.[1]

So many complaints had gone into headquarters, however, that the commander was still suspicious, if not of the governor, at least of the courts. On April 15th he had ordered that such criminal cases as could not be tried impartially in civil courts should be carried to his headquarters for trial before a military commission.[2] On April 27th he issued from Galveston the famous *Circular no. 13*, generally known as the " Jury Order ".[3] It ran as follows:

[1] Letters from Griffin, Good and others in MSS., *Exec. Corres.;* copies of Throckmorton's letters in *Executive Records, loc. cit.,* pp. 317-321.   [2] *Annual Cyclopædia,* 1867, p. 714.

[3] Printed in Sen. Ex. Doc. 40 C., 1 s., no. 14, pp. 208-209; *Texas Republican,* May 11, 1867, and in Throckmorton's *Address.*

The attention of the Commanding General of the District having been directed to the fact that persons disqualified by law are drawn to serve as jurors in the civil courts of the State of Texas, it is hereby ordered that hereafter no person shall be held as eligible to serve or to be sworn in as a juryman until he shall have taken the following oath:

Here followed the text of the iron-clad oath,[1] after which the order continued:

To prevent the exclusion of loyal citizens from the jury box on account of race or color, and for the guidance of officials authorized to impanel juries in the State of Texas, the following section of the Civil Rights Bill is published:

Then followed the second section of that act.[2]

Just what General Griffin meant by the assertion that persons " disqualified by law " were being drawn to serve as jurors is not easy to determine. It could not have been the state law that was being violated, for the courts were anxious to observe that. The Reconstruction Acts under which he was professedly acting had stipulated nothing as to jurors, unless jurors were to be regarded as officers of the state; and even in that case the only qualification de-

---

[1] *Supra*, p. 116, note 4.

[2] "Any person who, under cover of any law, statute, ordinance, regulation, or custom, shall subject, or cause to be subjected, any inhabitant of any state or territory to the deprivation of any right secured or protected by this act, or to different punishment, pains, or penalties on account of such person having at any time been held in a condition of slavery or involuntary servitude, except as a punishment for crime where-of the party shall have been duly convicted, or by reason of his color or race, than is prescribed for the punishment of white persons, shall be deemed guilty of a misdemeanor, and, on conviction, shall be punished by a fine not exceeding one thousand dollars, or imprisonment not exceeding one year, or both, in the direction of the court." —*U. S. Statutes at Large*, vol. xiv. p. 27.

manded was innocence of felony and the ability to take the oath prescribed by the Fourteenth Amendment—one not so stringent as the iron-clad oath. Indeed, it is difficult to find any legal warrant for an order prescribing the test oath except by construing jurors in this case to be " officers of the United States "—at best a strained construction—nor is it easy to see any point in the reference to the second section of the civil rights act; for nowhere in that act was jury service named as one of the civil rights to be secured to all citizens " of every race and color "; and debarring negroes from the jury could not be a violation of the act.

Copies of the order were sent the governor with directions that he distribute them to the judicial officers of the state and see that the order was " rigidly enforced ".[1] Throckmorton sent it out as required, and, in the circular letter accompanying it, admonished all officers that they should earnestly and diligently discharge their duties in order to secure a faithful and efficient administration of the laws. However, he stated that in view of the difficulties that must result from an observance of the order he would transmit a copy of it to the President for his consideration. In his letter to the President, May 2d, he stated that if the law should prove to be in accordance with the laws of the United States, it should be complied with without question; but, if otherwise, it was in the interest of justice that proper orders be issued for its discontinuance. He also pointed out that the federal judges in Texas had ruled that the petit jurors of their courts were not required to take the iron-clad test oath; and he stated the qualifications of jurors under the Texas law.[2] Finally, he insisted that the enforce-

[1] Griffin to Throckmorton, *Exec. Corres.*, quoted in full in Throckmorton's *Address.*

[2] The juror must be over twenty-one years of age; a white citizen, —of the state twelve months, of the county six months; a householder

ment of the order would necessarily stop the operation of the courts in many sections of the state.[1]

As might have been expected, this order threw the courts into the greatest confusion. The governor's office was flooded with letters from the county and district judges reciting their difficulties and asking for further information and advice. One question that arose immediately was whether the order set aside the qualifications required by state law or whether it was cumulative in effect—that is, whether taking the test oath was to be only an additional qualification, so that it would not be necessary to go back of the county jury list already provided. Several judges were inclined to act upon this latter interpretation, which was supported by the governor, and which, as it developed, General Griffin himself had expected to be followed.[2]

This view, however, resulted practically in disqualifying most of the white population by requiring the test oath; and in disqualifying nearly all of the negroes and most of the remaining whites by the demands of the state law. In consequence judge after judge reported that he had been unable to find full juries, and that except for such business as could be transacted without a jury, the work of the court had stopped.[3] Some few were able to get juries in certain

in the county, a freeholder in the state; and eligible to vote for members of the legislature. Negroes it will be seen, were debarred. This was by an act of 1858.—See Gammel, *Laws of Texas*, IV, p. 1076.

[1] *Executive Records, loc. cit.*, p. 323; also in Throckmorton's *Address.*

[2] R. A. Reeves to Throckmorton, May 8; John G. Good to Throckmorton, May 11; J. J. Holt to Throckmorton, May 13; Whitmore to Throckmorton, May 14; MSS. in *Exec. Corres.*; excerpt from *Flake's Bulletin* in *Weekly Austin Republican*, July 4, 1867; Throckmorton to Whitmore, *Executive Records, Register Book 85*, p. 115; Griffin to Sheridan, Sen. Exec. Doc. 40 C., 1 s., no. 14, p. 210.

[3] Various communications, Reeves, Templeton, Ector, Holt, Harrison, Good, Whitmore, Storey, Perkins, *et al.* to Throckmorton, MSS. in *Exec. Corres.*

counties of their districts, but not in others. Some suggested that the right to serve be extended to all registered persons, though this involved a departure from the state law.[1] Others, however, refused to do this because, in substituting disqualified for qualified jurors, they must disregard their oath of office, and, ceasing to be officers of the state, become mere agents of the military power, thrusting upon the citizens jurors who were irresponsible, ignorant, and incompetent, in cases affecting rights of property, life, and liberty.[2] The conservative newspapers denounced the order as full of mischief and danger. The *Texas Republican*, May 11, 1867, claimed that forty-nine-fiftieths of the white men of the state would be disqualified for jury service, and that the result would be to throw " the lives and liberty, as well as the property of the people into the hands of the negroes, who were themselves considered so imbecile as to require especial guardians in the shape of Bureau officers and supervising agents ". *Flake's Bulletin,* on the other hand, asserted that under the old system it had proved impossible to secure convictions for murder, especially of unionists, and that it had been decided by the commanding general, " after consultation with the highest jurists of the state ", that " the most simple, prompt, and direct remedy would be to compose juries of loyal men ".[3] This statement was evidently inspired by Griffin, who wrote Sheridan that the jury order was only " an attempt to open the courts of Texas to loyal jurors for the protection of all good citizens ".[4]

---

[1] Thos. Harrison to Throckmorton, May 14, Jas. G. Storey to Throckmorton, May 18, 1867, MSS. *ibid.*

[2] S. W. Perkins to Throckmorton, May 22, 1867, MS. *ibid.*

[3] Excerpt in *Weekly Austin Republican*, July 4, 1867.

[4] Sen. Exec. Doc., *loc. cit.*, pp. 209-210.

But whatever the motive or the justification, it is certain that the confusion and demoralization wrought in the court system by this " Jury Order " was responsible in a large degree for the undoubted increase of lawlessness in the latter part of 1867; although other causes, to be mentioned later, contributed to that end. The order seems to have remained in force until September 28th, when Sheridan's successor, General Mower, ordered that only persons registered as voters under the reconstruction laws should be eligible as jurors. The test oath was no longer required.[1] This greatly widened the class of persons from which jurors could be drawn; and though it included all negroes, it admitted most of the whites also, and was less dangerous than Griffin's order.

Whatever the part they played in launching the Jury Order, it is not difficult to detect the hand of the local radical leaders in the series of controversies into which the governor and the military officials were now plunged. One of these disagreements arose out of an act of the recent legislature. The constitutional convention of 1866 had provided for reducing the number of judicial districts and redistricting the state, for the sake of economy, and because the populated area of most of the western counties had shrunk before the continuous attacks of Indians. In pursuance of the plan there outlined, the legislature had abolished five districts—namely, the fourth, fifth, seventh, eleventh, and seventeenth—and had enlarged and renumbered the rest. It so happened that, in two of the districts abolished, the judges and attorneys were Union men, in the other three the officials were ex-Confederates.[2] Three

---

[1] Special Orders no. 151, copy in *Exec. Corres.*

[2] See statement of J. L. Haynes to Griffin, Sen. Ex. Doc., *loc. cit.*, pp. 221-222.

other Union men were left untouched, but the radical press
seized upon the fact that " loyalists " had been deprived of
office, and protests were lodged with Griffin and Sheridan.
On June 10th, the latter issued an order annulling the act
which had abolished the fourth and eleventh districts, and
reinstating Judges Thomas H. Stribling and W. P. Bacon,
who, being " strong Union men ", had been set aside solely
" on account of their political opinions, regardless of the
public interest ".[1] Throckmorton immediately called the attention of the President to all the facts in the history of the
case, pointed out that Sheridan's order did not restore the
three other districts or the judges who had been elected in
them, and showed how great would be the confusion re-
sulting from such action.   He took advantage of the opportunity further to show, by orders and communications which
he enclosed, how the military of all ranks were constantly
interfering with the action of the civil courts, requiring
judges and attorneys to dismiss prosecutions for criminal
offenses, and in some cases destroying court records and
papers.   He was careful to admit the power of the military
commanders under the acts of Congress to *withdraw* cases
from the civil courts, but questioned their right to *dismiss*
cases without trial.[2]   In this particular the governor
stated his contention with skill and discrimination, and perhaps a close and narrow construction of the acts of Congress would sustain him; but the intention of that body to
give the military supreme control over all civil processes
was too clear to leave hope of effective support to Throckmorton from the President.

By this time the process of registration of voters for the
future elections was in full swing.   The state had been

[1] Special Orders no. 65, *ibid.*   Also printed in Throckmorton's *Address.*

[2] *Executive Records, loc. cit.,* p. 340; also in Throckmorton's *Address.*

divided into fifteen registration districts, comprising from six to eleven counties each; and over each district were placed two supervisors. In each sub-district, generally a county, was a board of three registrars, which was to move from place to place in the county in order to facilitate the registration of voters. Upon completion of registration within the sub-district the registrars were to make out lists showing the total number of voters registered, the number of colored voters, the number of rejected applications for registration, and the reasons for the rejection; and finally to state whether they had reason to believe that all the legal voters in the sub-district had been registered, and, if not, the reasons for the belief.[1] In many counties considerable difficulty was experienced in securing for supervisors, registrars, and clerks, whites who could take the test oath required of all officials, and it was generally necessary to place negroes upon the boards; but the latter were in no way discriminated against, and quite frequently, it seems, they were appointed when whites were available. The work proceeded slowly, for although the freedmen were generally eager to exercise their new prerogative, many of the eligible white conservatives held back, sometimes because of indifference, sometimes because of repugnance to the policy of Congress, sometimes because they disliked to appear before a board of negroes. The governor and the conservative press generally urged upon all white citizens the " solemn duty " of registering in order that they might still have some share in the affairs of the state, which would otherwise fall entirely into the hands of the radicals and negroes.[2]

Soon, however, arose complaints that many persons apparently eligible under the laws were denied the privilege

---

[1] Circular no. 16, May 16, 1867, in *Exec. Corres.*

[2] *Galveston Tri-Weekly News*, June 9, 1867; *Texas State Gazette*, July 13, 1867.

of registration. At Galveston, for instance, the board was accused of denying registration to persons who had supported the Confederacy but had never previously taken an oath to support the Constitution of the United States.[1] The editor of the *Galveston News* was rejected because he had once been mayor of Galveston, the only office he ever held, and had later given aid and comfort to the rebellion. When he insisted that he was not disfranchised by the law, the board replied that he was by their instructions; " nor did they refer to the law but to their instructions for their authority ".[2] It developed upon inquiry that every one who had held an office from the highest to the lowest was thereby disqualified, if he had later supported the Confederacy. This was directly ignoring the construction of the law enunciated by the Attorney-General of the United States, and in defiance of the instructions given the military commanders by the President on June 20th.[3]

In fact, Sheridan had been acting upon his own construction of the law, and distrusting Johnson and Stanbery, continued, with Grant's connivance, so to do.   Early in April, when about to begin registration in Louisiana, he had asked Grant for instructions as to who were eligible for registration.   The question was submitted to the Attorney-General and Grant told Sheridan to go on giving his own interpretation of the law in the meantime.   The latter immediately drew up instructions for his registrars, employing the most stringent interpretation by applying the widest possible construction of the term " executive or judicial officer of a state ".[4]   When he had received the Attorney

---

[1] Communication from " J. S." in *Galveston News*, June 9, 1867.

[2] *Ibid.*, July 14, 1867.

[3] See Sen. Ex. Doc., *loc. cit.*, pp. 262-287.   Richardson, *Messages and Papers*, vol. vi, p. 552.

[4] Sen. Ex. Doc., *loc. cit.*, pp. 196, 199-200.

General's opinion, Sheridan complained to Grant of its embarrassing effects upon his " just course ", and asked if he should regard it as an order. He received the reply that it had not been issued in the manner of an order and that he should enforce his own construction of the law until ordered to do otherwise.[1]

These instructions or memoranda were not published and were evidently intended for secret use. Later, when Griffin began the work of registration in Texas, they were transmitted to his registrars also. It was impossible, however, to keep them secret, and as soon as Throckmorton discovered that the registrars were making use of them, he wrote General Griffin asking for copies of his instructions for guidance of registration. The commander disingenuously sent copies of other orders, none of them in the remotest degree related to the memoranda in actual use. Thereupon the governor sent a copy of the memoranda which had come into his possession, and asked if they met with his approbation.[2] Griffin made no reply, and to that extent displayed

---

[1] Sen. Ex. Doc., *loc. cit.*, pp. 236-237.

[2] Throckmorton's *Address.*—The memoranda ran as follows: " Memoranda of disqualifications for the guidance of the boards of registration under the military bill passed March 2, 1867, and the act of Congress supplementary thereto, passed March 23, 1867:

1. Every person who has acted as United States Senator or Representative.

2. All who have acted as electors of President or Vice-President.

3. Every person who has held any position in the army or navy of the United States.

4. All persons who held any position under the United States in which they were required to take an oath before they entered upon the duties of office; such as officers in the custom houses, post offices, mint, judges, and all officers of the United States court, United States marshals, and deputies.

5. All who have held any office in any state under the constitution and laws in force prior to February 1, 1861, such as governor, state senator or representative, secretary of state, treasurer, comptroller,

discretion; for it would have been difficult even for a lawyer to have argued for the construction which he and Sheridan placed upon these acts of Congress, and Griffin had the disadvantage of not being a lawyer. This, be it remembered, was before the second Supplementary Act of July 19th, which was designed to relieve the military commanders, particularly those of the Fifth District, of any embarrassment from excess of radical zeal.

It was daily becoming more and more difficult for the governor and other civil officials to continue friendly relations with the military authorities; and the Texas Radicals were doing their full share towards widening the breach.

auditor, commissioner of land office, surveyors and deputy surveyors, judges of courts, county commissioners, county treasurers, justices of peace, clerks of courts and deputies, sheriffs and deputies, constables and deputies, tax collectors, assessors, coroners, police jurors, auctioneers, pilots, harbor masters, recorders of conveyances and mortgages, county recorders, notaries public, and all commissioned officers in state militia; any person who has acted as mayor of any town or city, treasurer, comptroller, recorder, alderman, assessor, tax collector, administrator of the charity hospital, member of the board of health, commissioner of elections and his clerks, chief of police, lieutenant of police, town or city marshal, and all who have served on the police force, wardens and underwardens of county prisons or work houses; board of school directors, city surveyors and deputies, city attorney and assistant attorneys, superintendent of public schools, inspectors of tobacco, flour, beef, and pork, weighers and measurers, managers and superintendents or directors of asylums for deaf, dumb, blind, and lunatic, and sextons of cemeteries.

6. All who in 1862 or 1864 registered themselves as aliens, or who obtained protection papers from representatives of foreign powers.

Any person who at any time held any of the above offices and who afterward engaged in rebellion against the United States, or gave aid and encouragement to the enemies thereof, is disqualified from voting."

There followed a series of questions to be asked applicants for registration as to whether they had held any of the above named offices and had afterward been in any branch of the Confederate service. A slightly variant form of the above, designed for Louisiana, is printed in Sen. Exec. Doc., *loc. cit.*, and in Fleming, *op. cit.*, vol. i, p. 433-435.

The invalidation of the state government and the provision for registering the negroes as voters had been the signal for active reorganization in the Radical camp for the purpose of bringing the colored brethren into line and teaching them their duties and obligations to the party that had done so much for them. Organizations of the Union League,[1] devoted to this lofty purpose, sprang up wherever there were negroes to vote and " loyalists " to lead them. Throughout the latter half of April, May, and June loyal mass meetings were held everywhere for the purposes of effecting local organizations, arousing enthusiasm, and choosing delegates to a state convention at Houston. In practically all of them resolutions were passed pledging support to the recent legislation of Congress and the military officials, and declaring for full equality for all persons in civil and political rights. The freedmen greatly predominated in all of these meetings and exercised their new privileges with the greatest enthusiasm.[2] The state convention assembled at Houston early in July, with representatives from twenty-seven counties present. Ex-Governor E. M. Pease, who had recently returned from the North, presided. Like many others of his party, he had greatly changed his views since twelve months before when he had declared his opposition to negro suffrage. A state Republican party was organized; but the resolutions adopted were fairly moderate in tone. They ad-

---

[1] The first reference to the Union League in Texas that the author has seen is in a letter, dated April 26, 1867, from A. M. Boatright, who signs as " correspondent of the Union League of Goliad County," to General Griffin, complaining that there were " rebbles " in authority who should be replaced at once with good Union men.—MS. in *Exec-Corres.* ·There are numerous references to the League thereafter.

[2] For accounts of these mass meetings see *Flake's Bulletin, Southern Intelligencer*, and *Austin Republican*, for April, May, June, and July, 1867. The party name adopted varied,—Unionists, Unionist Republicans, Republicans and Radicals.

vocated free common schools and free homesteads out of the public lands to all without distinction of color, thanked the military for protection afforded to the people, declared the Conservatives to be disloyal and to have manifested a " contumacious spirit of hostility " in the opposition shown to the measures of Congress but denied that the Republicans had ever sought to have the Federal government deal harshly with them.[1]

During all this time the Conservatives had done nothing, for there was nothing that they could do but await the issue. It was not long in coming. The Radicals were not content with perfecting their organization and registering their followers in preparation for the elections to the convention. Insisting that the safety of loyal citizens and the proper carrying-out of the laws of Congress necessitated putting the control of the state into the hands of loyalists, and that the rewards of office should be reserved only for the faithful, they began a systematic attack upon the whole line of the state's officials, but concentrated chiefly against Throckmorton. A group of Radical leaders established at Austin a paper which speedily became the party organ, the *Austin Republican*. From its first issue on June 1, 1867, it leveled its guns against the governor. Through the Radical press and letters which poured into military headquarters from Union Leagues, his administration was accused of incompetency, inefficiency, and rank disloyalty. It was asserted, and Griffin eagerly reiterated the charge, that Throckmorton encouraged the oppression and murder of Union men and refused to do anything toward having the criminals punished.[2] It is but justice here to say that a careful examination and review of all the evidence accessible does

[1] See account of the convention in *Weekly Austin Republican*, July 11, 1867.

[2] *Ibid.*, July 25; Sen. Ex. Doc., *loc. cit.*, p. 194.

not in any way justify these accusations. Many cases cited and complained of had not even come to the governor's attention until brought up by the military, for the simple reason that the complaints had been filed not with the civil officials but with the military instead. In all other cases which came to him he showed the most evident anxiety to have the law enforced.[1]

By the middle of July it had become evident that the governor would soon be set aside. Griffin and Sheridan both wished it and only awaited full authority to take the step. Some small officials had gone already.[2] On July 19th the second supplementary Reconstruction Act became a law and bestowed full power of removal and appointment upon the military commanders, freeing them at the same time from any obligation to respect the opinions of the Attorney-General in construing the law.[3] The Radical press confidently prophesied the sweeping out of the whole administration.[4] One of his own party, a Conservative-Unionist, B. H. Epperson, who had remained at Washington since winter, wrote Throckmorton with regard to the effect of the new act of Congress:

[1] *Exec. Records, Register Book 85*, pp. 9, 17, 24, 35, 37 and *passim.* Subsequent to March 2 Throckmorton issued twenty-six proclamations for the arrest of murderers, of whom twenty-four were whites; during the same time he issued seven pardons for homicide, six being to whites, five of whom, however, were convicted before 1861, and eighteen pardons for theft, *etc.*, seven being to negroes. See *Exec. Records, Register Book 281.* It may be that this list is not complete, but the proportion will hold.

[2] On June 8, the entire police and detective force of Galveston was discharged by order of General Griffin. Several of the new appointees were freedmen. *Flake's Daily Bulletin,* June 9, 1867.

[3] *U. S. Statutes at Large,* vol. xv, p. 14; Fleming, *op. cit.,* I, pp. 415-418.

[4] See *San Antonio Express,* July 25, 1867; *Austin Republican,* July 25, 1867.

I consider it a settled fact that your head goes off; perhaps your decapitation will be completed before you read this letter. At all events it is but a question of time and the time is short. Pease has gone down to be at the proper place to supersede you. The program has been fixed up here, and a most desperate effort is to be made to radicalize the state. . . . The judiciary will go overboard, and in fact every office worth having in the state has to go into Radical hands.[1]

On July 30th Sheridan issued the following order:

A careful consideration of the reports of Brevet Major General Charles Griffin, U. S. Army, shows that J. W. Throckmorton, Governor of Texas, is an impediment to the reconstruction of that state under the law; he is therefore removed from that office. E. M. Pease is hereby appointed Governor of Texas in place of J. W. Throckmorton, removed. He will be obeyed and respected accordingly.[2]

No official notification of the governor's removal was received at Austin for about a week; but the news had traveled rapidly and the *State Gazette* disgustedly chronicled the " noisy demonstrations of joy made on Wednesday last [August 1st] by the negroes and a few Radicals, over the shameful degradation of the state ". On the 7th, Pease sent a polite note to Throckmorton, whose personal friend he was, enclosing the order, and asking if it would be convenient for him to deliver the office and its records at ten o'clock next day. An equally polite answer was sent that this arrangement would be perfectly convenient, and on July 8th, therefore, Pease formally took possession and notified General Griffin that he had begun the discharge of his duties.[3]

---

[1] July 14, 1867. MS. in private correspondence of Governor Throckmorton.

[2] Extract from Special Orders no. 105, copy in *Exec. Corres.*

[3] MSS. in private correspondence of Throckmorton and in *Exec. Corres.*

The deposed governor immediately prepared an *Address to the People of Texas,* in the form of an elaborate review of his relations with the military officials, in refutation of the charge that he had been " an impediment to reconstruction ". By quoting almost the entire correspondence, he made clear his own efforts to follow out the laws, aid the commanding general, and maintain the peace; and placed the onus of all the difficulties upon the military, whose harshness in the matter of appointments and interference with courts and juries had thrown the whole civil administration into disorder and had aroused bitterness and apprehension in the hearts of the people. Finally, he urged the people to abide by the laws, however unjust they might regard them, to be kind to the negroes, to refute by their conduct the Radical charges of disloyalty, to register if allowed to do so, and to elect good Union men to the convention.[1] The *Address* was widely and favorably commented upon at the time, and was, in fact, more than a refutation of the charge made by Sheridan.

[1] The *Address* was printed by the *Weekly State Gazette,* Aug. 10, 1867; by the *Dallas Herald,* Sept. 7, 1867; and as a pamphlet in 1873.

CHAPTER VIII

RADICAL-MILITARY RULE

1. *Radical Politics and Factions*

IT was, beyond question, exceedingly fortunate for Texas that, if Throckmorton must be removed, E. M. Pease should be his successor; for no other man among the Radicals, with the possible exception of A. J. Hamilton, combined to the same high degree his qualities of firmness, wisdom, and moderation. A native of Connecticut, but a citizen of Texas since 1835, he had taken an active part in public affairs for many years, and up to the eve of the war had been very popular, for his two administrations as governor, 1853-1857, were both progressive and successful; but in the stormy years that followed he cut himself off from public favor by an uncompromising opposition to secession and a constant adhesion to the Union throughout the war. However, unlike most prominent Unionists, he remained quietly at his home in Austin during the struggle. The course of events since the war had not restored him to popular favor. From the first he had been identified with the party led by Governor Hamilton, and had gradually come into opposition to President Johnson and into affiliation with the Radicals. Badly defeated by Throckmorton in 1866, he had joined the group of southern Radicals at Washington in the fight against the Johnsonian state governments. Now he returned in the guise, whether he desired it or no, of an exultant victor over his own people, to supplant by military power the man whom they had preferred over him. He was made to appear as the willing tool of a hated military despot, bartering the honor of the state for political power, and suspected in every action of the most unworthy motives. Truly, his position was in no way an enviable one. As was natural, Pease was judged more harshly by far than he deserved. He always insisted afterwards that he did not seek and did not want the provisional governorship, but that he could not refuse it when it was tendered without subjecting himself to the charge of being unwilling to give his aid to the state in a time of disorder and crisis.[1] It was well for Texas that he gave his aid even at the cost of his own political future, for he was the most moderate of all those who had the confidence of the military authorities; and, though he obediently followed out the measures of his superiors, his advice carried weight as Throckmorton's could not and saved the state from some of the worst consequences of a bitter and often mistaken partisanship.

One of the first as well as one of the most troublesome questions with which he had to deal was that of recommending to vacancies in the various state and county offices. For one reason or another a great many vacancies in elective offices had occurred during the last five months of Throckmorton's administration and many of them had remained unfilled, partly because of Griffin's distrust of the governor and the persons recommended by him, partly because of the scarcity of persons eligible according to Griffin's requirements and at the same time willing to accept office and its accompanying unpopularity. It was now the duty of Pease to find and recommend to Griffin, for he could not make the appointments himself, suitable persons to fill these vacancies, that is to say, Radicals who could take the test

[1] Message to Constitutional Convention of 1868, *Convention Journal*, p. 12. Also, his speech at Galveston, July 12, 1880 (printed by McKenna and Company, Galveston).

oath. In consequence, he was immediately overwhelmed with petitions, not always for offices already vacant, but more frequently for the removal of officials of "rebel" or anti-Congressional proclivities; for now it had become axiomatic with the Radicals that any person who opposed the Congressional plan of reconstruction was perforce a "rebel", perhaps a traitor, no matter what had been his previous attitude toward secession or the Confederacy. General Griffin at once began the removal of county and district judges, in order to finish the work, begun by his jury order, of putting the courts into the hands of "loyal" men. The Conservative heads of the various departments of state administration—the attorney-general, the treasurer, the comptroller, and the land commissioner, all elective—had been allowed to remain in their offices, but they too went out within a month.[1] In every part of the state the local Radicals, agents of the Freedmen's Bureau or correspondents of the Loyal Union League, were busily forwarding petitions for the removal of local officers and recommending suitable successors.[2] In many cases, however, it proved impossible to fill the vacancies thus created,

[1] By Special Orders, no. 160, August 27, General Griffin removed S. Crosby, land commissioner; W. L. Robards, comptroller; M. H. Royston, treasurer; and W. M. Walton, attorney-general, "on account of their known hostility to the general government"; and replaced them with Joseph Spence as land commissioner, M. C. Hamilton as comptroller, Jno. T. Allen as treasurer, and Wm. Alexander as attorney-general. Order in *Exec. Corres.;* printed in *Texas State Gazette,* Sept. 7, 1867.

[2] Some of these petitions from the Union League associations are curious documents. One from Dallas County, asking for the removal of district and county officers, has about eighty signatures, practically all in the same handwriting as that of the petition. It meant of course, that the petitioners were nearly all negroes taking the first steps of their political tutelage, if indeed they had even authorized the use of their names. MS. in *Exec. Corres.*

sometimes because there were not enough competent Radicals to go around, sometimes because those who were competent would not accept the positions. A. H. Latimer, a prominent unionist of Red River County, could find " only one true loyal man " in Bowie County.[1] Another unionist, Judge M. D. Ector, declared to Governor Pease that there were numerous vacancies in Shelby, San Augustine, and Harrison counties and that it was " practically impossible to find Union men to fill them, for the few who are qualified decline the positions ".[2] " There are not a dozen outspoken white Radicals in the whole Eighth Judicial District," wrote Judge C. Caldwell.[3] An agent of the Bureau admitted that it was " impossible to find enough loyal men qualified to fill the offices " in Robertson and Milam counties; and for that reason recommended that of the twenty-one officials in the former county, fourteen be retained, and of a like number in Milam, eight be retained.[4] A dozen similar statements, all from Radical sources, could be cited. Yet removals went on almost daily. The governor requested the removal of Judge J. J. Holt because, when serious disturbances in Goliad and Victoria counties, both in his district, required action, the judge insisted that his court had been closed by the jury order.[5] The death of General Griffin, September 15th, in the midst of the scourge of

---

[1] A. H. Latimer to Lt. Kirkman, A.A.A. General, Aug. 15, 1867, *ibid.*

[2] Ector to Pease, Sept. 13, 1867; *ibid.*

[3] Caldwell to Pease, Aug. 20, 1867; *ibid.*

[4] J. L. Randall, Sub. Ass't. Comnr., to General Griffin, Aug. 26, and Sept. 4, 1867. *Ibid.*

[5] Pease to Griffin, Sept. 5, 1867, *ibid.* Pease refused to believe that Holt could not get juries, because there had been a large registration in those counties. Not all qualified voters, however, could serve on juries, for the iron clad test oath was at that time required of the juror but not of the voter; and moreover, the requirements of the state law as to jurors was still in force. See *supra*, p. 157.

yellow fever that swept over the coast and far up into the interior of Texas that summer, did not stop the work of " purifying " the state. He was succeeded by General J. J. Reynolds, a less able and also a less scrupulous man, who was soon credited by the Radical organ, the *Austin Republican,* with having swept out the " rebel " officials in over sixty counties.[1]

It was to be expected, doubtless, that these removals would take place. Both the governor and the military officials felt that the progress of reconstruction would be facilitated by putting the administration of the country, even in local matters, in the hands of those who were in sympathy with the Reconstruction Acts. Then, too, they were constantly urged on by many who were either solicitous for preferment or actuated by rancor against political or private enemies. Nor can it be doubted that the old prejudice against unionists and the new prejudice against Radicals was too often manifested in the acts of civil officials, and gave color to the charge that better protection was needed for " loyal " citizens. Nevertheless, it was not a good thing for society, at a time when a recent political upheaval made it necessary that every facility possible should be offered for the preservation of order, that nearly one-third of the county offices should be vacant, and that some districts should be entirely without any peace officers. Texas in those days suffered greatly from violence even under normal conditions, and indeed retained some of the turbulence of frontier society for two decades longer; but it is pretty clear that the crime and disorder that reached such an alarming state during the administration of Pease, was due in a large measure to the mistaken policy of the military authorities.

Conditions had been improving up to April, 1867. Throckmorton had made earnest efforts to suppress lawless-

[1] Issue of Nov. 13, 1867.

ness, and had accomplished much; but with the issuance of the jury order which crippled the courts; with the constant interference, more frequent now, of the military in civil matters; and with the growth of party rancor, the lawless element seized upon its opportunity and an increase of crime was noticeable nearly everywhere. Then came, after the change of governors, the further crippling of the state's authority by the bestowal of vacated offices upon unpopular men, who were viewed not as representatives of the state but as the minions of an arbitrary military power, and by allowing to remain vacant many positions of the greatest importance to the peaceful ordering of society. Another complication in the southern and eastern sections was the confusion and demoralization wrought by the yellow fever scourge. Under all these conditions it was next to impossible for the officials to maintain order, not because the people were "disloyal" to the United States government, as the Radicals asserted, but because the very foundations of order had been taken away.

Hardly had the Radicals got control of the state administration when they fell out among themselves over the question of the validity of the constitution and legislation of 1866. Governor Pease had assumed that all state laws not in contravention of the acts of Congress or the Federal constitution, and not specifically annulled by order of the military commander, were, though provisional in character, actually in force and binding upon all state officials and citizens. In this he followed the example of Governor Hamilton in 1865, and had the express sanction of the military officials themselves.[1] It was clearly the only course that could have been taken in view of expediency, common sense, and custom. However, it soon developed that a small group of ultra Radicals at Austin, some of them members of the

[1] Sheridan, General Orders, no. 1, March 19, 1867.

governor's own official family, had conceived the notion that
the Reconstruction Acts of Congress not only had destroyed
the existing state government but also had rendered its acts
null and void from their inception. According to this
strange theory all legislation of whatever character since
March 1, 1861, was swept away, every public or private
relation based upon any law enacted during this period was
invalidated. The consequences of such a condition, the
doctrinaire authors of the theory themselves, perhaps, did
not clearly see; but, even granting the saving application
of the constitution of 1845, society must have been thrown
into the greatest confusion and uncertainty without advanc-
ing any necessary purpose of state policy.

The first intimation of the existence of such a body of
doctrine is in a scathing editorial in the *Austin Republican,*
October 23, 1867, denouncing the state supreme court for
rendering a decision to the effect that the state constitution
of 1866 and the laws passed under the authority thereof, in
so far as not abolished, modified, or superseded by the
United States or its officers, were valid and binding.[1]   The
Republican at this time was owned chiefly by local politicians, of whom Morgan C. Hamilton, a brother of Governor A. J. Hamilton, was one.   Soon afterwards control
of the paper passed into the hands of the moderates supporting Pease.   It was not long before the actual breach
came.   Just before this, M. C. Hamilton, as comptroller,
had refused to issue to certain state officials salary warrants
on the treasury in accordance with an act of the recent
legislature appropriating money for the support of the state
government for the years 1867 and 1868.   The opinion of
the attorney-general, Alexander, was invoked and he sus-

[1] This seems to have been the case of L. S. Shrader *vs.* The State
of Texas, 30th Texas Reports, 386. See also Smith *vs.* Harbert, and
Luter *vs.* Hunter, *ibid.*, pp. 669 and 688.

tained Hamilton.[1] Thereupon, the governor, in order to fix the law, issued, on October 25th, with the consent of General Reynolds but against the protest of Hamilton, Alexander, and Allen,[2] a proclamation declaring the constitution of 1866 and the statutes passed in conformity thereto, with certain exceptions, to be " rules for the government of the people of Texas and the officers of the civil government ".[3] Alexander promptly resigned and sent in to General Reynolds a lengthy protest against the proclamation, chiefly to the effect that the constitution of 1866 had never become valid because it had never been accepted either by Congress or by General Sheridan, and that the constitution of 1845 should be held as the real one.[4] Hamilton also protested to General Mower, then commanding the Fifth Military District, rehearsing much the same arguments used by Alexander; but he did not resign, for which display of " lack of taste " he was severely criticised by his former organ, the *Republican*.[5] Reynolds transmitted to Mower a copy of the proclamation and Alexander's protest against it; Mower agreed with Pease and submitted an opinion from J. P. Boyd, his attorney for civil affairs, who also sustained Pease.[6]

[1] D. J. Baldwin to Pease, Oct. 23, 1867; MS. in *Exec. Corres.* For Alexander's opinion, see appendix to *Convention Journal, 1868-9*, 1st Session, pp. 968-977.

[2] M. C. Hamilton to General Mower, Oct. 29, 1867; in *Austin Republican*, Nov. 13, 1867.

[3] *Annual Cyclopædia*, 1867, p. 715.

[4] *Austin Republican*, Nov. 16, 1867; also appendix to *Convention Journal*, 1868, 1st Session, 962-968.

[5] Issue of Nov. 13, 1867.

[6] Mower, by Col. W. T. Gentry, to Reynolds, Nov. 23, 1867; MS. in *Exec. Corres.* Boyd held that only laws passed in hostility to the United States government were null and void *ab initio*. The others, as the one in question, were only voidable at the will of the district

Though defeated, the *ab initio* Radicals did not give up the fight. They managed to get control of the local branch of the Union League long enough to formulate resolutions demanding of the state Republican party that new planks be added to the Houston platform:[1] one, declaring that emancipation of all slaves should date from January 1, 1863; one, that all ex-rebels should be disfranchised; another, that all legislation in Texas since 1861 had been null and void from the beginning and should be so considered.[2] The *Austin Republican* severely arraigned the "pronunciamiento" of the "misanthropic old bachelors" who were "attempting the formation of a negro party", and declared their resolutions "infamous", because they proposed

> to disfranchise all the whites of the state except a few of the elect, to strip them of their property, to exact back hire for negroes for the years 1863 to 1865; in a word to place all political power in the hands of the negroes and then vote themselves all the property in the state. . . . They are trying to lead the colored race to destruction. We do not believe that fifty whites or five hundred colored men in the state will endorse them, even with this stupendous bribe.[3]

Ex-Governor A. J. Hamilton, who returned to Texas at about this time as associate justice of the state supreme court, threw the whole weight of his influence into the scale against his brother and on the side of Pease.[4] These two brothers, so unlike in so many ways, soon became the

commanders. The distinction between "void absolutely" and "voidable" had been sanctioned by Congress and maintained in practice.

[1] *Supra,* p. 166.

[2] Printed in *Austin Republican,* Dec. 18, 1867.

[3] *Ibid.,* Dec. 25, 1867.

[4] See speech of A. J. Hamilton, *ibid.,* Dec. 18, 1867.

leaders of the rival factions which were to fight two years longer for the control of the state. A. J. Hamilton became in a short time the candidate of the Republicans of Travis County to the coming constitutional convention. The *ab initio* wing bolted and nominated Morgan C. Hamilton, but he afterwards withdrew from the ràce in Travis and announced himself as a candidate from the neighboring county of Bastrop. The two came face to face again in the convention.

2. *Removal of Sheridan and Reversal of Military Policy by Hancock*

Hardly had the Radicals got firmly in control of the state administration through the sweeping changes effected by Sheridan, when they were deprived of the watchful oversight of that zealous partisan. He had for a long time given offensive evidence of his sympathy with the political enemies of the President and had exerted all his influence to wreck Mr. Johnson's reconstruction policy. In the quarrels which he had waged with the governors of Louisiana and Texas the latter had succeeded in enlisting the sympathy of the President, who was convinced that neither had attempted to thwart the execution of the laws of Congress. The arbitrary and offensive manner in which Sheridan had exercised his authority, capped by the removal of Governors Wells and Throckmorton, further convinced Mr. Johnson that the testy general's presence in the South was itself an impediment to a peaceful and orderly reconstruction.[1] In spite, therefore, of the protests of Grant, with whom Sheridan was always a favorite, the President on August 17th ordered that General George H. Thomas should take the command of the Fifth Military District, and that Sheridan

[1] Washington correspondence of *Boston Post*, quoted in *Houston Telegraph*, Sept. 3, 1867.

should be sent to the upper Missouri. Grant, in issuing the order, endeavored to maintain Sheridan's policies by instructing General Thomas to continue to execute all orders he should find in force in the district, unless authorized by the General of the Army to annul, alter, or modify them. Some ten days later, however, General Winfield S. Hancock was substituted for Thomas, whose health was bad, and the President took occasion to direct that the new commander should exercise any and all powers conferred by Congress upon district commanders, thus intimating that he should have a free hand.[1]

Hancock did not proceed immediately to New Orleans, and the command devolved for the time upon General Griffin, who continued energetically along the lines that he and Sheridan had been following. Upon Griffin's death, September 15th, he was succeeded by General James A. Mower, then in immediate command of Louisiana, who followed a more moderate policy, until Hancock assumed command at New Orleans, November 29th. Hancock had done brilliant service as a corps commander during the war, and was popular in the North. He was, however, a Democrat, he disliked the Radical program, and strongly sympathized with the policies of the President. He believed that the white people of the South should carry through the process of reconstruction with as little interference on the part of the military as possible, and entertained the most cheerful view of the self-sustaining powers of the civil authority. In " General Orders, no. 40 ", announcing his assumption of command, he gave expression to this optimism and to his purpose to reverse the policies which Sheridan had followed.

The General Commanding is gratified to learn that peace and quiet reign in this Department. It will be his purpose to preserve

[1] Report of Sec'y of War, House Ex. Docs., 40 C., 2 s., no. 1, pp. 26-27.

this condition of things. As a means to this great end he regards the maintenance of the civil authorities in the faithful execution of the laws as the most efficient, under existing circumstances.

In war it is indispensable to repel force by force, and to overthrow and destroy opposition to lawful authority. But when insurrectionary force has been overthrown and peace established, and the civil authorities are ready and willing to perform their duties, the military power should cease to lead, and the civil administration should resume its natural and rightful dominion. Solemnly impressed by these views the General announces that the great principles of American liberty still are the lawful inheritance of this people, and ever should be. The right of trial by jury, the [right of the writ of] *habeas corpus,* the liberty of the press, freedom of speech, and the natural rights of persons and the rights of property must be preserved.

Free institutions, while they are essential to the prosperity and happiness of the people, always furnish the strongest inducements to peace and order. Crimes and offences committed in this district must be referred to the consideration and judgment of the regular civil tribunals, and those tribunals will be supported in their lawful jurisdiction. Should there be violations of existing laws which are not inquired into by the civil magistrates, or should failures in the administration of the courts be complained of, the cases will be reported to these headquarters, when such orders will be made as may be deemed necessary.

While the General thus indicates his purpose to respect the liberties of the people, he wishes all to understand that armed insurrections or forcible resistance to the law will be instantly suppressed by arms.[1]

This generous and enlightened policy could have been more successfully applied to Texas six months earlier when

[1] Report of Secretary of War for 1868, H. Ex. Docs., 40 C., 3 s., vol. i, p. 210.

the administration of the civil authority was more unified
and harmonious; for in the present disorganization and confusion, when there was a total lack of sympathy and of confidence between the new Radical appointees on the one hand
and the remaining Conservative officials, backed by the
great mass of the people, on the other, there was small
chance that it could be carried out in the spirit in which it
was conceived. Hancock's determination to respect the
regular civil tribunals seemed to threaten the powers of the
new state administration and brought him at once into conflict with Pease.

The occasion was this. In October, 1867, a Union man,
R. W. Black, had been murdered in Uvalde County, west
of San Antonio. The accused parties had been arrested and
confined in the county jail, when the district judge, G. H.
Noonan, a Radical, suggested to Pease that they be tried
by a military commission, for he thought it extremely doubtful whether they could be kept in confinement long enough
to be tried before a civil court in this thinly populated district. Pease agreed and sent Noonan's letter with his endorsement to General Reynolds, who naturally referred the
whole matter to his commanding officer. The governor
had failed to state very clearly the grounds for his request,
and Hancock replied that he could see no reason for violat-
ing the principle laid down in his recent proclamation, more
especially as it had not been charged that there was any in-
disposition or unwillingness on the part of the local civil
tribunals to try the case fairly. While it was not to be
denied that the act of March 2d conferred upon the military
commander of the district the power to organize military
commissions for the trial of criminals, it was nevertheless
an extraordinary power and from its nature should be exercised only in the extraordinary event that the local civil
tribunals were unwilling or unable to enforce the laws.
From this, Hancock went on to read the governor a lecture
upon the subject of civil liberties.

At this time the country is in a state of profound peace. The state government of Texas, organized in subordination to the authority of the government of the United States, is in full exercise of all its proper powers. The courts, duly empowered . . . are in existence. . . . That the intervention of this power [the military] should be called for or even suggested by civil magistrates, when the laws are no longer silent and the civil magistrates are possessed, in their respective spheres, of all the powers necessary to give effect to the laws, excites the surprise of the Commander of the Fifth Military District.

In his opinion it is of evil example and full of danger to the cause of freedom and good government that the exercise of military power through military tribunals . . . should ever be permitted when the ordinary powers of the existing state governments are ample enough for the administration of the law . . . [and the officers] are faithful in the discharge of their duties.

If the state authorities were not able to secure the confinement of the prisoners until trial, Hancock continued, sufficient military aid would be furnished; if the prisoners could not be fairly tried in that county, a change of venue should be made, as provided by the state law. The state possessed all the powers necessary for a proper and prompt trial of the prisoners, and a failure to exercise them must be due to the inefficiency of its officers; and in the case of any such failure it would become his duty to remove the officers in question and to appoint others. And if these should fail and it should become apparent that not enough could be found in Texas who would enforce the law, it would then become necessary for him to employ military commissions; but until such a necessity should be shown to exist, it was not his intention to have recourse to them.[1]

---

[1] See Report of Secretary of War for 1868, *loc. cit.*, pp. 244-246. A printed copy of the letter is in *Exec. Corres.*

On January 17, 1868, Pease replied, dissenting on purely legal grounds from the declaration that the state government of Texas was " in full exercise of all its proper powers ", citing the language of the reconstruction acts of Congress to show that such civil government as Texas had was provisional only. He also dissented from the statement that the country was " in a state of profound peace ", insisting that, although there was no longer any organized resistance to the authority of the general government, the bitterness aroused in a large majority of the population by defeat, the loss of slaves, and the policy of Congress, together with the demoralization wrought by civil war, had made it very difficult and often impossible to enforce the criminal laws. The greater part of his letter was an elaboration of this assertion. Over one hundred homicides, Pease said, had occurred in Texas during the past twelve months, but less than one-tenth of the offenders had been arrested and half of these had not been tried. Even the military had often been unable to arrest the guilty parties, although the latter were well known. Often the civil officials failed because not properly sustained by the citizens, and, after arrest, the criminals often escaped from custody because the jails were insecure and the counties were unable to furnish proper guards. Moreover, it often happened that grand juries failed to indict the accused and petit jurors to convict those finally brought to trial. All good citizens acknowledged there was but little security for life in Texas, and many of the loyal citizens had expressed the belief that it would have a good effect if military commissions could be employed to make examples in a few cases. In fact, the governor continued, the fear of military commissions had had a markedly deterrent effect upon crime until the publication of General Hancock's General Order no. 40, November 29th; since then there had been a very perceptible in-

crease of crime and manifestation of hostile feeling toward
the government.

If all these matters had been known to the Commanding General of the Fifth Military District, his surprise might not have
been excited that a civil magistrate of Texas, who is desirous
of preserving peace and good order and to give security to
person and life, should have applied to him as the chief
officer to whom the government of Texas is entrusted by the
laws of the United States, to do by military authority what
experience has proved cannot be done by the civil officers of
Texas with the limited means and authority with which they
are invested by law.[1]

Evidently nettled at the tone of Pease's reply, which had
been given to the newspapers, Hancock immediately telegraphed Reynolds to ascertain " in the most expeditious
manner " how many cases of crime were known to have
occurred in Texas since his (Hancock's) assumption of
command, how many had been reported by the civil authorities to Reynolds, how many by Reynolds to Hancock,
whose fault it was if criminals were running at large, and
how many applications had been made by the governor
upon the military for aid in arresting these criminals.[2]
Reynolds called upon Pease for such information as was in
his possession, and it developed that only eighteen cases of
homicide had been recorded for the period of Hancock's
incumbency, that in no case had the governor appealed to
the military to make an arrest, and that only four cases had
been referred to the district headquarters; furthermore the
eighteen homicides were all of such character as to pre-

[1] Pease to Lt. Col. W. G. Mitchell, in *Austin Republican*, Jan. 29,
1868. Also in Report of Secretary of War for 1868, *loc. cit.*, pp.
268-271.

[2] Hancock to Reynolds, telegram, Jan. 30, 1868, in *Exec. Corres.*

clude the charge that they were attributable to General Orders no. 40. In a final reply, Hancock pointed out these facts, and proceded vigorously to deny that lack of respect for the government and prevalence of crime constituted a war status or necessitated military courts, and to criticise the governor for his implied censure of the civil authorities, most of whom were now his own political friends, and for the " indications of temper " and " intolerance of the opinions of others " in which his letter abounded.[1]

This closed the correspondence but not the controversy. A strong backing by the military was absolutely essential to the efficiency of the Radical state administration, and, while in respect to most matters General Hancock stood ready to help, all possibility of sympathetic co-operation had been destroyed by the recent unpleasantness, in which, moreover, the commander's thinly-veiled antagonism to the whole Radical program had become sharply revealed. He became at once the object of a most bitter attack. The charges of Pease that he was responsible for the general increase of lawlessness were violently reiterated by the Radical papers, and a clamor, echoed in the North, went up for his removal. However, his tenure was not directly affected by this, for when he was relieved of the command of the Fifth District, March 28, 1868, it was at his own request.[2]

There is abundant evidence that there had been an increase of disorder and crime during the winter; but that it was due to the pacific policy of Hancock is not so easily apparent. By far the greater part had in no way grown out of political animosities but flourished in the confusion that Sheridan, Griffin, and Reynolds had wrought among the

---

[1] Report of Secretary of War for 1868, loc. cit., pp. 262-268.

[2] This request was due to Grant's revocation of his orders removing certain members of the board of aldermen of New Orleans. See Report of Sec'y. of War for 1868, loc. cit., pp. 208, 222-232.

courts and the peace officers. For this much the Radicals themselves were more directly responsible than their opponents. It is true, on the other hand, that political enmity had increased, that conflicts, riots, and outrages were not unusual, and that the Conservatives, or " rebels " as their opponents uniformly called them, were more often, though by no means always, the aggressors; but it is still to be remembered that the sources of this increase of bitterness are to be found in the humiliations forced upon the majority of the people in the execution of the Radical policy, and for this also the peculiar harshness of the military officials in the Fifth District were mainly responsible.

Long before Hancock's assumption of command the *State Gazette* had complained of the " incendiary publications " of certain radical papers as tending to inflame the minds of the negroes and " to disturb the friendly relations which ought to exist between the races ".[1] Later, reverting to the subject, it called attention to the fact that nearly all negroes were carrying arms, especially pistols and long knives, and were displaying them on all occasions.[2] To this the Radicals replied that the blacks had as much right to carry weapons as the whites, a proposition that did not readily commend itself to the majority of the latter, who beheld in the armed negro, insolent and swaggering, puffed up with new and indigestible theories of equality, the most intolerable of created beings. The appointment of negro registrars, who were frequently disposed to make too much of their new authority, increased the irritation. Negro political meetings, generally under the auspices of the local Union League, harangued by fervid orators and enlivened by parades and " Yankee " or " anti-rebel " songs, never failed to stir popular wrath. It is surprising, not that these de-

[1] September 28, 1867.   [2] November 20, 1867.

monstrations sometimes resulted in riots, but that the riots were not more frequent. Probably the disturbance of this sort that aroused the most attention, though it seems to have been far from serious, occurred at Marshall on December 30th, where a pistol shot fired by a drunken man broke up a negro gathering at the court house just after a radical speech by Judge C. Caldwell, of the state supreme court. The next day Caldwell, a man of excitable temperament, quarreled with the deputy sheriff, who seems to have been in no way responsible for the trouble, and obtained the arrest of nearly all of the local peace officers by the military. They were released, pending trial, by writ of *habeas corpus,* but before the trial came off they were again arrested, by orders apparently of General Reynolds. Hancock ordered that the writ be respected and that they should be tried by the civil courts, winning for himself renewed abuse from the Radical press.[1] Caldwell wrote wrathfully to Pease:

> None but a Johnson man would be tolerated here. He must *cuss Congress* and damn the *nigger.* . . . General Hancock is with the President *politically* and will only execute the letter of the law to escape accountability. . . . There is not an intelligent rebel in all the land who does not so understand him. . . . He might regard such an interpretation of his course as an affront, but it does not alter the fact.[2]

Complaints of strong anti-radical sentiment came from various quarters. In Fannin County the numerous executions issued for the public sale of landed property were paralyzing the country, the secessionists using the machinery of the courts " to come down upon Union men with

[1] See Report of Sec'y of War for 1868, *loc. cit.,* 253, 254-258 for Hancock's order and the report of special inspector, W. H. Wood. See accounts in *Austin Republican,* Jan. 8, 15, 1868.

[2] January 2, 1868, MS. in *Exec. Corres.*

much vim and apparent satisfaction ".[1]   A rather panicky official wrote from Palestine of petty persecutions he suffered there and declared his belief that there was a secret organization of " rebels " there to murder all Radicals and office-holders of Unionist proclivities.[2]   The Bureau agent at Sherman asserted that the people in that region had been well disposed until they had been persuaded by General Orders no. 40 that the civil authorities were superior to the military.   Now there could be no protection or justice if the troops should be removed; more cavalry was, in fact, desirable; and the *Sherman Courier* should be suppressed.[3] Another Bureau agent in Dallas County reported that the " rebels " were very bitter and continually making threats.[4] A more measured statement of the difficulties in the way of executing the criminal law in one district, was that of Judge Thornton, of Seguin.   " Where the black man alone is concerned, there can be no cause of complaint; if guilty, he will probably be convicted, if innocent, he will be acquitted." Such, however, was not the case with white men charged with the higher crimes of violence against the person.

From my experience I regard it as almost an impossibility under existing arrangements to convict a white man of any crime, the punishment for which involves his life or his personal liberty, where the proof or any *material part of the proof* depends upon the testimony of a black man, or where the violence has been against a black man; and as to convicting a

---

[1] Samuel Galbraith to E. M. Pease, Jan. 23, 1868, *ibid.*

[2] Judge Tunstall to Gen. J. J. Reynolds, March 26, 1868, *ibid.* Tunstall must have found comfort in office, nevertheless, for he was both county judge and postmaster, and later became secretary of the constitutional convention.

[3] Report of H. E. Scott, Sub. Ass't Commissioner, to J. J. Reynolds, March 31, 1868, *ibid.*

[4] Wm. H. Horton to Reynolds, Dec. 11, 1867, *ibid.*

white man of the crime of murder in the first degree on any
kind of testimony, it is almost out of the question. . . . I can
suggest no means by which I think the civil courts can remedy
the evil without a change in the public sentiment of the
country.[1]

Much of the evidence presented on the subject of lawlessness is of a most partisan and untrustworthy character. A
noteworthy instance of the way in which facts were distorted for political purposes is to be found in what purports
to be the report of the district clerk for Blanco County—
printed in the *Austin Republican,* March 4th, and copied by
the *New York Times,* March 18, 1868—of the state of the
criminal docket of that county. In brief the statement as
printed was that since June, 1865, the grand juries had
issued 178 indictments, of which 83 were for murder and
61 for theft and robbery, while the registered vote was only
120, due to the number of murders. The clerk, however,
indignantly declared that his report had been falsified, that
not a single murder had been committed in Blanco since the
date given, but that all of the 83 indictments had been returned by "loyal" juries for the killing of seven "bushwhackers" during the war, and that most of the other
offences charged had likewise been committed before June,
1865. The small number of registered voters was due, he
declared, to the ignorance and politics of the registrars.[2]

No county or district in the state, however, was wholly
free from these disorders, and though they seem to have
been most prevalent in the north and east, all sources of
information fully attest that they were quite too numerous
everywhere. Yet it may not be amiss to repeat here that the
evidence fails to show that more than a very small per-

[1] J. J. Thornton to Pease, Feb. 10, 1868, MS. in *Exec. Corres.*
[2] *San Antonio Daily Herald,* June 10, 1868.

centage of the cases of actual violence at this time originated in differences of political opinion. The continuous and peculiarly offensive activity of branches of the Union League and the Grand Army of the Republic among the negroes with the view of securing political control through the black vote, had brought into existence the counter organization of the Ku Klux Klan. This last had but recently appeared in Texas; it could not have been very extensive as yet, nor did it deserve the sinister reputation that it later acquired; but it grew rapidly both in membership and reputation during the following summer. Its operations, however, had from the first called forth the bitterest invectives from its enemies, who were quick to see its dangerous possibilities and to threaten retaliation. The *Austin Republican* declared that

the Union League and the Grand Army have learned many valuable lessons from the Rebels and it will not take them long to learn another. Their organization is as perfect as that of the *Ku Klux Klan,* and if driven to extremities they can do as effective work.

The radical papers and politicians continued to charge all their troubles to Hancock's encouragement of " disloyal malignancy ", and appealed to the coming convention to do something to stop the " saturnalia of blood ".[1] The matter of lawlessness was, in fact, one of the first things taken up by the convention, and it will be necessary to revert to the subject again in narrating the history of that body. We must now turn our attention to the preparations for assembling this convention, which was to carry out the will of Congress and of the " loyalists " of Texas.

[1] The *Austin Republican,* April 1, and 22, May 13, and 20, 1868; *Exec. Corres., passim,* for spring of 1868. Unreasoning partisanship could go no further than to call a man with Hancock's record a " copperhead " and " rebel ", yet it was done habitually.

It will be remembered that the process of registration of the voters had been begun by General Griffin early in the summer of 1867, and that the registrars had been governed by secret memoranda which rigidly excluded many citizens who believed themselves entitled to registration under the law. The work went on slowly from May to the end of August, generally without interruption, though disturbances and threats against the registrars were reported from several places. By order of Griffin, the offices of registration were again opened in each district from September 23rd to 28th to enable any who had been neglectful of the privilege to avail themselves of a last opportunity.[1] That a relatively small number of conservatives had registered was due in no way, therefore, to lack of time, nor was it wholly because of the zeal of radical registrars, although the latter was no inconsiderable impediment.[2]

Many of the whites were at first plainly indifferent.[3] Some believed that it was the settled purpose of Congress to shut them out of political power and that it would be useless to try to participate in political affairs. Others held

[1] Special Orders, no. 163, Sept. 2, 1867, copy in *Exec. Corres.*

[2] " The boards in this district have been extremely rigid, and the secessionists have been excluded almost without exception." — H. C. Pedigo (Radical) to Pease, Oct. 1, 1868, MS. in *Exec. Corres.* " In this district lawyers, on account of their oaths as attorneys, have been refused registration. The most impertinent questions have been asked of others—as to which party they sympathized with during the war, —if they would support the present and future laws of Congress,—if they think negroes their equals, *etc.*; and if the answers were not in accordance with the notions of loyalty of these petty scoundrels, the parties were refused registration."—J. W. Throckmorton to Ashbel Smith, Sept. 21, 1867, printed in the *State Gazette,* Oct. 26, 1867.

[3] In Titus County by the end of August only 500 out of 1200 had registered; in Fort Bend only 110 out of 500; and in Harris the total of whites was between 500 and 600 short. Other counties frequently made as bad showing. *Houston Daily Telegraph,* Sept. 5, 1867.

that participation in reorganization under the recent laws would be equivalent to consenting to them, and that the congressional radicals would be encouraged to make further demands in order to give the Texas radicals and negroes the full control of the state. Some seemed to think at first that by a refusal to register they could defeat immediate reorganization and await a better opportunity; meantime, military rule would be preferable to the radical-negro rule they would be subjected to under the Reconstruction Acts.[1] It was soon discovered, however, that this plan would avail nothing, since the calling of a constitutional convention hinged not upon the number registered, but upon whether or no half of the total registration voted afterwards. Should the registration be left wholly to the radicals, who were sure to vote afterwards, there would be no doubt whatever that Texas would be " reconstructed ". Hence, the better way to defeat it would be to register all the voters possible and then to stay away from the election in the hope that less than half of the votes would be cast. Conservative papers unceasingly urged the whites to follow this plan.[2] The *Houston Telegraph* sounded the warning that unless the full strength of the whites should be enlisted there would be no reason to expect that Texas would not be completely in the hands of the negroes, who had as keen a relish for offices as had the whites, and who would satisfy their ambition to own land by taxing it out of the hands of the present owners.[3]

[1] See the public letter of J. W. Throckmorton to Ashbel Smith, *loc. cit.*, in which opposition to immediate reconstruction is urged in the hope of a favorable reaction in the North. Danger of suffering harsher measures, especially confiscation, is declared a "phantom."

[2] The *State Gazette*, Oct. 26, 1867, gave a list of Conservative papers that advocated this plan, including all those of prominence except two, —the *San Antonio Herald* and the *Clarksville Standard*. The *Austin Republican*, Nov. 5, stated practically the same thing.

[3] Sept. 5, 1867.

Probably the known dislike of General Hancock for the extreme radical program and the news of the slight reaction against the radicals in the northern elections during the summer and fall of 1867, had much to do with the growing opposition to reorganization according to the congressional program. But notwithstanding the accusations of his enemies, the commander showed no disposition to play the partisan. He refused to accede to a request of the conservative leaders that he set aside the registration in Texas because of alleged errors of the boards of registrars.[1] In view of the fact that the boards of registrars were left unchanged, it could hardly be accounted a partisan act that on January 11th he announced his dissent from the construction given to the disqualifying clauses of the Reconstruction Acts by Sheridan's " memoranda " and " questions ", and ordered that these boards should no longer be governed thereby, but should " look to the laws and to the laws alone ", which they were to interpret for themselves. Their decisions were to be final, except in cases appealed to the commander of the district. It is not probable that a very great number of cases were affected by this order, for in a considerable number of those that were appealed the boards were sustained. It would be hard to find fault with the reversal of their decisions in the other cases.[2]

On December 18, 1867, Hancock ordered an election to be held at each county seat from February 10th to 14th to determine whether a constitutional convention should be called and to select delegates to the same; and in accordance with the law he also ordered that the registry lists should be

[1] See his answer to John Hancock of Austin, in Report of Sec'y of War for 1868, I, 243; and comment on both letters in *Austin Republican*, Jan. 22, 1868.

[2] See for example a list of Hancock's decisions in Report of Sec'y of War for 1868, I, 239-241.

reopened and revised during the last five days of January.[1]
Voters of both parties who had neglected to register in the
previous summer now hastened to add their names to the
lists. Nearly five thousand were registered during this
time, with the two parties about equally represented, for
two-fifths were negroes. The total registration as stated in
April by General Buchanan, Hancock's successor, was
109,130.[2] The number of those disqualified was not officially estimated but was variously placed from 7500 to
12,000.[3] From the fact that the total white registration
was very close to the total vote in the exciting Throck-
morton-Pease campaign of 1866, it is evident that the
number actually disfranchised was not as high as the Conservatives themselves claimed. The proportion of negroes
seems excessive in view of the census of 1860,[4] but it was
claimed by the radicals that this could be accounted for by
the fact that over a hundred thousand negroes had been
brought into Texas for safety during the war.[5] But even
so, it is doubtful if the list of registered blacks should have
been within 6,000 to 8,000 of the total given.[6]

---

[1] *Op. cit.*, 215-218.

[2] Sen. Ex. Docs., 40 C., 2 s., no. 53. The *Austin Republican*, which
enjoyed facilities for obtaining official information, gave, on November 27, 1867, the total registration, except for a few unimportant
counties, at 104,096; while the total given in the *Annual Cyclopædia*,
evidently taken before the January revision, was 104,259,—56,678 whites
and 47,581 colored. The final registration showed 59,633 whites and
49,497 colored.

[3] *Austin Republican*, Nov. 27, 1867.

[4] The census of 1860 gave the population of Texas as 421,294 whites
and 182,921 colored; that of 1870 gave 564,700 whites and 253,475
colored.

[5] *Austin Republican*, Nov. 27, 1867.

[6] There is no doubt whatever that in many cases the registrars
knowingly allowed negroes under twenty-one years of age to register;

Although it had come to be the general understanding that the conservatives would refuse to vote at all in the election, some of the leaders, not knowing what the final registration returns would show as to their strength, began to fear that with this plan they ran too great a risk of putting their opponents in control. On January 2d, a call was issued from Houston for a general conference of conservatives at that place on the 20th, with the view of agreeing upon a definite program. Most of the press fell in with the idea, though some expressed the fear that a sudden and late change of the plans would create uncertainty and division when unity was most necessary, and thus play into the hands of their enemies.[1] The time was so short that, when the convention met on the day appointed, less than twenty counties were represented. However, resolutions were passed declaring that the one issue before the people of the state, rising above all questions of party, was that of African equality, and that, since it was the declared intention of the radicals in securing a constitutional convention to Africanize the state, it was recommended that all persons entitled to register vote first *against* a convention and then *for* delegates who would frame a constitution without negro suffrage. A state central committee was appointed to establish local committees and to push the work in every county. A special committee, of which John H. Reagan was chairman, issued a public address stating that although the people of Texas were anxious to have the state restored to the Union, necessity demanded that they prevent the incorporation of negro suffrage into the organic law. Disclaiming any intention of giving offense to Congress, they

but on the other hand it was often impossible to know the exact age of a negro, for he usually did not know it himself. In such cases the tendency was to place it sufficiently high.

[1] *Houston Telegraph* quoted in *Texas Republican*, Feb. 1, 1868.

rejoiced " that the terms of reconstruction were to be submitted to them for their approval without Africanizing the
state." Their convention, they said, had adopted a course
which offered to the people three chances to save themselves
and their children from such a fate: first, by defeating the
call for a convention; second, by controlling the convention;
third, by rejecting a constitution that embodied negro suffrage. Reconstruction under the acts of Congress would
be far worse than any military rule. Again the committee
was careful to state that the action of the conservatives was
based upon no spirit of factious opposition to Congress or
of hostility to the negroes.[1]

There was not time enough to canvass the state for the
new program, and in fact, if the election could have been
carried through on the line laid down, it would have availed
little. The *Austin Republican* derided the hopes of the conservatives and expressed the well-founded opinion that even
if the voters of the state should refuse the terms of Congress because the Reconstruction Acts admitted negroes to
the ballot, Congress would not therefore accept *their* terms
and disfranchise men on account of their color; rather, it
would disfranchise enough " rebels " to make certain the
result of future elections. " Negro suffrage is *here*—it is
no longer a question and the failure of a convention would
be just as great a victory for the loyal men as its success." [2]

The election passed off more quietly than might have
been expected. The soldiers had explicit orders from General Hancock to stay away from the polls unless called upon
by the civil officers to assist in keeping the peace. The

---

[1] The minutes of the convention and the resolution are in the
Texas Republican, Feb. 1, 1868. The address of Reagan's committee
is in the issue of Feb. 8. A brief account of the convention is in the
Annual Cyclopædia, 1868, p. 729.

[2] Feb. 5, 1868.

registry boards acted as the officers of election and made returns directly to Hancock's headquarters. The returns failed utterly to justify whatever hopes the conservative leaders may have had. Most of their followers were out of reach of their tardy appeal and refused or at any rate failed to vote at all. The radicals were overwhelmingly victorious; 44,689 votes were cast for a convention and only 11,440 against it.[1] The total vote was slightly more than half the total registration, and the only effect of the Houston convention had been to bring out just enough votes to make the constitutional convention a certainty. The defeated whites relapsed into sullen, despairing inactivity; the conservative papers were filled with the gloomiest forebodings as to the future of both business and political freedom.

[1] The vote as tabulated by General Buchanan was as follows:
For a convention — whites, 7,757; blacks, 36,932; total, 44,689. Against a convention—whites, 10,622; blacks, 818; total, 11,440. Total of vote cast, 56,129. Persons registered who failed to vote, 41,234 whites; blacks 11,730, total 52,964. Sen. Exec. Docs., 40 C., 2 s., no. 63.

CHAPTER IX

THE RECONSTRUCTION CONVENTION OF 1868-1869

1. *First Session*

THE constitutional convention elected under the authorization of Congress—generally known as the "reconstruction" convention, but stigmatized by the Conservative press as the "mongrel" convention—assembled in Austin on June 1, 1868. The delegates were ninety in number, the same as the lower house of the legislature in 1860 and apportioned as nearly as possible in the same way. Six had been in the convention of 1866. Of the twelve Conservatives only one, Lemuel Dale Evans, an exiled Unionist during the war, had been of more than ordinary political prominence. All twelve were from the eastern and northeastern counties, some of which had a heavy negro population. Too weak to carry through any of the principles of their party, they were able to make themselves felt only by holding, when they could, the balance between the two wings of their opponents; though they generally allied themselves with the moderates. Their leaders were L. D. Evans and James Armstrong, of Jasper. On the Radical side the upper councils of the party were well represented. Their delegates included three members of the supreme court, namely, A. J. Hamilton, acknowledged leader of the moderates, and his able supporters, Colbert Caldwell and Livingston Lindsay; also A. J. Evans, of Waco, A. P. McCormick, E. J. Davis, who with M. C. Hamilton, the comptroller, led the ultra-radicals, Armstrong

of Lamar, E. Degener, leader of the Germans of the southwest, G. W. Whitmore, J. W. Flanagan, and F. A. Vaughan.
At least half a dozen of the Radicals had served in the Confederate army, while some fifteen or twenty had been in the
Federal service. Most of these latter were *bona fide* Texans;
not more than six or eight were of the true carpet-bag
variety. The carpet-baggers, none of whom showed conspicuous ability, were led by R. K. Smith, of Galveston, a
Pennsylvanian; they supported the faction of Morgan Hamilton and Davis. There were only nine negro delegates, all
save one from the black districts bordering the Brazos and
Trinity rivers. The exception was G. T. Ruby, of Galveston, a county preponderantly white. Ruby was a mu-
latto carpet-bagger from New England, a man of some
ability and fair education, who generally led the negroes
and threw his influence with the white carpet-baggers for
the ultra-radical policies. He soon became the head of the
Loyal Union League in Texas and was destined for fifteen
years to be the political leader of his race in the state.

Though the lines were not as yet closely drawn between
the two radical factions, each began manœuvering for control and presented its candidate for the presidency of the
convention. E. J. Davis, put forward by the Morgan Hamilton or *ab initio* party, was elected over Judge C. Caldwell,
the candidate of A. J. Hamilton and the moderates, by a
vote of 43 to 33. Davis's career has already been indicated,
as a Federal judge in the southwest before the war, an opponent of secession, colonel of the First Texas (Union) Cavalry and brigadier-general, serving both in Louisiana and
Texas, and delegate to the convention of 1866. He was one
of the first in Texas to espouse the cause of negro suffrage
and was always one of the most radical of the Radicals.
Able, well-known, and popular within his own party, it was
conceded by the *Austin Republican* that only one other man

in Texas, A. J. Hamilton, could have beaten him for the presidency of the convention.

The first two days were consumed in completing the organization of the body. On the third day a message was received from Governor Pease. After referring to the conditions of "extreme difficulty and embarrassment" under which the provisional government had been placed, both because it was distasteful to "the majority of the people who had formerly exercised the political power of the state," and because the commander of the Fifth Military District (Hancock) to whom its powers were subordinate, had sometimes withheld his co-operation and assistance, the governor went on—by inference connecting the two facts— to declare that crime had never been so prevalent as at that time. Since the first of December there had been reported to him, from sixty-seven out of the one hundred and twenty-seven organized counties of the state, two hundred and six homicides. Few of the guilty parties had been punished by the law, and the dereliction of the courts had given rise to mobs and lynching. The first step toward remedying this condition of affairs would be the re-establishment of civil government by renewing the proper relations of Texas with the Union. That was now the work before the convention; but from the temper manifested by the public press, the majority of the white people had not yet profited by their experience, were still scornful of the mild terms offered by the United States, and seemed determined to risk bringing upon themselves harder terms. While not empowered to make recommendations to the convention, the governor ventured to suggest certain lines of action which it was expected would be followed in forming the new constitution. The pretended act of secession and all laws in aid of rebellion or repugnant to the Constitution of the United States should be declared null and void from their inception, and

all laws making any discrimination against persons on account of their race, color, or previous condition, should be
repealed; payment should be provided for the state debt
owing at the beginning of the war, but the payment of all
debts incurred in aid of the rebellion or for the support of
the rebel government should be prohibited; equal civil and
political rights should be secured to every inhabitant of the
state who had not forfeited them by participation in rebellion or by conviction for crime; but a sufficient number
of those who had participated in rebellion should be temporarily disfranchised, in order to place the political power
of the state in the hands of those loyal to the United States
government.   Other measures were recommended, as liberal provisions for public free schools for every child in the
state, granting of a homestead out of the public domain to
every citizen without one, and encouragement of immigration.   With regard to the proposition for a division of the
state, so much discussed of late, the governor expressed the
opinion that the population of the state, only about 800,000,
was not sufficient to bear the expense of two or three governments, and that such a division would not only weaken
the efforts of the government to carry out a system of public
education and other needed measures, but would retard the
re-admission of Texas into the Union, since the Reconstruction Acts provided for only one state in this territory.   A
sort of counter proposition was offered, namely, that the
state government be authorized to sell to the United States
government that portion of Texas lying west of a line
drawn from the mouth of the Pecos river to the northwest
corner of Hardeman County, that is, the southeast corner of
the Panhandle.   The governor thought this region would
never be of great value to the state and that the money derived from its sale could be used very profitably in supporting public education and internal improvements.   The total

amount of money in the treasury at this time and applicable
to ordinary expenses of the state government was some
$203,000, practically all of which was United States cur-
rency. It was believed that $90,000 would cover all the
expenses of this convention, since the convention of 1866
had sat fifty-five days and used only about $70,000. In
such case it would not be necessary to levy the additional
tax contemplated by the Reconstruction Acts.[1] It will be
noticed that the governor showed no disposition to recede
from the position which he had earlier taken in refusing to
consider all acts of the *de facto* governments from 1861 to
1867 and all acts done under their authority as null and void
ab initio; but that he did put himself on record as favoring
the political proscription of enough of the Conservative
whites to enable the Radicals to control the government.

A resolution was carried to require all members to take
the test oath, but when it was found this would exclude a
number of good Radicals, it was hastily reconsidered, and
then the whole subject was postponed indefinitely. The
per diem of members furnished matter for a long wrangle.
A resolution, introduced by Webster Flanagan, to fix the
pay at $15 per day, with mileage to and from the conven-
tion at 25 cents per mile, was rejected in committee, and a
recommendation of $8 per day and $8 for every 25 miles
of travel was substituted.[2] Several efforts to raise the pay
above this amount were defeated, notwithstanding the plea
of one prominent Radical that " the bill would be paid by
the rebels " and that he " would like to handle their money."
The recommendation of the committee was carried.[3] In

[1] *Convention Journal,* 1st sess., 12-17.

[2] This was the pay received by the members of the convention of
1866. They had raised it from $5 because of the depreciated condition
of the currency.

[3] $4 per day was allowed for each clerk, but the official reporter
received $15 per day.

the same resolution the commanding general was requested to authorize an appropriation of $125,000 for the expenses of the convention. This appropriation was approved on July 2d, by General Buchanan, to the extent of only $100,000—ten thousand more than Governor Pease deemed necessary.[1]

But if careful not to be too generous with themselves the members did not forget to be indulgent toward some of their friends. The Radical papers were clamoring for patronage, and when a proposition was brought forward to furnish newspapers to the delegates, a most unseemly quarrel arose between the *Austin Republican* and the *San Antonio Express*. The former had the advantage of location, but the latter had one of its proprietors, Jas. P. Newcomb, in the convention; and when it was proposed to subscribe for 1,800 copies of the *Republican* only, on condition that it print the journal, so bitter a squabble began, so full of personalities, that the president, E. J. Davis, induced the convention to extend the subscription to the papers of Newcomb, who, it chanced, was one of his staunch supporters. As it turned out neither had much cause for complaint; for the *Republican* was allowed $160 per day for 2,000 copies, and its competitor $72 per day for 400 copies of the *Express* and 500 copies of the *Frei Presse*.[2] *Flake's Bulletin*, left out of the patronage, expressed the greatest disgust at this " plundering of the public treasury for the benefit of party newspapers—for which the authors ought to blush ", and furnished its own paper to the members gratis.

The convention was a long time in getting down to the task of making a constitution. There was much preliminary work to be done by the committees, and there was the temptation constantly at hand to bring up matters in no way

[1] *Convention Journal*, 1st sess., 33, 35-38, 46-48, 110, 129, 232.

[2] *Ibid.*, 1st sess., 28, 29, 39, 49-51, 59, 61-63, 75-76, 78.

related to constitution-making. It was generally understood that the constitution of 1845 should be the basis of
the new one, and it was the desire of many members to sim-
plify the task before them by modifying the older constitution only in so far as changes incident to the war had rendered it necessary;[1] but as time went on political exigencies
forced this idea aside.

The question as to the powers possessed by the convention was prolific of debate in the early days of the session.
A strong minority endeavored without success to hold the
body to the doctrine that, since its powers were derived
solely from the Reconstruction Acts and not from the people,
it should restrict itself to the framing of the new constitution. The majority determined that it was a question for
the convention alone to determine what ordinances, declarations, and resolutions were " necessary and proper to carry
out the expressed will of Congress," and thus, though there
seemed to be a general desire to stick to the chief work
before them, the way was opened for the consideration of a
number of extraneous and time-consuming subjects.[2]

The real contest was waged about the *ab initio* question.
Since the controversy aroused by the stand taken by Governor Pease in the previous October, the extremists had been
vigorously at work making converts, and they were now
able to muster a considerable number of the ablest delegates.
These included the president, E. J. Davis, Morgan C. Hamilton, the acknowledged leader of the faction on the floor,
E. Degener, A. J. Evans, an able lawyer and debater, and
G. W. Whitmore, a lawyer and judge who had been long in
politics. Most of the " carpet-baggers " also were *ab initio*
men, such as R. K. Smith and the negro Ruby. Opposed
to them were A. J. Hamilton, Colbert Caldwell, Livingston

[1] *Convention Journal,* 1st sess., 75, 185, 217, 735.

[2] *Ibid.*, 32, 54, 55, 56, 75, 77, 137.

Lindsay, the two Flanagans, Vaughan, H. C. Pedigo, and the able young lawyer, McCormick.

The conflict between the two factions was not to be long delayed. A preliminary trial of strength had given the extremists control of the chair. On June 5th, A. J. Evans precipitated the issue by proposing a resolution asserting the theory that the people of the United States and not the states established the government of the United States; that no local, territorial, or state government could exist in the United States without the express sanction of Congress; and that the convention would not recognize or sanction the ordinance of secession " or any bill, law, ordinance, act, resolution, rule, or provision, made or enacted since March, 1861, as having now or ever having had validity in the State of Texas." The committee on federal relations, to which it was referred, divided, the majority reporting favorably on the whole resolution, the minority dissenting from the last clause and desiring so to amend it as to confine its application to those laws and acts passed in aid of the rebellion and conflicting with the Constitution of the United States. The majority report [1] aroused a long and bitter debate, and led to a renewal of the quarrel between the *Austin Republican* and the *San Antonio Express,* the latter of which had become the organ of the *ab initio* faction. A vote was not reached until June 29th, when a substitute offered by A. J. Hamilton was adopted in committee of the whole, declaring, in essence, that only the secession ordinance, laws in contravention of the constitution or laws of the United States, or in aid of the rebellion, and laws designed to benefit disloyal men at the expense of the public or of loyal men, were null and void from the beginning; and that such laws as only regulated the domestic concerns

[1] *Convention Journal,* 1st sess., 28, 53.

of the people and were not in contravention of the laws of the United States should be respected by the courts. The Conservatives, who had supported the substitute in committee of the whole, joined with Morgan Hamilton when it came before the convention and succeeded in tabling the whole matter by a vote of 46 to 43.[1]

Feeling ran too strong, however, for the subject to be more than temporarily disposed of in this way. Two days later, E. J. Davis introduced for incorporation into the general provisions of the new constitution, a declaration embodying the *ab initio* doctrine, but with provisions appended for validating and establishing such laws, parts of laws, and acts, passed or performed since secession, as should be deemed necessary and worthy to be preserved and respected.[2] But Morgan Hamilton, as chairman of the committee on general provisions to which the resolution was referred, reported the committee unwilling to accept as valid or to validate " any pretended law, however inoffensive its character ", passed by those in rebellion against the government.[3] However, in their report the section dealing with this subject provided

that the acts of the so-called officers in solemnizing marriages, in taking acknowledgments, and recording deeds and other instruments of writing, the decisions of so-called courts, and all contracts between private parties subject to the laws of the United States since the 28th day of January, 1861,

should be declared valid and binding. In other words, all laws and official acts passed since 1861 had been null and void from the first, but certain acts involving only private

---

[1] *Convention Journal*, 1st sess., 53, 120, 126, 157, 161, 176; *Austin Daily Republican*, June 27, 30, July 6.

[2] *Ibid.*, 188.   [3] *Ibid.*, 234.

relations should now be validated nonetheless. The acts of the convention of 1866 and of the eleventh legislature, were without sanction of legal authority and should be respected only so long as the commanding general should enforce them as rules of action under his government.[1]

It was not until August 20th that the convention reached this section of the report, and in the interval the subject had been fought over elsewhere. The Republican state convention met in Austin from August 12th to 14th, with most of the members of the constitutional convention as delegates or alternates. The *anti-ab-initio* party had about two-thirds of the delegates and therefore secured control of the organization. The majority of the platform committee reported resolutions pledging adherence to the national platform, the reconstruction laws, and the prospective state constitution, and made no mention whatever of the local controversy. E. J. Davis, in a minority report, offered additional resolutions embodying the doctrine of his faction. After a vigorous debate the minority report was overwhelmingly rejected, whereupon Davis and a large number of the *ab initio* delegates withdrew and formed a convention of their own with Jas. P. Newcomb as chairman. The regular convention endeavored to find some middle ground upon which to stand with the bolters, and drew up additional resolutions that went so far as to concede that the rebel legislatures, which they had always insisted had the force of *de facto* governments for the passage of laws governing the private relations of citizens, had " had no legal capacity to enact laws binding upon the people of Texas." The " Newcomb convention " refused as a body to make the compromise, but the fear of the consequences of a permanent party split so worked upon certain individuals among them, their comparative paucity and hopelessness outside the regu-

[1] *Convention Journal*, 1st sess., 234, 241-242.

lar organization upon others, that many of their members, the leaders excepted, found their way back before final adjournment.[1] Thus the *anti-ab-initio* faction was able to go on in the constituent body with the prestige of regular party approval; and they did not fail to claim in addition the support of the military commanders, of Grant, now Republican nominee for the Presidency, and of the national platform, since this last did not at any rate raise the issue.

On August 20th the convention reached the *ab initio* section in the report of general provisions. Morgan Hamilton was now in Washington on mission to Congress, but it is doubtful if his presence could have availed his followers much. After a stormy wrangle the whole section was tabled by a decisive vote, 52 to 27, and a new section offered by Caldwell was adopted over a substitute by Davis, 45 to 28. The greater part of the Conservatives voted against all the propositions. The section now finally adopted simply took the familiar ground of the moderates, that secession, the whole state debt contracted during the war, and all acts of the " rebel " state government in contravention of the constitution and laws of the United States were null and void from the beginning; that the legislatures which sat from March 18, 1861, to August 5, 1866, had no constitutional authority to make laws binding upon the people of Texas; provided that this should not be construed to inhibit the authorities of the state from respecting and enforcing such " rules and regulations " as had been prescribed by the said legislatures, and were not in violation of the constitution and laws of the United States, or of Texas, or in aid of the rebellion, or prejudicial to loyal citizens—nor to prejudice private rights which had grown up under these rules and regulations, nor to invalidate official acts not in aid of the

[1] For proceedings of this Republican convention see *Austin Daily Republican*, Aug. 13-15, 1868.

rebellion.   The eleventh legislature (1866) was declared provisional only, and its acts were to be respected in so far as they were not in violation of the constitution and laws of the United States, or were not intended to reward participants in the rebellion, or to discriminate between citizens on account of race or color, or to operate prejudicially to any class of citizens.[1]

There would seem to be but little difference in the practical application of the two theories, since the one proposed to validate by special acts what the other proposed to regard as already valid for reasons of public policy and social stability.   Only an abstraction now separated the two factions; but neither was willing to go further, and the split continued despite efforts at conciliation.   The *Austin Republican* made an earnest plea for party harmony and urged the danger of division in the face of their Conservative enemies. who were, in fact, very jubilant over the Radical split.[2]

That the issue was still alive was shown just three days before the final adjournment when a negro delegate, Ralph Long, of Limestone, offered a resolution annulling certain decisions of the provisional state courts, among which were those that declared the government of the Confederacy and of the rebel states *de facto* governments, and held that emancipation did not take universal effect at the time of Lincoln's proclamation.   The resolution was promptly rejected, 40 to 22.[3]   Davis and his followers gave no sign of surrendering or even of modifying their views, but on the contrary threatened to oppose the adoption of the new constitution and went about building up an organization of their own in opposition to the " regulars ".

[1] *Convention Journal*, 1st sess., 793-798.

[2] *Austin Daily Republican*, July 16, 18, Aug. 19, 21; *San Antonio Daily Herald*, June 22; *State Gazette*, Aug. 17, 1868.

[3] *Convention Journal*, 1st sess., 920.

The proposition to divide Texas into two or three states brought about another sharp fight that helped to widen the breach and intensify the bitterness between the two factions; for the alignment here was nearly the same as in the *ab initio* controversy. The Davis faction favored division almost to a man and on this issue gained over a sufficient number of A. J. Hamilton's followers to secure a slight majority. The division question, however, was not strictly a party issue, for both Conservatives and Radicals were to be found on each side. It was rather sectional than political. Nor was it a new thing; for the idea had been entertained and occasionally brought forward from the time Texas had first become a member of the Federal Union. The terms of her admission in 1845 had provided for a future division into five states; and the problems at that time incident to her vast territorial extent had kept the question alive. The lack of railroads, except for a few short lines, inadequate means of travel and communication, the long, harassed frontier line, the peculiar grouping of the population, had made the problem of administration a difficult one for the state government even before the war. Now there were additional incentives. It was urged by many of the Radicals that the arm of the state government was too weak to reach into the far-out districts and preserve order, that only by a division into separate states could the people be assured of security and peace. East Texas was then the wealthiest part of the state and complained of bearing more than its share of the public burdens; it was also the stronghold of the Conservatives, many of whom were doubtful of their ability to control the whole state with the foreign and the negro vote against them. The south and the southwest were peopled largely by Germans and were predominantly Radical or Republican; hence political interests also seemed to call for separation. But more potent reasons, perhaps, in the convention of 1868, were the ambitions of political leaders. Three states would offer more opportunities for political advancement than one; and moreover the faction opposed to A. J. Hamilton feared that he could not be eliminated from the control of the Republican party in the state, which would surely mean political subordination for themselves. If Hamilton could not be thrust out of the leadership of the party, he might be eliminated, so far as the most of them were concerned, by so slicing up the state as to leave him the central region only. It was perhaps this fear of Hamilton's dominance that led E. J. Davis, of Nueces, to come to terms with Lemuel Dale Evans, the able Conservative from East Texas, on the matter of division. Both were ambitious, each represented a section upon which he might confidently reckon for support, but neither enjoyed much of a prospect for support in sections other than his own. The southwest delegation was solid for division and a large number of Republicans from the eastern districts supported it also. What sort of understanding there was between them and L. D. Evans in the event of the success of the measure is not clear, but it is almost certain that some agreement existed.

In addition to the certain and powerful opposition of A. J. Hamilton, the plans of the divisionists were embarrassed by two other propositions. One of these was the proposal submitted by Governor Pease to sell the northwest territory to the United States; the other was the petition brought by W. W. Mills, a young delegate from El Paso, for Texas to cede that remote corner of her territory to the United States, provided it should be joined with the county of Dona Anna, New Mexico, in a territorial government.[1] Neither of these propositions suited the divisionists of the

_____
[1] *Convention Journal*, 1st sess., 135, 758-761.

southwest, for either would subtract a substantial portion
from the state of which they dreamed. In the meantime,
however, the divisionists had secured help in another quarter. As early as December 3, 1867, Thaddeus Stevens had
introduced a resolution into the national House of Representatives directing the reconstruction committee to enquire
into the expediency of dividing Texas into two or more
states. Considerable pressure seems to have been brought to
bear at Washington—by whom, it is difficult to say though
it is easy to conjecture; for the idea cropped up now and
tnen during the spring.[1] Just before the convention assembled, Beaman, from the reconstruction committee of
Congress, reported a bill to divide Texas into three states.
One line was to cut the state along the San Jacinto and
Trinity rivers, up to the East Fork of the Trinity and thence
to the Red river along the western boundary of Fannin
County. The other was to follow the Colorado river to the
thirty-second parallel of latitude, thence west to the Rio
Grande along the northern edge of El Paso County. The
bill further provided that the Texas convention should
divide itself into three conventions representing respectively
three new states, East Texas, Texas, and South Texas.

On June 9th, a special committee of fifteen was appointed
to consider the subject of division. The Beaman bill, still
before Congress, was telegraphed for, referred, and on June
24th, favorably reported, with a few trifling amendments,
and the request that it be recommended to Congress for
speedy action.[2] An effort to get rid of the whole matter by
referring the subject of division to the legislature was un-
successful. Since the divisionists had a slight majority,

[1] L. D. Evans had been in Washington until the spring of 1868, and
was accused by the *Austin Republican* of having intrigued in the
matter.

[2] *Convention Journal*, 1st sess., 51, 106, 144-148.

their opponents determined either to prevent a decisive vote by filibustering, or to divide the forces of the three-state party. The latter manœuver was tried first. A. J. Hamilton introduced a substitute proposing other lines of division, namely, to make the Brazos the boundary between East and West Texas and to create a third state north of the thirty-second parallel of latitude. It was hoped, not that this substitute [1] would really be adopted, but that it would divide and confuse the advocates of division. It was finally voted down.[2] But Congress had not yet acted upon the Beaman bill, and until that should be passed it was urged that the convention had no authority to pass finally upon a subject of such paramount importance, one that had not been contemplated by the Reconstruction Acts nor by the people of the state in the election of the delegates. Some of the lukewarm divisionists, too, were beginning to fear that the subject was being made paramount to the proper work of their body, and that it was only driving further asunder the two wings of the Republican party in Texas; and on July 16th, several of them voted for a resolution by Thomas that no question relating to a division of the state would thereafter be entertained unless by the authority of Congress. It was carried, 47 to 37; the Republican vote standing 39 to 35.[3] Two days before adjournment an attempt was made to bring the matter up again, but it failed. The subject was revived, however, in the next session and precipitated a most violent conflict. Governor Pease's proposition to sell the northwest had, in the meantime, been quietly shelved. The El Paso cession, championed by the energetic Mills, seemed on the point of going through, but it suc-

---

[1] *Austin Daily Republican*, July 6, 1868.

[2] *Convention Journal*, 1st sess., 309.

[3] *Ibid.*, 391, 409-11. *Austin Daily Republican*, July 18, 1868.

cumbed finally to a combination of divisionists, chiefly from the southwest, and a few anti-divisionists, by a vote of 38 to 32.[1]

A subject that claimed a great deal of the time and attention of both sessions of the convention was that of railroads; but, although it was one of great importance to the state, it does not come sufficiently within the province of this essay to warrant more than the briefest discussion here. Some half dozen railroads, by an act of 1856, had borrowed large sums from the state school fund, and the total of principal and accumulated interest now amounted to a little more than two and a half millions of dollars.[2] During the war all of the roads had suffered great deterioration, from which they had hardly begun to recover, and in order to secure their debts to the school fund, those that seemed hopelessly insolvent were ordered to be foreclosed upon and sold by the governor, while those that showed signs of reviving were given more time.[3] As it turned out, none were actually sold by the state, for the convention failed to appropriate any money for the expenses of the sale. All the existing roads were short lines that reached but a little way into the state and were wholly inadequate to the needs of the interior population. It was generally felt that not only more roads, but especially a number of trunk lines were needed; and in addition to granting extensions to existing lines, several new roads were chartered. Some suspicion hovered over certain of these grants; for in several of them prominent members of the convention figured as directors of the companies, eliciting in one case an ironical proposal " to amend by adding the remaining members of the convention as in-

[1] *Convention Journal*, 1st sess., 758-761.

[2] *Ibid.*, 270-275, 482-485.

[3] *Ibid.*, 848-850; Gammel, VI, 47, 48.

corporators."[1] One of the new roads that excited particular controversy was the International Pacific, later known as the International and Great Northern, about which centered one of the scandals of the twelfth legislature.[2]

If the *ab initio* question and the proposed division of the state had created dissensions and bitterness within the Republican ranks, there was still one matter upon which they stood as a unit. Ever since the close of the war they had complained of lawless violence and of persecution—that their condition everywhere was precarious and sometimes unbearable; and never had their complaints been louder or more persistent than since the machinery of the state government had passed into the hands of " loyal " men. It had been confidently asserted before the assembling of the convention that one of its duties would be to take measures for the suppression of lawlessness and for insuring protection to the members of the Republican party.

Hardly had the convention completed its organization when Judge Colbert Caldwell, whose experiences at Marshall have been mentioned, offered a resolution for the appointment of a select committee to investigate and report upon the conditions of lawlessness and violence in the state.[3] The committee did not make its formal report for nearly a month, but the convention did not wait for that. On June 13th, a resolution was introduced by Lippard tendering to the state commander, General Reynolds, " a sufficient number of loyal men in each county, as in his opinion may be necessary, to aid and assist in the suppression of crime and the protection of life and property and the enforcement of the laws ". The resolution was reported favorably, but a substitute offered by A. J. Hamilton was accepted and

[1] *Convention Journal*, 2nd sess., 163.

[2] See speech of E. Degener, in *Austin Daily Republican*, July 22, 1868.

[3] *Convention Journal*, 1st sess., 30, 34.

passed, requesting Congress to allow the convention to organize a militia force in each county to act in conjunction with and under the direction of the military commander (Reynolds).[1] A number of the Conservatives protested against the resolution on the grounds that the rumors of lawlessness were greatly exaggerated, " that the organization of such a force by a political party would only tend to exasperate the public mind and in all probability have the effect to produce conflicts of races," [2] that the officers of the provisional government, if they would do their duty, would be able with the help of the military to bring all transgressors to punishment, and that the resolution was an implied censure of and an affront to the commander of the Fifth Military District, in that the granting of such a power would invest the state commander, through the convention, with power over the district commander within the limits of the state.[3] This was followed up by another resolution appropriating \$25,000 to enable the governor to offer suitable rewards for the arrest of desperadoes and to employ detectives to ferret out their hiding places. Before the resolution was passed an amendment was tacked on, providing that none of the money so appropriated should be used unless the state commander should first be authorized to organize military commissions for the trial of offenders— an undisguised attack upon General Buchanan, who held to Hancock's opinion of military commissions, and all the more strangely out of place, since any resolution appropriating money had to be sent to that officer for approval.[4]

---

[1] *Convention Journal*, 1st sess., 108, 111.

[2] A sensible conclusion, for most of the "loyalist" militiamen would of necessity have been negroes.

[3] *Convention Journal*, 1st sess., 131. The district commander had in general followed the policy of Hancock and was disliked almost as much by the Radicals.

[4] *Ibid.*, 124, 132, 134, 136.

As should have been expected, Buchanan refused to approve the measure, on the ground that it was unauthorized by the Reconstruction Acts under which the convention was assembled, that it was properly a subject for the consideration of the state legislature, and that the proviso with reference to military commissions, " intended as a gratuitous indignity to the Commanding General," displayed a spirit of which he could hardly be expected to approve.[1] Shortly afterwards, however, when General Reynolds became commander of the Fifth Military District, confined now to Texas, the resolution was again passed and submitted to him for approval, as one in whose " loyalty, ability, and patriotism the people of Texas repose full confidence." [2]

On July 2d, the committee on lawlessness and violence made its report, which it supplemented three weeks later with more complete statistics.[3] The committee had had access to three sources of information: the records of the state departments, particularly the official reports of the clerks of the district courts; the records of the Freedmen's Bureau; and the sworn statements of witnesses from various parts of the state. It was claimed that none of these furnished complete information; the first, because only about forty counties were represented and only those offenses were taken notice of for which indictments had been found; the second, because the records of the Bureau covered only about sixty counties and dealt only with the outrages upon freedmen; and the last, because it was difficult to get witnesses to testify, through fear of assassination, while those who did testify had to rely wholly upon memory. It was also claimed that no report had been accepted that did not bear the marks of veracity and that every statement made

[1] *Convention Journal*, 1st sess., 510.
[2] *Ibid.*, 616, 619-21.   [3] *Ibid.*, 193-203, 500-505.

was warranted by the facts. The committee had been compelled to restrict its investigations to the homicides committed since the rebellion, and to take no note of the numerous assaults, robberies, and other outrages, which would have imposed " an endless task ". The homicides from the close of the war to June, 1868, were tabulated as follows :[1]

Killed in 1865, whites,	47 ;	freedmen,	51 ;	total	98.
" " 1866 "	75	"	95	"	170
" " 1867 "	173	"	174	"	347
" " 1868 "	182	"	137	"	319
" Year unknown "	32	"	29	"	61
" Race unknown				"	40.
	509		486		1035.

More than ninety per cent of the total were asserted to have been committed by white men, while little more than one per cent were by negroes upon whites.[2]

Though admitting at the outset that many of these homicides were committed for the purposes of plunder and robbery, the principal conclusion that the committee endeavored to deduce was that the chief cause of these crimes was " the hostility entertained by ex-rebels toward loyal men of both races." In support of this was cited the large number of negroes killed by whites as against the small number of whites killed by negroes, so that " the war of races " was all against the blacks; and also, that a large proportion of the whites slain were unionists, and that they had been killed for their unionism by men who " with remarkably

[1] This table is taken from the supplementary report of July 25, which was claimed to be more accurate than the first. See *Convention Journal*, 1st sess., 194, 501.

[2] The statement in the report of July 2 that only 48 freedmen had been killed by freedmen during the three years is incredible; but whether a correction on this point would reduce the number attributed to whites or simply swell the total, cannot be said.

few exceptions were and are disloyal to the government."
It is impossible to accept in full the conclusion of the committee on this point. In the first place, few or none of the
negroes killed during 1865 and 1866 were killed for their
unionism—the negro was not then a political factor—but
chiefly on account of labor disputes and other private quarrels. Since the formation of the Union Leagues in the
spring and summer of 1867, irritation against the blacks
had developed rapidly, but even during this time the political
question was more often the remote than the immediate
cause of trouble. At the same time there is no doubt whatever that negroes were sometimes killed because of their
connection with the League, and in many cases murdered
most brutally and wantonly for no real cause whatever. As
to the large proportion of unionists among the whites killed,
the evidence is in no way conclusive; for other evidence
shows that many of the " union men " were not unionists
at all, and that in a number of cases where they were, private quarrels lay at the root of the trouble.[1]   On the other
hand, nothing is more certain than that Radicals were not
popular in many sections of Texas, and that an aggressive
activity in the Union League was the occasion, direct or in-
direct, of much retaliatory violence and a number of homicides. The committee's report, however, made conditions
appear worse than they seem to have been in reality. The
constant challenge of the Conservatives that the individual
cases of murdered loyalists be specified was answered with
a list of twenty-three whites and fourteen blacks; but of the
total only eight victims were named or otherwise identified
—though it should have been easy to give the names of all
or nearly all—and of the eight, four proved to be incorrectly

---

[1] See minority report of Mullins, *Convention Journal*, 672-79.

given, a fact which cast suspicion upon the accuracy of the remainder of the list.[1]

That there were organizations of " disloyal, desperate men " in several sections of the state, was another conclusion reached by the committee. These organizations were believed to be widespread and to exist for the purpose of driving out or murdering Union men, of intimidating the freedmen, and of protecting their own members from the military and the courts. In some districts these combinations were too strong for the civil authorities and openly defied them. In others the county officers were themselves involved in their acts of violence, or connived at them, and wilfully neglected to make arrests. In several cases the sheriffs were leaders of the gangs which infested their districts. However, even if arrested, bad men had little to fear from the civil courts; for it was notoriously difficult to secure a conviction for murder upon any evidence, sometimes because of the sympathy of the jury with the criminal, sometimes through their fear of his confederates. This laxity in the civil courts was ascribed chiefly to " that animosity toward the government and its friends so prevalent everywhere. . . . It is our solemn conviction that the courts, especially juries, as a rule will not convict ex-rebels for offenses committed against Union men and freedmen."

Special stress was laid upon " the increase of crime within the last seven months ", and the responsibility for this condition was ascribed to Generals Hancock and Buchanan. It was claimed that since the publication of Hancock's " General Orders No. 40," November 29, 1867, which had relieved criminals of the fear of military commissions, crime had fearfully increased. Figures were adduced to

[1] Supplementary report, *Convention Journal*, 500; *Austin Daily Republican*, Aug. 24, 1868.

show that to the date of Throckmorton's removal murders had averaged eighteen per month; falling off to only nine per month during the first three months of Pease's administration; and rising to thirty in the first month of Hancock's command, December.

In other words, according to the lowest calculation, the peace administration of Generals Hancock and Buchanan has to account for twice the number of murders committed under the Sheridan-Throckmorton administration, and three times the number committed under the Sheridan-Pease administration. Moreover, fuller reports show that since the policy of General Hancock was inaugurated, sustained as it is by President Johnson, the homicides in Texas have averaged fifty-five per month; and for the last five months they have averaged sixty per month. It is for the Commander of the Fifth Military District to answer to the public for at least two-thirds of the 330, or more, homicides committed in Texas since the first of December, 1867. Charged by law to keep the peace and afford protection to life and property, and having the army of the United States to assist him in so doing, *he has failed.* He has persistently refused to try criminals, rejected the prayers of the Executive of the State and of the Commanding General of the District of Texas for adequate tribunals, and turned a deaf ear to the cry of tried and persecuted loyalists. And knowing whereof we affirm, and in the face of the civilized world, we do solemnly lay to his charge the death of hundreds of the loyal citizens of Texas—a responsibility that should load his name with infamy, and hand his very memory to coming years as a curse and an execration.

The report closed with an appeal to the United States government for protection, and a resolution that copies of the report be sent to Congress to that end.

It was a skilfully drawn and an impressive document, though most obviously partisan both in the arrangement of its matter and in its conclusions. The committee bent every effort to place all the blame for the lawlessness in Texas, which was certainly bad enough, at the door of their political opponents. To this end they appear to have exaggerated the popular hostility, which naturally existed, toward their party, while they wholly ignored the fact that the radical program of reconstruction was itself responsible for the political excitement, the administrative confusion, and the general unrest which had so encouraged lawlessness. It was true that convictions for homicide were difficult to obtain; but that had been true before the war, as it continued to be true in Texas long after the period of reconstruction had closed, and was due more to the old code and influences of the frontier than to any other cause. As for the bitter charge against General Hancock, his refusal to organize military commissions had been coupled with a promise to furnish military assistance for the arrest of criminals and to strengthen the hands of the civil authorities whenever called upon to do so; and it does not appear that, after their disagreement relative to the military tribunals for Uvalde County, Governor Pease ever made any request for help of Hancock himself. The increase of crime in 1868—and that it had greatly increased is not to be disputed—can not be justly laid wholly to the charge of the military commanders; the Radical leaders themselves must bear a part of the responsibility.

On the day after the report was received, E. J. Davis introduced a resolution providing that Morgan Hamilton and Judge Caldwell, chairman of the above committee, should go to Washington without delay to

lay before Congress the conditions of lawlessness and violence prevalent in this state and urge the immediate necessity for action on the following matters: *first,* the adoption of some law or regulation that will secure the filling of all state provisional offices with competent and loyal incumbents; *second*, the organization of a loyal militia, to be placed under the direction and control of the loyal provisional authorities of Texas; *third*, the appointment by this convention of registrars of voters previous to the coming election.[1]

On July 6th, the resolution was passed and the delegates named proceeded immediately to the national capital.[2]

Before passing to the general provisions of the constitution upon which the convention finally got to work during the last days of the session, some mention should be made of certain miscellaneous measures which occupied much time and attention. Some were of importance, while others merely illustrated the prevailing temper of the delegates. Such was the effort made to induce Congress to transfer from the commander of the Fifth Military District to the convention the control over the appointment and removal of registrars for ascertaining and recording the qualified voters.[3]   Another was a provision granting lands out of the

---

[1] *Convention Journal*, 1st sess., 212-213.   The third clause was added later.   See the *Journal*, 221.

[2] The publication of the report on lawlessness, followed by the sending of a committee to Washington for the purposes avowed in the above resolutions, aroused the ire of the Conservatives.   The *Houston Telegraph*, July 14, closed a wrathful editorial on the prospect of a negro militia with the words: " No man ever hung in Texas by lynch law was ever half such a criminal in the sight of God or man as the man who seeks to plunge his country into a war of races, the most savage of all wars, which would result in the extermination of the blacks and in the ruin of the state.   We say it solemnly, such men [Hamilton and Caldwell] ought to die."   For this the convention requested General Reynolds to arrest the editor, Gillespie, try him before a military commission for counselling and advising assassination, and suppress his paper.   *Convention Journal*, 435; *Austin Daily Republican*, July 21, 22, 23, 1868.

[3] *Convention Journal*, 40-42.

public domain and a bounty in money to Texans who had served in the Federal army.[1]   A list of Republicans, "loyal citizens," disfranchised by the reconstruction acts, was very carefully prepared and Congress was petitioned to have their disabilities removed.[2]   Several of these were members of the convention.   The condition of the state penitentiary was examined into, its financial management under the Throckmorton administration condemned, and a large number of convicts, mostly negroes, alleged to have been convicted unjustly or for trivial offenses, were recommended for executive clemency.[3]   Finally, an effort was made to have Congress indemnify the settlers on the frontier for their losses at the hands of Indians since the war, and to appropriate money for the ransom of captives held by the savages.[4]

Progress upon the constitution itself was very slow, chiefly because so much time was taken up with controversies over the *ab initio* doctrine, the division of the state, railroads, and a score of minor matters, some of them purely legislative in character and therefore not proper to a constitutional convention.   Reports were made by all the important committees having parts of the constitution under consideration, but the convention did not succeed in passing upon them all.   The introduction and first section of the "bill of rights" clearly illustrate the new Radical view of the condition of the state government:

[1] *Convention Journal*, 173, 186, 294-296, 845-847.   Gammel, VI, 45.

[2] *Ibid.*, 141, 143, 226-227, 232, 512-526, 925-939.

[3] The recommendations seem generally to have been based upon the statements of the convicts themselves. *Convention Journal*, 534-554, 627-628, 771-775, 803-809, 864-869.

[4] *Ibid.*, 76, 395, 593.   The language of these resolutions shows that the Unionists of Texas did not share Sheridan's skepticism as to the danger from Indian attacks.

That the heresies of nullification and secession which brought the country to grief may be eliminated from future political discussions; that public order may be restored, private property and human life protected, and the great principles of liberty and equality secured to us and our posterity, we declare that:

Section 1. The Constitution of the United States, and the laws, treaties made and to be made, in pursuance thereof, are acknowledged to be the supreme law; that this Constitution is framed in harmony with and in subordination thereto; and that the fundamental principles embodied herein can only be changed, subject to the national authority.[1]

A marked tendency toward centralization of authority was manifested by extending the governor's appointive power and lengthening the terms of nearly all state officials. It was provided that the governor should hold office for four years, and that he should appoint the secretary of state and the attorney-general; and an attempt was made, though it ultimately failed, to give him general control over and power to remove not only those officials, but likewise the comptroller, treasurer, and land commissioner, who were elective. It was agreed that he should appoint the justices of the supreme court for terms of nine years each, and district judges for terms of eight years. A strong effort was made to have district attorneys, clerks and sheriffs made appointive also, the first by the governor, the others by the district judges, but these were finally all made elective.[2] The county courts were abolished. These changes were probably for the purpose of injecting more vigor into the courts and the peace officers with a view to checking lawlessness. It is a curious fact that this centralizing policy was championed by the moderate Republicans and opposed

[1] *Convention Journal*, 1st sess., 235; Gammel, VII, 395.

[2] *Ibid.*, 1st sess., 477-482, 465-470. Gammel, VII, 410-415.

by the faction of E. J. Davis, in whose hands it later became so odious.

Action on the report from the committee on education was postponed until the next session. The most noteworthy features of that report were the provisions for increasing the existing permanent school fund by adding to it all money to be received from the sale of the public domain, and for applying all the available fund to the education of all children within the scholastic age—from six to eighteen years — without distinction of race or color.[1] The convention was careful to wipe out all such distinctions wherever they had previously existed.

The very important question as to suffrage qualifications was reached only on August 26th. Since the great differences of opinion on this subject precluded the possibility of settling it in the few remaining days of the session, its consideration was postponed until after the recess.

It had been evident for some time that an adjournment would be inevitable before the work was finished. The extreme Radicals became more and more dissatisfied as they saw the opportunities steadily diminishing for carrying through their measures, and from the middle of July they began to demand a recess until the next session of Congress; but on August 10th their opponents succeeded in crowding through a resolution shutting off consideration of the subject for the next two weeks. In the meantime, however, the appropriation for the pay and expenses of the convention, approved by General Buchanan to the extent of $100,000, had been exhausted; and a resolution was passed, August 20th, requesting the new district commander, Reynolds, to approve the balance ($25,000) of that appropriation. Reynolds refused, pointing out that the convention had already

[1] *Convention Journal*, 609-614; Gammel, VII, 417-418.

been in session eighty-five days and had expended $100,000, while the low state of the treasury, the rate at which money was coming in, and the prospective wants of the state government forbade further outlay.[1] It was absolutely necessary, however, to find means of paying for another session unless the constitution was to be left hanging in the air, unfinished. The Radical extremists were so dissatisfied with it that they expressed a cheerful willingness to see it hang there, and the Conservatives manifested a similar feeling. These factions were not strong enough, however, to have their way. As soon as it was known that the additional appropriation would not be granted, the moderates agreed to an adjournment from August 31st to the first Monday in December.[2] The day after the receipt of Reynolds's reply, an ordinance was passed levying the tax provided for in the Supplementary Reconstruction Act of March 23, 1867. The rate was fixed at twenty cents on the hundred dollars valuation, and the proceeds were required to be in the state treasury by December 1st.[3]

The convention had been in session ninety-two days when it adjourned with its work still uncompleted.[4] It had already cost the state nearly fifty per cent more than did the convention of 1866, which sat only fifty-five days and was severely criticised because of its slowness.

[1] *Convention Journal*, 780, 798, 858.   [2] *Ibid.*, 851-53.

[3] *Ibid.*, 860; Gammel, VI, 52.

[4] Another reason for taking a recess, but hardly worth consideration because evidently brought forward to cover up the real one, was offered by the *Austin Republican*: namely, that there was so much danger of a "renewal of rebellion" by the disfranchised Democrats who were threatening to go armed to the polls and vote against the constitution, that it was necessary to avert a collision by postponing the completion and submission of the constitution until the election and inauguration of Grant should make all things safe. See issue of August 31, 1868.

2. *Conditions during the Recess—the Presidential
Election*

Despite the fact that Texas was now under the unhampered control of General Reynolds,[1] the late summer and fall of 1868 saw no apparent abatement of the general disorder and lawlessness. The negroes here and there were beginning to show the effects of the teachings of reckless carpet-baggers and " scalawags "; and though in the abstract the assertion of their new rights may seem just enough, the manner of the assertion was often such as to bring them into immediate collision with the whites. At Millican, on July 15th, a riot occurred because a mob of negroes, who were attempting to lynch another negro, refused to disperse at the order of a deputy sheriff. A posse of whites was gathered, a fight ensued, and a number of negroes were killed. Another difficulty, almost identical in circumstances, occurred at Houston, but here the patient determination of a number of prominent citizens prevented a general battle. There was trouble also at Tyler. The *Texas Republican* (Dem.) declared that these conflicts went to prove that the two races could not live together in harmony on a basis of equality. To the Radicals they were evidence of a plan for the deliberate extermination of the loyal citizens and " a renewal of rebellion ".[2] This belief was strengthenen by an affair which occurred at Jefferson early in October. Geo. W. Smith, a carpet-bagger from New York, had become the leader of the negroes in that community, where they outnumbered the whites two to one, and by his conduct had aroused the bitter enmity of the latter. The

---

[1] Louisiana had been turned over to the new state government in June, 1868, and this left Texas alone to constitute the Fifth Military District.

[2] *Texas Republican*, Aug. 7, 1868; *Austin Republican*, July 22, 1868.

Jefferson Times declared that he had lived among the negroes on terms of social equality, had encouraged them in all manner of evil, and by incendiary speeches had constantly stirred up animosity and trouble between them and the whites. He was a member of the constitutional convention, and, on his return from its session, he became involved in a dispute with a white man. Smith brought up a gang of negroes to his support, wounded several white men, and then fled to the protection of the military, who turned him over to the civil authorities. He was jailed and strongly guarded by both citizens and soldiers, but a large body of armed men overawed the guard, entered the jail, and killed him, along with two or three negroes taken with him. Under the caption, " Murder of an Infamous Scoundrel ", the *Jefferson Times* gave an account of the lynching and sought to justify it.

Though condemned in the eyes of the law, [the lynching] was an unavoidable necessity. The sanctity of home, the peace and safety of society, the prosperity of the country, and the security of life itself demanded the removal of so base a villain.[1]

The Radical press, however, hailed Smith's death as that of a martyr to the Union and to free speech, and this was the version that was accepted at the North. Reynolds sent additional troops to Jefferson, proclaimed martial law there and arrested some thirty prominent citizens on the charge of murder. He held them in close confinement for about ten months for trial before a military commission, and ultimately five were convicted.

In portions of northeastern Texas the general disorder was made worse by a series of feuds that involved whole

[1] Quoted in *Texas Republican*, Oct. 16, 1868.

communities. The most noted of these was the " Lee and Peacock War " in Hunt and Fannin Counties. The Peacock party was or claimed to be unionists, the Lees had been secessionists. From all accounts the former were the aggressors, though politics had nothing to do with the quarrel. Through the distorting medium of the Radical press the feud appeared as another effort of an armed band of rebels to exterminate Union men. The Peacocks made an advantageous alliance with the military, and General Reynolds offered a reward of $1,000 for the capture of Bob Lee, the head of his faction. In and about Hopkins County a great deal of trouble was caused by two bands of guerrillas under the leadership of B. F. Bickerstaff and Cullen Baker. They were strong enough to offer fight to the troops stationed in that vicinity; they plundered several supply trains on the way to the soldiers; and they were therefore set down as evidence of prevailing disloyal sentiment and credited to the account of the Democratic party, though they had no discoverable political affiliations and were tolerated by the people generally only through fear. Large rewards were offered for their arrest, more troops were pushed into that region, and these bands were soon broken up.[1]

Bands of Ku Klux made their appearance in nearly all parts of the state, especially where the Loyal Union League had produced restlessness among the blacks. Sometimes giant horsemen, shrouded in ghostly white, some of them headless, passed at midnight through the negro settlements, disarming and frightening the superstitious freedmen out of their senses, but otherwise doing no harm. A community thus visited was usually quiet for some time thereafter. Sometimes, however, the matter did not stop with these

---

[1] *Texas Republican*, August 14, Sept. 11; *Austin Republican*, Sept. 15, Oct. 2, 1868.

comparatively harmless pranks. Now and then negroes and Radical whites, whose political activity made them particularly obnoxious, received written warnings couched in mysterious and sanguinary terms, and embellished with fearful symbols. Though some of it was but " fantastic foolery ", some of it was not; and if the warnings went unheeded, the offender was likely to be taken out and whipped, or even murdered. It is but fair to say, however, that in many cases the guilty parties proved to be reckless and irresponsible persons masquerading under the name of Ku Klux; and they only helped to bring the name of the organization into disrepute and to furnish campaign material to the Radicals.[1] The Ku Klux in Texas seem not to have been a part of the general organization which operated east of the Mississippi, but rather imitative, local, and independent companies, generally of brief existence.[2]

Other means were sought for overcoming Radical influence with the negroes. Democratic clubs passed resolutions to the effect that they would not give employment, assistance, or patronage to any man, white or black, that belonged to or acted with the Radical party.[3] Negro Democratic-Conservative clubs were formed in opposition to the Union League and the Radicals, and special favor was shown in the way of employment and protection to the negroes who went into them.[4] But it could hardly have

[1] See report of Gen. J. J. Reynolds on affairs in Texas for 1868, in *Austin Republican*, Dec. 19; in *Houston Telegraph*, Dec. 17, 1868. Also printed in *Convention Journal*, 2nd sess., 110-112.

[2] W. H. Wood, " The Ku Klux Klan," in *Texas Historical Quarterly*, IX, 262-268.

[3] *Texas Republican*, Aug. 21, Oct. 30, 1868; *Austin Daily Republican*, Nov. 25, 1868.

[4] *Texas Republican*, Sept. 18, 1868; J. H. Fowler to E. M. Pease, MS. in *Exec. Corres.*

been expected that many freedmen would long be satisfied in the party that was so desperately bent upon shutting them out of participation in politics, and the superior attractions offered in the Radical camp gradually enticed most of them away.

On October 5th, General Reynolds ordered a special election in the counties of Falls, Bell, and McClennan to fill a vacancy in the convention caused by the death of Wm. E. Oakes. New boards of registrars were appointed in each county, headed by officers of the army, with directions to revise the lists of voters registered in that district. The importance of this lay in the fact that the commander issued to the registrars a set of instructions very similar to the secret memoranda used earlier by Sheridan and Griffin. In fact it gave more explicit directions as to the persons to be forbidden registration, under the acts of Congress of March 23d, and July 19, 1867, by enumerating every office created by state law since 1845.[1] Reynolds's instructions were wholly within the law, as Sheridan's were not when first issued; but they rigorously went to the very extremity of the law in the way of disfranchising the whites. The *Austin Republican* expressed great satisfaction with the order because a similar one could be expected at the next general state election, and invited the disfranchised rebels to " howl to their heart's content " over the fact that it was a condensation of all of Griffin's orders, including the secret circular. The rebels did " howl ", but without effect.[2]

---

[1] Special Orders, nos. 49 and 51, printed in *Austin Daily Republican*, Oct. 8, 1868. It will be remembered that the second Supplementary Reconstruction Act had declared any person disqualified from voting who had ever held any Federal or state office and afterward engaged in rebellion, " whether he had taken an oath to support the Constitution of the United States or not."

[2] *Austin Republican*, Oct. 9, Nov. 25; *Houston Telegraph*, Oct. 14, 15, 1868.

The impending Presidential election overshadowed for a time in interest and importance all other political matters. State politics, in fact, were at a standstill. With no immediate local campaign in sight the parties were doing little but prepare their organizations for a future trial of strength. The Democrats held a convention at Bryan, July 7th and 8th, where was adopted the usual string of resolutions attacking radicalism in both state and nation, but no state ticket was nominated. The Republicans held their state convention at Austin on August 12th to 14th, as has already been noted, and adopted a platform in conformity with the national platform of their party; but because the new constitution was as yet uncompleted and their own party was splitting in two, they also refused to put out a ticket. All eyes were turned northward on the struggle between Grant and Seymour, for upon its outcome depended to a very great degree the immediate political future of Texas. The election of Grant would mean not only national endorsement of the reconstruction policy of Congress, but the perpetuation of Radical power in the state. If, on the other hand, the Democrats should succeed in carrying Seymour into the presidency and secure a majority in the lower house of Congress, it was certain that the South would get more liberal treatment. Many believed it would result in declaring invalid and setting aside the acts of the " Rump Congress ", from which the representatives of ten states had been excluded—especially the acts which particularly affected those states—and that, in Texas, not only the radical constitutional convention would never re-assemble, but Pease and his fellow officials would be swept away and the Throckmorton administration restored.

In the presidential election Texas could have no part, since, by a joint resolution of Congress passed July 20, 1868, all states not reorganized under the Reconstruction

Acts and readmitted to the Union, were to be excluded from
the electoral college. However, the resolution did no. expressly forbid the holding of an election for presidential
electors, and the idea grew up that the election should be
held anyway on the chance that somehow the votes might
be counted, especially if the election should be a very close
one. It is hard to see how any one expected any result of
this kind without a resort to force—though some may have
been willing to go to that extremity—but it is possible that
the plan was encouraged by certain northern Democrats.[1]
The Democratic state executive committee itself nominated
a full ticket of electors for Texas, which the party papers
carried at the head of their columns. The manner in which
the election was to be called and held presented considerable
difficulty. An act of 1848 governing elections made it the
duty of the governor to issue a proclamation requiring the
chief justice of each county to cause the election to be held
in each precinct; but this Pease would, of course, refuse to
do, nor could it be expected that without his order the county
justices would take any action themselves.[2] It was urged
by some Democratic papers that, in the event of Pease's refusing to act, the Democratic executive committee should
suggest the manner provided by law in which the people
themselves should hold the election; and some others went

---

[1] "About your being allowed to vote, be not alarmed; we shall see
that Texas is represented. Vote, by all means." From letter of Geo.
H. Pendleton (Ohio) to S. Kinney, August 21, 1868, printed in
Houston Times, Sept. 13, 1868, and quoted in *Austin Republican*, Sept.
30, 1868. It is proper to state that this letter was later denounced by
Pendleton as a forgery.

[2] The *Austin Republican* insisted that an act of 1861 changing the
law of 1848 to fit the Confederate system, in fact repealed it without
substituting a valid one in its stead; and that therefore there was
now no Texas law in existence governing the subject. See issues of
Sept. 1 and 28, 1868.

so far as to demand that Throckmorton, as the rightful governor, should issue the necessary proclamation.[1] The former plan was adopted, and on September 28th, W. M. Walton, who had been attorney-general in the Throckmorton administration and was now chairman of the executive committee, issued a circular " to the qualified electors of the State of Texas ", reciting the law, the failure of the governor, and the probable failure of the county justices to perform their duties as prescribed by the law, and recommending that the said electors peaceably assemble at their usual voting places on November 3rd, appoint a presiding officer to act at the election and proceed without any violence or disturbance to vote for electors for President and Vice-President of the United States, and that the presiding officer make duplicate returns of the votes cast, one to the county-justice, the other to the executive committee. On the same day Walton sent a letter to General Reynolds, inclosing his circular and requesting that, as there was no law actually forbidding the election, that he himself either order it or have Governor Pease do it, or else allow the people to hold it themselves. Reynolds promptly refused to do any of these and on the next day issued a special order reciting the joint resolution of Congress above mentioned and adding thereto:

No election for electors of President and Vice-President of the United States will be held in the State of Texas on the third of November next. Any assemblages, proceedings, or acts for such purpose are hereby prohibited, and all citizens are admonished to remain at home or attend to their ordinary business on that day.[2]

As it was useless to go further, Walton issued another

[1] *Texas Republican*, Oct. 9, 1868.

[2] Special Orders no. 44, Sept. 29, printed in *Austin Republican*, Sept. 30, 1868.

short circular advising his fellow Democrats of Reynolds's
attitude and stating that it was now their duty not to attempt to vote. Their dejection was for a short time turned
to joy by the news that President Johnson had caused
Grant, as General of the Army, to issue an order reciting a
law of Congress forbidding the military to interfere in elections. It was rumored that this was intended to counter-
mand Reynolds's order and " put a wet blanket over military despotism in Texas "; but it was soon discovered that
the order had reference only to the states recognized by Congress as in the Union, and that Special Orders no. 44 would
stand.[1] The Democrats derived a certain satisfaction soon
afterwards from the publication of orders relieving General
Reynolds from command in Texas and naming General E.
R. S. Canby, recently in command in the Carolinas, as his
successor.[2]

In the meantime both parties were awaiting with some
apprehension the elections in the North. The result was
foreshadowed in various elections held in doubtful states in
October, but the Democrats seemed wholly unprepared for
the avalanche that came on November 3rd. They saw Radicalism triumphant, and themselves demoralized, helpless.

[1] For circulars of Walton and correspondence with Reynolds see
Texas Republican, Oct. 23, 1868; also *Austin Republican*, Oct. 5, 13
and 22.

[2] What the reasons were for Reynolds's removal, or whether there
were any outside of the mere routine of the war department, was not
divulged; but numerous conjectures were indulged in. One was that
he had aroused the powerful hostility of army contractors; another,
that his instructions to the registrars of Bell County to disregard
special pardons by the President in cases of disqualified persons applying for registration, had aroused Mr. Johnson's resentment; and
still another, that his interference with the action of a district court
in Washington county, in the case of the heirs of J. C. Clark, in order
to continue the case, was the cause. *Austin Republican*, Nov. 6, 7, 10,
13 and 24, 1868.

" All our hopes for a return to good government [in Texas] have passed away," said the *Texas Republican.* Its Radical namesake, on the other hand, professed that it was

with no feeling of exultation but with devout thankfulness that we publish the great victory of yesterday. It relieves us of the most painful apprehensions of persecution and outrage; and it assures us of the existence of a moral force in the nation not only able but determined to protect the loyal men of the South.

Now that the election of Grant had assured their power for the next four years at least, the Republicans of Texas were better able to turn their attention once more to the reconstruction of the state. The convention was to reassemble early in December, and there was much to be done before that time in the way of harmonizing, if possible, the discordant factions of their party. When the first session ended, there seemed to be a genuine desire on the part of members of both factions to come to some sort of agreement, but the weeks passed without tangible result. Even the heat of the national campaign was not sufficient to weld the severed parts. The Davis faction still grumbled over the rejection of their *ab initio* doctrine and of the division of the state, and threatened to oppose any constitution not embodying their ideas. The quarrel between the two factional organs, the *San Antonio Express* and the *Austin Republican,* had never been made up, but constantly grew more bitter. Private quarrels that boded ill for any general harmony had grown up between certain members of the convention. Morgan Hamilton had returned from his Washington mission as bitter as ever against his brother and his brother's following. Nor were all the hard words on one side. The regulars, as the Jack Hamilton faction termed themselves, denounced the bolters from the state convention who were

now threatening opposition to the new constitution, as deserters and political bushwhackers, who would jeopardize the
welfare of the party and the state to satisfy private grudges
and ambitions. Each faction still maintained its own state
executive committee and refused to recognize that of the
other.

Besides this unyielding factional antipathy another factor that promised to be a disturbing one was the question of
suffrage, or rather the extent to which the rebels should
be disfranchised. Governor Pease, as has been stated, recommended in his first message to the convention that
a sufficient number should be denied the suffrage to
place the state government in the hands of the "loyal",
and the subject was reported on by committee, but was not
reached in debate before adjournment. The general disposition at that time had been to follow out the suggestion
of Pease, but the sweeping national victory seemed to admit of a more generous policy, and several of the moderate
leaders, such as A. J. Hamilton, Caldwell, and J. L. Haynes,
chairman of the "regular" Republican executive committee, had become convinced that the best interests, not only
of the state but also of their party, demanded no further
restriction of the franchise than that already provided in
Amendment XIV to the Constitution of the United States.
The Davis faction was, of course, almost solidly opposed to
this policy, as were not a few of Hamilton's own friends, of
whom the most influential perhaps was A. H. Longley, editor of the party organ, the *Austin Republican.* It was
argued by the latter that to admit the rebels to the ballot
would endanger the supremacy of the Republican party and,
therefore, of truly republican institutions; that their undying
malice, manifested in persecutions and assassinations, their
bitter opposition to negro suffrage, the bulwark of the

"loyal" party, and to any constitution embodying that principle, should not be rewarded by giving them a chance to seize upon political power. The recent action of the Democrats in the Georgia legislature in unseating all the negro members of that body was cited in warning of what the Democrats of Texas might be expected to do. It was claimed that " if the late election meant anything, it meant that the loyal people of the United States were unwilling for the late rebels to exercise power in this Republic." [1] The advocates of the liberal policy answered that, in the first place, disfranchisement would almost certainly involve the defeat of the constitution unless Congress could first be induced so to amend the Reconstruction Acts as to prevent the rebels from voting upon it; and Congress would not be likely to do a thing so contrary to the policy of the Republican party, as expressed in the great Amendment and the Acts. In the second place such a measure would arouse the bitterest discord when quiet was most desirable, and leave a heritage of hatred against the Republican party that would ruin its future in Texas. Lastly, nothing could be more dangerous to the welfare of the state and of the negroes themselves than to give all political power into the untrained hands of these new citizens and a few white office-seekers. It would narrow the struggle to one of races, and would inevitably in a few years result in the overthrow of the negro and in *his* disfranchisement in retaliation.[2]

The difference of opinion on this question was not likely to cause serious division among the regulars, but it endangered their control of the convention until they could agree among themselves. The Democrats had no part in this

---

[1] *Austin Republican*, Sept. 10, Oct. 19, 27, Nov. 23 and Dec. 2, 1868.

[2] For an able summary of the arguments against disfranchisement, see Article of J. L. Haynes in *Austin Republican*, Dec. 2, 1868.

controversy, but had to confine themselves to gloomy prophecies of disfranchisement, helpless protests against negro suffrage, and now and then pleas for a qualified negro suffrage based upon either property or education.

3. *Second Session*

Unreconciled and full of mutual suspicions, alternating between offensive innuendoes and appeals for harmony, the two factions of Republicans came together in December to finish the constitution. The attendance was never as full as in the previous session. During the recess one member had died, another had been killed, four had resigned; four others never returned to their duties, and several others were delayed until very late.[1]

The beginning of the session was not auspicious for harmony, despite the appeal of the *Austin Republican* to the factions to avoid, in the interest of party success, " the bickerings, the heart-burnings and the wrangling " that characterized the first session. When it was proposed to renew the subscription to newspapers, a personal encounter was almost precipitated between Caldwell and Morgan Hamilton because the latter bitterly attacked the political affiliations of the *Austin Republican*.[2] Immediately afterwards a committee was appointed, with Morgan Hamilton chairman, to consider a general reduction of expenses of the convention,

[1] Died, W. H. Mullins (Dem.) ; G. W. Smith (Rep.), killed at Jefferson; resigned, Talbot (Rep.), Crigsby (Rep.), Boyd (Dem.), and Muckleroy (Dem.) ; absent, Johnson, Coleman, Foster and Yarborough. Johnson soon resigned, Foster and Coleman left the state, the latter, a carpet-bagger, under charges of bigamy and horse-theft. W. W. Mills returned only for the last week of the session.

[2] *Convention Journal*, 2nd sess, 14-15; *Austin Republican*, Dec. 11, 12 and 14, 1868. Just before this, Morgan Hamilton had made offensive allusions to a public speech of Caldwell's delivered in Jefferson just after the killing of G. W. Smith, who was of the Davis faction.

and when it reported its chairman was able to get in another thrust at the organ of the other party. These comparatively trivial things were enough to awaken the old hostility, which never slept again.

It was known before the convention assembled that the question of division of the state would come up again. Upon this question the Davis faction had resolved to make their fight. *Ab initio* appeared hopelessly dead; but division had commanded a slight majority in the summer session until it began to crowd out other matters, and it seemed a promising issue. From the very start, therefore, a fight was begun to secure reconsideration or rescission of the Thomas resolution, passed in July, setting aside the subject. On December 10th, Newcomb of Bexar moved to rescind. Thomas replied with another motion to the effect that the convention would entertain nothing that did not relate to the formation of the constitution. A trial of strength on this last resulted in its rejection by 35 to 24. The antidivisionists resolved, therefore, to filibuster against all attempts to rescind the original Thomas resolution, and when Newcomb's resolution came up next day it was met by a " call of the house." [1] Sixteen members were absent, most of whom had never reported for this session. In a rage, Newcomb moved to adjourn *sine die*, and was supported by twelve other members. Every time the resolution came up thereafter for nearly three weeks, it was checked in the same way.[2] Feeling was rapidly rising. An effort of

---

[1] Under no. 55 of the convention rules, fifteen members could sustain a " call of the house" on any measure. No further consideration of this or any other measure could be had until all the members absent without satisfactory excuse had been brought in. Designed to secure action by all the members, it was used solely to obstruct measures.

[2] One whole day, December 15, was spent in calls of the house and voting by " yeas" and " nays" on motions to adjourn. *Convention Journal*, 2nd sess., 51-65.

McCormick to amend the rules so as to allow consideration
of other matters pending a call was voted down by the angry
divisionists.[1] Possibly foreseeing that they could not hold
out forever, the " anti's " endeavored to secure the passage
of a resolution binding the convention to submit the question
—along with the constitution—to a popular vote. This also
was voted down by the suspicious divisionists, for fear
that it might in some way embarrass them later.[2]

It was urged in extenuation of reviving the question that
the members of Congress had indicated that Texas must
take the initiative before the national legislature could act,
and that the popular sentiment for division had grown
enormously since the summer session. It was argued on the
other side that the convention was restricted solely to the
powers granted it by the Reconstruction Acts, and that these
had given it no authority whatever to consider such a
question; that by the Constitution of the United States, the
matter must be passed upon by the state legislature; and
that before anything was done the people should be allowed
to vote upon it, since the creation of additional states would
entail heavy expense for duplicating buildings and offices.
The southwestern delegates, among whom were Davis,
Degener, Newcomb, Varnell, and Morgan Hamilton, were
determined not to depend wholly upon the convention and
appointed a committee of seven to draft a constitution for
" West Texas," to be submitted to Congress for approval.[3]
It does not appear that they expected to submit it to their
people first, though they asserted that west Texas had a

---

[1] *Convention Journal*, 2nd sess., 73.

[2] *Ibid.*, 95, 97-8; debates in *Austin Republican*, Dec. 30 and 31, 1868.

[3] This Committee of seven is given by the *Austin Republican* as
Davis, Degener, Newcomb, M. Hamilton, Keuchler, Jordan, Varnell.
See issue of Jan. 4, 1869, also of Dec. 21, 23, 30, 31, 1868.

right to separate itself from the rest of the state without waiting for the permission of the people in the other parts, —a statement of the right of secession that must have sounded strange from the lips of radical unionists. In this they seem to have received the sanction of the divisionists of east Texas, and together they agreed to prevent the convention from completing the constitution until it had agreed to division. The way was opened for them on December 29, when, a call of the house having failed, Newcomb's motion to rescind the Thomas resolution finally came to a vote and was passed. The question now took a sudden turn, to explain which necessitates a slight digression.

Much had been said in the press and on the stump of the disorder in the state, and of the hostility manifested toward radicals. Maintaining that rebel intolerance would not permit of free discussion or a fair and free vote, many influential Republicans were of the opinion that no general election should be held either to vote on the constitution or for officers under it, until the fall of 1869. On December 16, J. R. Burnett introduced a resolution providing for the appointment of a special committee of thirteen to enquire into and report upon the condition of the state in this respect; and in case they found conditions unfavorable, to report what additional legislation was necessary to effect the speedy reorganization of a loyal civil government that would protect the people in their lives, liberty, and property, and meet their present necessities for special and general legislation. The resolution passed.[1] Of those appointed, eight were for division, five against it; of the latter, two were Democrats. The report of this committee, rendered December 23, was based upon statements of General Reynolds, Governor Pease, Bureau officers, judicial and

---

[1] It was foreshadowed in *Austin Republican* of Dec. 14 and 16, 1868.

other civil officials, and private citizens, and asserted that no fair and impartial election could be held at this time and probably not until several months after the inauguration of Grant, though it was admitted that there was general evidence of a decrease of crime and lawlessness and of better feeling toward the government. With regard to the additional legislation necessary, a resolution was reported calling upon Congress to give the convention the powers of a state legislature; provided that every act passed by the convention should be approved by the provisional governor before it should take effect, or else be passed by a two-thirds vote after his veto, and that the provisional governor should make removals and appointments of state officers and that no other oath should be required of such officers except that prescribed in the Reconstruction Acts for electors and the oath of office prescribed by the state constitution. The reason assigned for setting aside the test oath still required of all appointees, was that it shut out many competent and loyal persons and left the offices to become vacant or to remain in the hands of the disloyal. What relations this anomalous government was to have with the military was not stated, but the effect would have been virtually to supplant the district commander by the governor. The proposition is curious as a declaration from Republicans that the Reconstruction Acts had failed.[1]

Two minority reports were made. One by Armstrong and Kirk, the two Democrats, denied at some length the allegations of the majority with respect to the wide extent of lawlessness and the absence of freedom of speech and of the press,—citing against the last ten very radical papers then flourishing in various parts of the state. The other

[1] This statement was frequently made in debate by members of the Davis faction.

minority report was by James P. Newcomb, the rabid divisionist, who insisted that the temper, loyalty, and conduct of the people living west of the Colorado River,—in the proposed state of West Texas,—were exceptionally good, and that those people should be allowed a separate state government, or else that the dual form of military and civil government, which was a manifest failure, should be replaced by a territorial government in order that the United States might be able to maintain order and peace.

As soon as the reports were taken up, it became evident that the majority report was not acceptable to the Davis faction, who had no intention of prolonging and increasing the power of Pease's administration, and who were not so much concerned about a general election as about their project of division. A substitute, therefore, was offered by Davis, declaring that the extent of the territory, the conflicting sectional interests and general disorganization rendered, in the opinion of the convention, a division of Texas necessary; and that six commissioners elected by the convention, one each from the northern, eastern, middle, and western sections, and two from the state at large, should be sent to Washington to acquaint Congress with these conditions and necessities. Nothing could make clearer the determination of this party to force division upon the convention as the paramount issue. For two weeks the subject was thrashed out in a committee of the whole, consuming during that time almost exclusive attention. On the night of January 13 the substitute was reported from the committee, and a furious fight began to get it adopted over the majority report. The anti-divisionists filibustered successfully until nearly daylight.[1] The next day the president

---

[1] *Convention Journal*, 2nd sess. 267-278.

wrote to General Canby,[1] explaining the impossibility of getting a vote under a " call of the convention " until four absent members should arrive, lamenting the consequent waste of time, and requesting the commanding general to apply whatever remedy he was authorized to use.[2]

In the meantime, the filibustering continued and the divisionists decided to amend the rules. Under cover of making inquiry concerning the tardy delegates, a committee was appointed to propose the necessary change and immediately reported a new rule to the effect that only those members who had been present within five days preceding a call should be counted. The report came up for passage on January 16, and was promptly met by a call. Here the president, Davis, clearly violated the rules by entertaining the resolution anyway,—reporting the convention as full despite the four absentees,—and hurrying it to a vote. Immediately the body was in an uproar. The anti-divisionists saw the ground cut from under their feet by these tactics, and three of them,—Bryant of Grayson, A. J. Hamilton, and Cole, a Democrat,—refused to vote and were placed under arrest. The last two agreed to vote, and Bryant resigned.[3] The new rule was declared adopted by a vote of 42 to 28. Thus armed against a call, the divisionists hurried immediately to a vote on the more important measure and succeeded in substituting Davis's resolution for the majority report of Burnett's committee.[4] It came up

---

[1] General Canby had assumed command of the District about the middle of December.

[2] Four delegates were still absent: Mills, Foster, Coleman and Yarborough. *Convention Journal,* 2nd sess. 287-288.

[3] He was later allowed to withdraw his resignation.

[4] *Convention Journal,* 2nd sess., 300-304. See *Austin Republican,* Jan. 18, 1869.

again for final passage on the 20th, and probably in anticipation of a " call ", one anti-divisionist, Sumner, deliberately walked out in order to prevent a vote. When the call
was made and he could not be found, the majority forth-
with expelled him by a vote of 38 to 32,—the president ruling, again in defiance of parliamentary law, that a vote of
two-thirds was not necessary to expel.[1] The Davis resolution was then finally passed, and the next day was fixed
for electing the commissioners for which it provided. Unable any longer to make use of the call, the minority ab-
sented themselves next day and broke the quorum. On the
second day they returned and A. J. Hamilton read a protest,
signed by thirty members, against Sumner's expulsion, but
the majority would not allow it to be spread on the minutes
and themselves appointed a committee to give their own
version of the affair.[2] Excitement was at white heat. Attention was now turned upon the election of the six commissioners to Washington. The majority succeeded on the
first ballot in electing, as the two delegates at large, E. J.
Davis and J. W. Flanagan. On the second ballot for the
representative from north Texas, they also won, electing
Whitmore. The minority offered no further candidates and
allowed Burnett and Morgan Hamilton to be elected from
east and central Texas; but by uniting upon Varnell, a
divisionist, they beat Newcomb for the western district.

The victory of the divisionists was not without qualifica-

[1] Objection was made that the resolution to expel was out of order
because the convention could not transact other business while under
a call. This also Davis overruled. *Convention Journal*, 325. See comment in *Austin Republican*, Jan. 21, 1869.

[2] *Convention Journal*, 2nd sess., 330-331. Hamilton's protest is
printed in *Austin Republican*, Jan. 23. The answer to it, *i. e.* the committee's report, is in the *Journal*, 521-524.

tions. While they were holding back every other important measure until division could be accomplished, every newspaper in the state, except the *San Antonio Express,* was either denouncing the measure or at least refusing its support, and the citizens of San Antonio, the proposed capital for " West Texas," and of New Braunfels, the second largest town in that district, declared against it in mass-meeting.[1] Although in entire control of the commission, the divisionists were weakened somewhat by the fact that in no form or manner had the wishes of the people been consulted on this important subject, while the action of the convention in considering it was wholly outside the duties contemplated by the Reconstruction Acts. Moreover, a reaction was threatened against the high-handed methods by which the victory was won. *The Austin Republican* announced the next day after the commissioners were elected that the fight was not over and that a delegation from the other side also would go to Washington.

Now that the troublesome question of division was out of the way, the delegates were free to turn their attention to other things. More than a month and a half had been consumed in fighting over that subject; the only other matters considered had been of a special and legislative character, and not a thing had been done towards completing the constitution except to appoint a committee to correct and revise so much of it as had been engrossed at the previous session.[2] There had been much criticism of the body even by Republican journals, because of its apparent disregard of its proper business. *Flake's Bulletin* had expressed disgust

---

[1] *Texas Republican,* Dec. 18, 1868; *Houston Telegraph,* Jan. 14; *San Antonio Daily Herald,* Jan. 14, 1869; *Austin Republican,* Jan. 13 and 18, 1869.

[2] *Convention Journal,* 255, 260.

with its methods in the preceding summer and now reiterated the advice to the members to adjourn and go home.
The Austin Republican criticised the delegates for "their
waste of time and money, their frivolous and long debates
upon foreign issues, their indiscriminate and lavish legislation, their long delay in the formation of a constitution,"
which had "brought reproach upon the Republican party
of our state "; and especially censured them for the vast
amount of legislative work they had presumed to do:

They have assumed to erect new counties; on the faith of
their action, court houses have been built; they have authorized
the levy and collection of taxes under which interests have
grown up; they have chartered railways and immigration companies, in which large amounts of capital have been, or soon
will be invested.[1] In a hundred ways they have put under
pledge to support any constitution they may present a hundred
powerful interests.

The Democratic press was more contemptuous in its com-
ments, and only one paper, the *Houston Telegraph*, showed
any disposition at this time to make the best of a bad situation and treat the product of the convention with less than
open hostility.

But though the way was now open for work on the constitution, many of the Davis faction showed no desire to
take up that subject, for they were not pleased with that
part already completed, and most of them were even more
opposed to the liberal suffrage views now rapidly gaining
adherents.   Possibly, too, they expected their commis-

---

[1] The Liverpool and Texas Steamship company was granted $500,000
in six per cent state bonds and half a million acres of land, the last to
be given as subsidy for bringing immigrants,—forty acres for each im-
migrant. Gammel, *Laws of Texas*, VI, 126-129.

sioners to Congress to bring about a division of Texas into
several states, in which case there was no need of framing
a constitution now. The commissioners were elected on
Friday, January 22. On the following Monday, a resolution was introduced by Adams for the purpose of shutting
out any new legislative topics and confining attention to
the constitution and such other matters as were already
taken up. It passed, but against the opposition of most of
the divisionists.[1] The next day the latter made an effort
to adjourn the convention on February 1st, "to be reassembled at any time by the Commanding General, or by a
majority of the committee to Washington." This revealed
too much of their designs, and a substitute was offered to
the effect that no adjournment should take place until a
constitution had been framed for submission to the people
and that no other business should be in order until this was
done. The vote of 34 to 25, adopting the substitute, expressed approximately the feeling for and against the constitution.[2] Under the operation of this resolution the convention began work, January 27,—just ten days before it
was to adjourn,—upon the engrossed parts of the constitution as revised by the special committee.

Two days later the question of suffrage was reached, and
here began the second great battle. The committee, controlled of course by the Davis or "ultra" faction, had reported a stringent provision disfranchising all who had
previously been disqualified by the laws of the United
States or by participation in the rebellion, and all who could
not take a prescribed oath [3] almost as difficult as the famous

[1] *Convention Journal*, 2nd sess., 359-361.

[2] *Ibid.*, 378-380.

[3] "I, ——, do solemnly swear (or affirm), . . . that I have not been
disfranchised for participation in any rebellion or civil war against the

iron-clad oath.   On this issue, ex-Governor A. J. Hamilton, as champion of a most liberal and generous policy, performed one of his greatest services to the state.   He set himself squarely against any and all attempts to disfranchise the late rebels further than was already done by the Fourteenth Amendment.   His following at first was comparatively small: many of his friends who had supported him in other questions left him on this; the one newspaper that had always acted as the organ of his party remained silent throughout the struggle; but the sentiment for conciliation that had begun to spread after the election of Grant came to his aid; and as the northern Republicans, one after another, gave expression to conciliatory views, his following increased.   After some preliminary skirmishes, in which a proposition of the Democrats to exclude negroes from the ballot, and another, by Mundine, for woman suffrage, had been overwhelmingly voted down, the real fight began on a substitute offered by Thomas to the committee report, granting unrestricted suffrage.   This was laid on the table

United States, nor for felony committed against the laws of any state, or of the United States; that I have never been a member of any state legislature nor held any executive or judicial office in any state and afterwards engaged in insurrection and rebellion in the United States or given aid or comfort to the enemies thereof; that I have never taken an oath as a member of the Congress of the United States, or as an executive or judicial officer of any state, to support the Constitution of the United States, and afterwards engaged in insurrection and rebellion against the United States, or given aid and comfort to the enemies thereof; that I have not voted as a member of any convention or legislature in favor of an ordinance of secession; that I was not a member of any secret order hostile to the Government of the United States; that as a minister of the Gospel or editor of a newspaper, I did not advocate secession, nor did I support rebellion and war against the United States, so help me God." Disabilities could be removed by a two-thirds vote of the legislature or by Congress. See *Convention Journal*, 1st sess., 568-579.

by a close vote, 34 to 31. Filibustering could not prevent
the adoption, then, of the committee report, but Hamilton
did not despair. The small group of Democrats came
solidly to his side under the leadership of L. D. Evans.
All his eloquence and all his powers as a parliamentary tac-
tician and leader of men, he threw into the struggle.
Helped perhaps by a reaction against Davis's methods, only
four days later Hamilton commanded a clear majority, and
under cover of a substitute for the provision relating to
the registration of voters, he reopened the whole question.
His substitute was as follows:

Section 1. Every male citizen of the United States, of the age
of twenty-one years and upwards, not laboring under the
disabilities named in this Constitution, without distinction of
race, color or former condition, who shall be a resident of this
State at the time of the adoption of this Constitution, or who
shall thereafter reside in this State one year, and in the county
in which he offers to vote sixty days next preceding any
election, shall be entitled to vote for all officers that are now,
or hereafter may be, elected by the people, and upon all questions submitted to the electors at any election; *provided,* that
no person shall be allowed to vote or hold office who is now or
hereafter may be disqualified therefor by the Constitution of
the United States until such disqualifications shall be removed
by the Congress of the United States; *provided,* further, that
no person while kept in any asylum, or confined in any prison,
or who has been convicted of any felony, or who is of unsound
mind, shall be allowed to vote or hold office.

An attempt to table was defeated by an overwhelming majority, as was another to make more stringent the clause
relating to disqualification. The Radicals struggled hard
to secure other amendments, but the substitute was finally
made a part of the constitution by a vote of 30 to 26, and

the victory was won.[1] The patriotism which could rise high enough to disregard the question of party advantage was not without its reward, if the gratitude of the white people of Texas for their rescue from political proscription may be accounted a reward.[2]

Another important part of the constitution, the article on education, was already disposed of between times. Two provisions of importance were added: one increasing the revenue for schools by imposition of a poll tax, and setting apart for the same purpose one-fourth of the annual state taxes; and the other directing the investment of the principal of the school fund in United States bonds. These measures were chiefly the work of A. P. McCormick.[3]

Two things now remained to be done. Provision must be made for printing the constitution and for ordering a general election at which the voters of the state should accept or reject the constitution and vote for officers for the new government. Here troubles arose again. The *Austin Republican* had been publishing the journals of the conven-

[1] *Convention Journal*, 2nd sess., 482-486.

[2] *The Houston Telegraph* (Dem.), of Feb. 25, 1869, paid a glowing tribute to Governor Hamilton: "He stood as a break-water between us and the floods of ruin. He moved among breakers, shoals, and quicksands. He had to steer between Scylla and Charybdis, with the heavens overcast with clouds, and the storm howling all around him. . . . If we reflect that he labored to give the ballot to those who had bitterly opposed him, that he placed himself in opposition to extreme members in his own party, and even to his own brother; that he labored for a people who he believed had wronged him; that a large number of newspapers in the state were pouring abuse upon him even while he was laboring for the people; that he clothed us with the ballot at the imminent risk of having it used against himself, and that all of passion and even promise pointed out to him the opposite course as the one most for his interest, then indeed does he stand before us a *patriot, firm, tried, and true,* deserving the gratitude of our whole people of all parties."

[3] *Convention Journal*, 2nd sess., 417-422.

tion daily and was endeavoring to get the contract for printing the bound volumes of the journal and the new constitution; but its ardent support of the moderates, especially its
opposition to state division, had so angered the Davis faction that they were determined the contract should go elsewhere. They therefore proposed that the Washington
delegation should have the printing done somewhere in the
North, and by filibustering, with the president's aid, they
prevented the other proposition from coming to a final vote.[1]
They likewise opposed every move to have the constitution
submitted to the people; and when, nevertheless, February
5, an ordinance was crowded through, providing that the
election for the constitution, and for state, district, and
county officers, and members of Congress, should be held
during the first week in July, they entered a written protest
against the constitution itself.[2] This remarkable document,
which seems to have been the work of Morgan Hamilton,
attacked the constitution in two points, *viz.*, its omission
of the *ab initio* doctrine and its extension of the right of suffrage to all those who voluntarily became the public enemy
of the United States.

The majority of the convention have deliberately removed
from the constitution every safeguard for the loyal voter,
white and black. They have stricken from that instrument
the whole system of registry; they have repudiated the oath of
loyalty contained in the reconstruction laws; they have spurned
the test of equal civil and political rights, and we do most
solemnly call upon the registered voters of Texas to vindicate
the national honor and the cause of right and justice by their
votes.[3]

---

[1] *Convention Journal*, 2nd sess., 437-441, 524-527; *Austin Republican*,
Feb. 6, 1869.

[2] *Ibid.*, 199, 509-510, 517-520.

[3] *Ibid.* Those signing the protest were, in order: M. C. Hamilton,

This was the declaration of war between the two factions, and here was the issue presented before the people. The convention was now seething with excitement. The bickerings and quarrels of the first session were as nothing compared with the animosity and altercations of this one. The two wings of Republicans had long since, as Davis himself said, come to hate each other with a bitterness they had never felt toward their rebel and Democratic opponents, and the situation had steadily grown worse as the session progressed. If the apparent triumph of division and the expulsion of Sumner had greatly excited the Jack Hamilton party, the defeat of disfranchisement, added to that of *ab initio*, had infuriated their opponents no less. An incident will illustrate how far one side, at least, was carried away. One member, C. W. Bryant, of Harris County, a negro preacher, was indicted in Austin for rape upon an eleven-year-old colored girl, and the examining trial made his guilt perfectly evident; yet in the face of this evidence, the Davis faction, to which he belonged, resisted every effort to expel the brute, for no other apparent reason than that they desired his vote. However, he was finally expelled.[1] A number of personal encounters occurred and added to the general ill-feeling.[2]

The closing scenes formed a fitting climax to the story of party rancor and strife. The passage of the ordinance pro-

J. P. Butler, H. C. Hunt, G. H. Slaughter, James Brown, A. Downing, J. P. Newcomb, J. H. Lippard, S. Mullins, N. M. Board, J. Keuchler, N. Patten, J. H. Wilson, E. Degener, R. K. Smith, E. J. Davis, Ralph Long (col.), G. T. Ruby (col.), W. Johnson (col.), B. F. Williams (col.), A. P. Jordan and W. F. Carter.

[1] *Convention Journal*, 2nd sess., 398-9, 441-44, 455, 459, 462-63; *Austin Republican*, Jan. 25, Feb. 1; *Houston Telegraph*, Feb. 11, 1869.

[2] *Convention Journal*, 2nd sess., 445-447; *Austin Republican*, Feb. 2, 3; *Houston Telegraph*, Feb. 11, 1869.

viding for an election and for submitting the constitution
to the people and the protest of the ultra-radicals had occurred on Friday morning, February 5. The passage of
the resolution to give the printing to the *Austin Republican,*
the last subject for controversy, was prevented by the president's declaring the convention adjourned. At the opening of the evening session only a few of Davis's supporters
were present, and at first there was no quorum. A call of
the house secured one. Thereupon the president had the
secretary read a letter from General Canby to the effect
that if the printing of the constitution were not provided
for by the convention, he himself would attend to it. Mills
accused Davis of influencing General Canby to write the
letter and arraigned him severely for plotting to break up
the convention in order to defeat reconstruction under the
new constitution. He was called to order but refused to
take his seat, and was ordered under arrest by the president,
who over-ruled an objection that this required the authority
of the convention. In the hubbub, Williams, a negro member in the Davis faction, resigned, and was followed by
Ruby, and then by Newcomb, who declared the sittings
were being prolonged " for the purpose of subsidizing a
venalized press." The effect was to reduce the number
present below the usual quorum, as was evidently intended;
but Governor Hamilton raised the point that a majority of
the actual members only constituted a quorum. Davis over-
ruled it. A motion to adjourn was voted down, and a call
of the house made; but Davis declared no call could be sustained unless he concurred,—a most highhanded ruling,—
and declared the house adjourned until ten o'clock the next
morning. As he left the chair, pandemonium broke loose,
but the majority held together and elected M. L. Armstrong
of Lamar as president *pro tem.* Hamilton, white with

anger, took the floor and poured forth upon Davis, who had not been allowed to leave the hall, such a torrent of invective as no man but Jack Hamilton was capable of delivering. Then an adjournment was had until 9.30 next (Saturday) morning.

Only the delegates of the Hamilton faction assembled in the morning. Davis would not come, even when sent for, and they proceeded without him. A committee was appointed to confer with Canby about the printing; nothing else was done. The committee reported in the afternoon that the general advised the delegates to attend to whatever business there was and adjourn in due form. A committee of fifteen was then appointed to take charge of the records and the constitution and see that they were properly placed in the hands of the Commanding General. It was found that the papers had disappeared and that they were in the hands of an assistant secretary, A. J. Bennet, who was acting under the order of Davis. Bennet was arrested and gave up the papers. It was then decided to adjourn over to Monday. On Saturday evening, at the usual hour, Davis with two or three members of his faction came to the hall and declared the convention adjourned *sine die*. The same was done on Monday morning by the other party.[1]

Forty-five delegates, a fair majority of the membership at the close, signed the constitution.[2] The records were

---

[1] *Convention Journal*, 2nd sess., 527-529, *Austin Republican*, Feb. 6, 8 and 10, 1869. All the minutes of the proceedings Friday night, after the resignation of Ruby, and of the sessions of Saturday morning and afternoon and Monday morning were suppressed in the permanent journal printed under the auspices of Davis's administration in 1870. They are given, however, in the *Austin Republican* of Feb. 8. For an account of the closing scenes, see also *Houston Telegraph*, Feb. 11, and *Galveston News*, Feb. 14, 1869.

[2] The names are given in Gammel, VII, 430.

found to be in such confusion that General Canby appointed a special commission, consisting of J. W. Thomas of the one side, Morgan Hamilton from the other, and one of his staff officers, to assist the secretary, Tunstall, in putting them into shape for printing.[1]

The two sessions of the convention had cost the state more than $200,000 for five months of wrangling, not more than one month of which was spent in actual consideration of the constitution.[2]

---

[1] Ten thousand copies were printed for distribution. The *Austin Republican* got to print them after all.

[2] The list of appropriations made and approved is as follows:
First Session:

Mileage, per diem, and contingent expenses........$100,000

Second Session:

Mileage and per diem........................... 50,000
Publishing completed parts of Constitution........   3,600
Contingent expenses 15,000
Printing and contingent expenses.................   6,000
Mileage and per diem........................... 20,000
Delegation to Washington   6,000

Total...................................$200,600

CHAPTER X

THE CAMPAIGN AND ELECTION OF 1869

1. *The Appeal to Congress*

FOR the present there was no thought of reconciliation on either side. Though foiled in the convention, the radicals,—a name now enjoyed exclusively by the Davis party, —still hoped to defeat the constitution and divide the state through their control over the commission elected to Washington. The moderates, or conservatives, were determined to prevent this by sending a delegation of their own. Within less than a week after the convention adjourned, both were on their way, and political interest was anxiously centered upon their work at the national capital.[1]

The rival delegations arrived in Washington about the last of February, and at once sought interviews with General Grant and the congressional leaders. The issue between them is very clearly defined in the memorials which they each laid before Congress. That of the radical delegation, dated March 2, was drawn up by Morgan Hamilton, generally accounted the ablest as well as the most fanatical of that party. After explaining their authority to act in

---

[1] The radical delegation consisted of E. J. Davis, Morgan Hamilton, J. W. Flanagan, Varnell and Burnett, official delegates of the convention, and Newcomb, Degener, H. Taylor, Ruby and C. W. Bryant, who was still under indictment. The moderates were more numerous, the list of their delegates including A. J. Hamilton, Jas. H. Bell, J. L. Haynes, C. Caldwell, Geo. W. Paschal, M. L. Armstrong, McCormick, Sumner, Buffington, Alexander Rossy and Donald Campbell. *Austin Republican*, March 16, 1869.

the name of the convention, the memorialists declared that'
the condition of society in Texas " has been, and is still, very
desperate ". In support of this statement the statistics, tabulated months before by the convention committee on lawlessness and violence, were cited, as were the report of
Reynolds and the statement of Governor Pease made in
December; [1] and it was declared that conditions had steadily grown worse since Grant's election. This was to prove
that no fair election could be held in Texas. Because these
conditions had been due to " Johnson's policy ", it had been
believed that a convention elected under the acts of Congress would bring about a solution satisfactory to the loyal
people, a hope that had not been realized.

A considerable number of members, calling themselves Republicans, did not in their actions come up to that firmness for
Republican principles which their constituents had a right
to expect. A constitution was framed which gives no satisfaction or security to the loyal people of either color, but which
is heartily endorsed by the Democratic or rebel party and a
few (so-called) Republicans. This new constitution recognizes
the validity of rebel legislation, so far as not prohibited by the
constitution and laws of the United States, thus putting the
legislation during the rebellion on the same footing as that of
the most loyal states. . . . [It] abolishes the wise safeguard offered by the reconstruction acts with regard to the right of
suffrage, allowing in this respect the utmost latitude to the
disloyal.

That the constitution would be accepted by the white rebel
majority, the memorialists regarded as certain, since a fair
canvass could not be made of the colored voters. The
legislative, executive, and judicial departments would be
filled with " ex-Confederates and so-called Republicans."
Such a fearful condition cried aloud for a remedy:

[1] *Supra*, p. 245.

The new constitution should not be submitted to the people
at such an early date as the resolution contemplates [July 5],
if it is to be submitted at all. . . . Our only hope rests [in a
postponement of the election] until genuine peace is restored,
and . . . [Congress intervenes] . . . to secure a remodeling
of the constitution, in consonance with the necessities and spirit
of the times.[1]

The memorialists then went on to an argument for the division of Texas into three states, as another part of the remedy,
—urging the diversity of interests and population of the
various sections, and the fact that a majority of the convention had endorsed the plan.   However, the chief reason urged in favor of division was that it would offer the
loyalists a better chance to get entire control, since smaller
administrative divisions would be more easily reduced to order, and a full vote of the loyal blacks could be had, sufficient, it was believed, with the loyal whites, to carry any
election.   As an alternative to immediate organization of
the three states, Congress should create three territorial districts and hold them under military control until civil governments could be safely established.

The memorial bore the signatures of Davis, J. W.
Flanagan, M. C. Hamilton, Varnell, and Burnett; but the
last named declared that his name was placed there without
his consent and presented a spirited memorial of his own,
protesting against classing the opposing wing of the Republicans with rebels, insisting that conditions had grown
better rather than worse since Grant's election, defending
the new constitution as satisfactory to the loyal people of
Texas, and praying for the election to be held in July.   He
concurred with his colleagues only in the matter of state

---

[1] This meant, of course, the adoption of the *ab initio* doctrine and
disfranchisement.

division, and in that for reasons other than those which they urged.[1] It was not anticipated, in fact, when these delegates were elected, that they would petition for anything but state division.

The moderates presented their "Statement and Memorial" on March 16. It was an eloquent summary of political conditions and measures in Texas from the close of the war to that time.[2] Particular attention was given to the origin of the *ab initio* doctrine, its rejection by Governor Pease, by the military, by the constitutional convention and the Republican state convention. The history of the attempt to divide the state, the failure of the divisionists to agree upon the lines of division, and the expense it would bring upon the people of Texas, who were generally poor, were briefly but clearly set forth. The section of the constitution granting suffrage to the late rebels was defended in language both eloquent and generous:

We are of the opinion that it is not the part either of wisdom or justice to perpetuate disabilities in our state constitution. . . . Those who have been temporarily clothed with power in the lately rebellious states, wisely and for necessary ends, are too much heated by the friction of the contest through which they are passing, and are under too strong a temptation to punish their opponents, and to preserve power to themselves, to be the best judges of what a wise and just policy requires to be done on such a subject. . . . We wish to sit down by our hearthstones once more in peace. We do not wish to prolong a contest which, if prolonged, can produce only the bitter fruit of settled and implacable hate.[3]

[1] For these two memorials, see *Austin Republican*, March 31, 1869.

[2] It was written by Judge Jas. H. Bell.

[3] This memorial was signed by twenty-four Texas Republicans, twelve of whom had been members of the convention. *Austin Republican*, March 30, 1869.

It soon became evident that only a few of the most extreme of the Republican leaders in Congress looked with any favor upon the designs of the Davis committee, and none openly espoused their cause. General Reynolds, who had influence with Grant, was credited with declaring " division " a ridiculous proposition; at any rate, neither congressmen nor the Northern press took up the idea readily. Nor did the *ab initio* doctrine, soon to receive its deathblow at the hands of the Supreme Court of the United States,[1] gain many adherents. They were not more successful in the matter of suffrage, for Northern politicians had grown weary of carrying the burden of a disfranchised South so long after the war had ended. The general disposition was to hurry up reconstruction and get it over with. Finding there was small chance of getting Congress to interfere in their behalf on these points, the radical leaders fell back to the question of postponing the election until fall, which would give them more time to determine upon their future policy. In this there was greater promise of success; for whether their accusation that the moderates had " sold out to the rebels " found many believers or not, there was some uneasiness among Grant's supporters as to how the elections in Pennsylvania and other doubtful states would go in the early fall, and a desire to hold back Texas and Mississippi until these elections were over. Meanwhile they interposed successful resistance to the efforts of their opponents to have Congress remove before adjournment the political disabilities of some two hundred citizens of Texas, among whom were such prominent unionists as Jas. H. Bell, Thos. H. Stribling, W. E. Jones, and G. H. Noonan.[2] After passing an act which left the Presi-

[1] *Cf.* Texas *vs.* White, 7 Wall., 700-743.

[2] *Austin Republican,* April 8, 12, 13, 14, 1869.

dent to order elections in Virginia, Mississippi, and Texas, at such times as he should see proper, for voting upon the constitutions and the officers thereunder, Congress adjourned April 10; but the two delegations lingered with Grant and his cabinet, seeking Federal patronage, until Grant informed them that the patronage would be divided equally between them. It was distributed, however, chiefly upon the advice of General Reynolds, who at this time seemed to favor the conservatives, and the latter got the larger share.[1] On the whole, the contest at Washington resulted in favor of the Hamilton Republicans and to the discomfiture of the radicals, who returned to Texas disorganized and discouraged.

One change had been made in Texas with which neither party had anything to do, though it must have seemed an additional advantage to the conservatives. Grant sent General J. J. Reynolds back to the command of Texas, transferring Canby to Virginia. No reason was assigned except that it was a matter of justice to Reynolds to allow him to finish up what he had begun.[2] Canby's rule had been vigorous and firm, but just, and he was looked upon by the people generally, that is, the whites, with more favor than Reynolds, who was regarded as unjust and arbitrary. Though the whole administration of the state practically centered at his headquarters, and was transacted largely through his special orders, Canby was careful to follow the state law as far as possible and to interfere but little with the peaceful pursuits of the people. His most unpopular order was not of his own making. It was the promulgation of a joint resolution of Congress directing that all persons holding office under the provisional governments of

[1] *Austin Republican*, April 4, 9, 10, 11, 13, 24, 30, May 7, 1869.
[2] *Ibid.*, March 5, 1869.

Virginia, Texas, and Mississippi be required to take the
iron-clad oath, failing which their places should be filled by
persons who could take the oath. This was carrying out to
its extremity the policy laid down by Griffin in 1867 and
followed ever since with respect to appointments to office.
It was easier to apply such a rule now than earlier, when
the prevalence of grave disorder made necessary the retention
of many officials in whom the people had confidence; but it
does not seem unfair to assume that the sole motive was to
get the offices and their perquisites into the hands of Republicans. Canby did not remain long enough to complete
the transfer of offices, and the task was left to Reynolds,
who assumed command on April 8.

2. *The Formation of Tickets*

Now that it was positively known that the constitution
would be submitted to the voters and state officers elected,
interest in the election deepened, though Grant had not indicated when it would be called. The late convention had
barely adjourned when considerable discussion arose among
the Democrats as to what should be their attitude as a party
toward the new constitution and the offices. At first they
diverged widely. The *Houston Telegraph* declared for
the constitution, as the best that could be expected under
the conditions of the times, and for Jack Hamilton for
governor. The *State Gazette* favored the constitution, but,
as the party organ, refused to commit itself to any candidate until a Democratic convention should be held and a
ticket put out.[1] The *Telegraph* vehemently opposed calling any convention, putting out any candidates for state
offices, or organizing in any way,—very sensibly urging
that if a Democratic ticket were elected it would defeat the

[1] Issues of Feb. 17, March 1, 3, 5 and 10, 1869.

readmission of the state as it did in 1866, and that if the
new officials must be Republicans, the Democrats should
throw their entire strength to the moderate party and in
such a way as not to lend countenance to the cry that the
latter had " sold out " to them.[1] The *San Antonio Herald*
sided with the *Telegraph*; some of the smaller papers demanded a straight Democratic ticket, but practically all
were for the constitution. At one time Walton, chairman
of the executive committee, announced that a convention
would be called, but soon withdrew the announcement,
fearing that participation in the contest by an organized
Democracy would result either in a victory for the radicals or rejection of the constitution by Congress. A ten-
tative proposition to fuse with the moderate Republicans
on the state ticket was at once rejected, and abandoning that
field thereafter the Democrats put forward only county and
legislative candidates. The *State Gazette* urged that a
Democratic legislature was necessary to save the state from
the ruinous effects of radicalism, since the rest of the government was already surrendered to the Republicans.[2]

The constitutionalist Republicans were slow to get their
ticket formed. It was evident from the first that A. J.
Hamilton was the general choice of their party for governor, but his name was not formally put forward until
it became evident that the constitution would not be set aside
by Congress. On March 18, he announced his candidacy
in a telegram from Washington, and on the next day his
associates in that city drafted a state ticket with his name
at the head. The state executive committee was called to
meet in Austin on April 20. A few of the conservatives

[1] *Weekly Telegraph*, Feb. 25, March 4, 11, 18 and April 1, 1869.
[2] *State Gazette*, April 19, 31, June 7, 18, 25, 1869.

held out for Pease, but he promptly declared he would not
be a candidate. Two questions now confronted this party.
Should they join forces with the Democrats on a fusion
ticket? and should they call a state convention for the
purpose of agreeing upon their ticket? The first, we have
seen, was decided in the negative; the other was debated at
great length. The *Austin Republican* opposed a convention, as did most of the leaders, on the ground that there
was not time; that the people would not respond because
there was not a big enough contest in sight to interest them;
and that a convention would be attended only by aspirants
for office. It was not a strong argument, but with the
strong combination of leaders back of it, it was sufficient to
prevent a convention. The consequence was that some dissatisfaction arose and accusations were made that the
"Austin ring" was manipulating affairs in its own interest; considerable difficulty was experienced in getting a
ticket that all of their own party would agree upon; and,
more than either of these, it deprived the conservatives
of that appearance of regularity which such an organization
would have given them in the struggle against their radical
brethren for recognition at Washington.

At first, however, the radicals did not seem dangerous.
They had returned from Washington defeated in practically
every issue they had raised. *Ab initio* was dead, division
was dead, and there was no hope for disfranchisement.
Greeley had informed them, with respect to the last, that it
was time for the southern Republicans to cease " hanging
around the neck of the North ", that they must take care
of themselves, and after the Fifteenth Amendment secured
the suffrage to the negroes it would be " Root hog, or die!" [1]

[1] Quoted from *New York Tribune* by *State Gazette*, June 9, 1869.

In all of Texas at this time there was not a single paper of importance that openly espoused their cause.[1] To continue the fight against the adoption of the constitution was already hopeless, and there was before them a choice of three things: to go down in defeat against the constitution; to give up the contest and disintegrate as a party; or to repudiate their former declarations, accept the constitution and either become reconciled to the other faction, or go into the field against it upon a similar platform. The first and second being out of the question, a hint was feelingly thrown out to the Hamilton party that reconciliation could be had by placing some of the radicals upon the ticket.[2] The former, however, were confident of success and distrustful of their opponents and refused to displace any of their candidates. In the meanwhile, Morgan Hamilton, who was no party to the reconciliation idea, issued a call for a radical Republican convention to meet at Galveston on May 10. It was poorly attended, only about twenty delegates with some twenty-five alternates and proxies from a score of counties being present—and many appear to have been self-appointed. None of the radical leaders were present except Ruby; and nothing was done except to attack General Reynolds for telling Grant that there were not enough Union men in Texas, under the operation of the iron-clad oath, to fill the offices, and to refer certain resolutions to another convention which J. G. Tracy, editor of

---

[1] *The San Antonio Express* had recently passed under the editorial control of E. M. Wheelock, Superintendent of Education, and a close friend of Pease. The *Houston Union* and *Flake's Bulletin* were as yet neutral Republican.

[2] E. M. Wheelock to Governor Pease, June 11, 1869, MS. in *Exec. Corres.* The *Houston Union*, now gravitating to Davis, proposed him for lieutenant-governor. See *State Gazette*, May 12. See also letter of Jas. McKean to J. L. Haynes in *Austin Republican*, June 12, 1869.

the *Houston Union*, had called to meet in Houston on June 7.[1]

The outlook was not auspicious, for the abortive Galveston affair had weakened their position and little could be hoped of another such attempt. But it seems that in the latter part of May the radical leaders began to receive encouragement from northern radicals, such as Boutwell and Sumner, who stood close to national headquarters, and who were already helping them to secure the postponement of the election. Whatever the understanding, the Davis party were made to see that in opposing reconstruction they were holding to an impossible position, and cutting themselves off from Northern help; and they came the more easily to the last alternative—to effect an independent organization on a liberal platform.[2]

When, therefore, the Houston convention assembled, consisting of about thirty-five delegates and forty alternates from seventeen counties, their plans were taking form. The platform adopted involved a complete reversal of policy and principles. It made no reference to state division; it said not a word of *ab initio* principles. It accepted and promised to sustain the reconstruction acts of Congress, which had so often been declared a failure, and the constitution, which heretofore had been so impossible, was now declared " to propose the main object of constitutional government, *viz.,* the equal civil and political rights of all persons under the law. This convention therefore recommends the ratification of the same." The only issue raised against their opponents, the conservatives, was embodied in a warning to " the

[1] Proceedings of the Galveston convention in *Flake's Daily Bulletin,* May 11 and 12, 1869.

[2] See *Houston Union,* June 1, 1869; quoted in *Austin Republican,* June 4, 1869.

loyal people of Texas that opposition to the organization of the Republican party is the result of an insidious design of the enemy purposing the practical surrender of the state to the disloyal." [1] There was, in fact, no essential difference between this platform and that of the state convention of August 12, 1868, upon which the conservatives stood. E. J. Davis was nominated for governor and J. W. Flanagan for lieutenant-governor. The ticket, however, was not completed, and that task was left in the care of the chairman of the new state executive committee. To this position had been called J. G. Tracy, president of the convention, a most thorough-going spoilsman and one destined to play a large part in the history of the radical administration. Less than a year before he had been the publisher of the *Houston Telegraph*, at that time one of the most violent Democratic sheets in the state; but anxious only for power, place, and profits, he was ready to act with any political party that promised them. He had been supporting Hamilton in a neutral sort of way, and his sudden adhesion to Davis, who was desperately in need of an organ, strengthens the presumption that some understanding had been effected between the latter and the radicals of the North.

There was one member of the party, however, who was not prepared for so complete a face-about of principles, and that was no less a person than the dominating, splenetic, but able Morgan Hamilton, whom one of his opponents called " the spinal-column of the Davis party." He had not attended the convention and he now refused to act on its new executive committee. In a long letter to Tracy he reviewed the history of the faction to which he belonged and the principles which had called it into existence, and then went on to say :

[1] The platform in full is given in the *Austin Republican*, June 14, 1869.

The platform adopted is a clean surrender of all the issues which separated the two sections of the Republican party. It sinks out of sight and out of hearing everything upon which our appeal to Congress was made and upon which we can go before the country. . . . I have no stomach for further work in the cause. . . . I have been so generally characterized by " all liberal minded men," *i. e.* conservatives, as impracticable, illiberal, fanatical, vindictive, blood-thirsty, and by many other choice epithets distinguishing the savage, that I can not well afford to have superadded those of knave or fool.[1]

3. *The Canvass—The Radicals Endorsed by Grant*

All parties now hurried to complete their legislative and Congressional tickets, and to this end conventions were held in various districts, though in some the ticket was simply agreed upon without a convention. The canvass grew more spirited. The only issues, aside from the bitter personalities that characterized the time, have already been indicated. The radicals still insisted that the conservatives had " sold out to the rebels ", or Democrats, and that the loyal people would suffer in the sale: the conservatives held up and derided the recent conversion of the radicals, declaring their inconsistency proved a lack of political principle, and stigmatized them as a negro-supremacy and carpet-bagger party.[2] One other question there was which was fought out elsewhere, the date of the election. The Davis party had everything to gain by delay, the Hamilton nothing to gain. The former continued to represent at

[1] Tracy for a time refused to publish this letter, though specifically requested to by its author, and not until Hamilton threatened to send out copies to other papers did he print it at all. It is given in full in the *Austin Republican*, July 6, 1869. Later on, Morgan Hamilton went back into the fold of the Davis faction.

[2] On this, see *Austin Republican, Flake's Bulletin, Houston Union, San Antonio Express, passim.*

Washington that political intolerance and assassination of union men, *i. e.* radicals, were terribly prevalent in Texas and that as yet they would not be allowed a free vote; the latter insisted that Texas had grown very peaceful and that there was no reason whatever for longer delay.[1]

It must have been about this time that another, and, for obvious reasons, a powerful factor entered the struggle in the form of an alliance between the Davis party and General Reynolds, who had been the subject of their bitter attacks and complaints since the origin of the *ab initio* controversy in the fall of 1867. Whether Reynolds had secret ambitious designs, when he induced President Grant, his old friend and West Point classmate, to send him back to Texas, can not be determined, but he was not long in acquiring an itch for political office. He had always professed sympathy with the moderate and liberal faction, and now he approached J. L. Haynes, chairman of their executive committee, intimated a desire to be elected United States senator from Texas, and suggested that his influence with Grant would insure a speedy reconstruction of the state, and, therefore, the triumph of Hamilton. Haynes was willing to accept the arrangement, but Reynolds tried to exact a pledge from Hamilton himself, who not only refused but denounced the bargain publicly. Rebuffed and humiliated, Reynolds secretly allied with Davis, and apparently on the same terms, for he was a candidate for the United States senate before the legislature the next winter.[2]

[1] It is very amusing to note the conservative Republicans employing identically the same arguments on this point that the Democratic-Conservatives, then their opponents, had used three years before. A different ox was being gored now.

[2] Much information on this point was contributed by Mrs. W. W. Mills, a daughter of A. J. Hamilton. Hamilton himself refers to it in his *Memorial* to Congress of February, 1870, concerning frauds in the recent election.

Thus began a career of duplicity and fraud that was to cover with reproach a hitherto honorable reputation. Soon afterwards, it appears, he wrote Grant advising a postponement of the election which Hamilton's supporters still hoped would be held in August or, at latest, September. Both parties were manœuvering for the support of the President, but the radicals were gradually getting the advantage. In the first place their organization had the appearance of regularity, because they had held the only state convention that called itself Republican since the year before, and they had the sympathy of men like Butler, Boutwell, Sumner, and Creswell, and by no means least in influence, Reynolds. They had a number of active agents in Washington who were endeavoring to secure the official recognition of their organization, and in this they finally succeeded.[1] On July 7, Governor Wm. Claflin of Massachusetts, chairman of the national Republican executive committee, officially directed that the Davis committee be recognized as the regular one in Texas. This petition being sustained by several of the members of his cabinet, Grant, who had hitherto refused to take sides, now announced to the radical leaders that, it having been decided which was the Republican party in Texas, he was " ready to make any changes necessary to the success of reconstruction in that state." [2] The conservatives seem to have been fighting in the dark. Pease, bearing a letter of commendation from Reynolds, who was not yet suspected of duplicity, went to Washington early in July to prevent the

[1] Among those agents were W. B. Moore, late of the *S. A. Express,* Judge C. B. Sabin and even L. D. Evans, a Democrat.

[2] The circumstances attending this recognition, especially his own part in it, are told by W. B. Moore in a printed circular written May 20, 1871.

postponement of the election. He could do nothing. On July 15, President Grant issued a proclamation fixing the election for November 30.[1]

Meanwhile several things occurred to alarm the Hamilton party. The stand taken by the President in the contest in Mississippi, where he openly espoused the cause of the radicals against his own brother-in-law, was an uncomforting precedent.[2] Then rumors flew about that several of the friends of Hamilton holding federal appointments were to be displaced by Davis men. The first to fall was W. W. Mills, collector of customs at El Paso and Hamilton's son-in-law, who was replaced by D. C. Marsh, a carpet-bagger from Michigan and a supporter of Davis. The Davis organs were soon prophesying the removal of others, and in September the changes began. The post offices at important places were given to prominent Davis men; revenue and customs officers, United States marshals and other federal appointees who were known to be Hamilton's supporters, were ousted.[3] This interference by Grant's cabinet was resented bitterly by the conservative Republican press in Texas, but was denounced as well by such Northern papers as the New York *Tribune* as " little short of idiotic," because calculated to endanger the ratification of the Fifteenth Amendment by alienating many of the Hamilton party.[4] These removals were as yet confined to federal offices. But

[1] *Ann. Cyclop.*, 1869, p. 674.

[2] Garner, *Reconstruction in Mississippi*, 241.

[3] J. G. Tracy was made postmaster at Houston, Swante Palm at Austin. Among other changes, J. H. Haynes was replaced as collector of customs for the Galveston district by Nathan Patten; A. H. Longley, assessor of internal revenue, by W. B. Moore. See *Austin Republican*, June 15, Sept. 27, 28, 30, 1869.

[4] Quoted in *Austin Republican*, Oct. 8, 1869. See also issues of Sept. 23 and 30.

following the example of the cabinet, Reynolds, when ill-feeling was aroused by the news of his alliance with Davis, soon began the decapitation of state officers.

The General's change of heart seems to have remained generally unsuspected by his late Hamiltonian friends until the telegraphic despatches of September 25 gave out part of his letter, "Personal No. 2," of September 4, to the President. Within two weeks the whole text of that remarkable letter was in their hands. It charged the failure of reconciliation between the factions wholly upon the Hamilton party, which had held aloof from any organization; and declared the only organized Republican party in the state was that headed by E. J. Davis; and that the reason for this action of the Hamilton faction was to be found in Democratic support of Hamilton for governor. Furthermore, the radical wing acted out their professions of adherence to the reconstruction laws by presenting for office men qualified under those laws; while the conservatives nominated men who could not qualify but were acceptable to the Democrats.[1]

The circumstances all considered, I am constrained to believe that the coalition which has been charged as existing between the Conservative, or A. J. Hamilton Republicans, and the Democrats (generally ex-rebels) does exist. . . . The success of the A. J. Hamilton faction, as it will be produced by Democratic votes, will be the defeat of Republicanism in Texas, and will put the state in the hands of the very men who, during the entire period of the rebellion, exerted every nerve to

[1] Reynolds cited as examples, Stribling of San Antonio, candidate for Congress, and McFarland of Austin, candidate for state senator. Yet Degener, the Davis candidate against Stribling, could not take the test-oath, and Whitmore, Davis candidate for Congress in North Texas, was disqualified by the Reconstruction Acts. There were quite as many ex-Confederates, though Union men, on the Davis ticket as on the other.

destroy the Union, and who have uniformly opposed the reconstruction laws with a persistency worthy of a better cause.[1]

The publication of this letter aroused a storm of angry
protest from the Hamilton party. As soon as its substance
had been made public, Governor Pease addressed an indignant but courteous letter to Reynolds tendering his resignation. The General's opinions, he said, were not warranted
by the course of the two parties; his endorsement of Davis
and the efforts of the national administration to assist in
the election of that factious element left no alternative.[2]
Pease now plunged into the campaign for Hamilton. It
was rumored that Davis or Morgan Hamilton would be
appointed to succeed him, but it was not done. Indeed
there was now little need for a governor, for the military
commander had gradually absorbed all his important
functions.

Although they saw the cards stacked against them, the
conservatives redoubled their efforts. Here and there
changes were made in the ticket, several candidates resign-
ing in order to concentrate upon one man. Stribling, candidate for Congress from the 4th or western district, who
ran some risk of disqualification, gave way to J. L. Haynes,
against whom nothing damaging could be urged. Speakers were sent out to all parts of the state. Nor were their
opponents idle. Though unable to command a like array of
able speaking talent—for Pease was right in saying that
eight-tenths of the educated Republicans were with Hamilton,—the radicals could appeal with peculiar force to the

---

[1] The full text of this letter may be found in *Ann. Cyclop.*, 1869, pp.
674-5; in *Austin Republican*, Oct. 8, 1869; and in appendix to Hamilton's *Memorial*, of Feb. 6, 1870.

[2] *Austin Republican*, Oct. 2, 1869. *Executive Records, Register Book*,
no. 283, pp. 427-8.

negroes through the Loyal Union League of which Ruby was president. In July, this officer had levied a special tax of twenty-five cents upon each member of the organization for campaign purposes.[1] It was represented to them that Hamilton and his friends had " sold out to the rebels " and intended to disfranchise the blacks, and as proof of this was cited the administration's endorsement of Davis. It was soon to be seen that the majority of the negroes were safe for the radical ticket. As they so overwhelmingly outnumbered the whites in the Republican party, it was evident that to win, Hamilton must secure a large number of Democratic votes. So great was the repugnance of the average Democrat to radical rule, that, as has been seen, most of them were willing to support him. However, many wavered and some extremists there were who would not vote for a Republican under any circumstances. These were encouraged by the radicals to take an independent stand, since such a course would weaken Hamilton. Indeed it is hard to acquit some of these extreme Democrats of having willingly played into the hands of the radicals. On September 29, a small group of Democratic editors assembled at Brenham and nominated Hamilton Stuart, editor of the Galveston *Civilian,* a man of the highest personal character, for governor, with a full ticket of state officers. The movement was engineered by a group of self-styled " careful thinkers ", who apparently had no hope whatever of electing Stuart, but expected to pull over enough wavering Democrats from Hamilton to defeat him. In this they were planning not for the present, but for the future. The election of the proscriptive radicals, controlled by carpet-baggers and negro leaders, would destroy the future

[1] The order is printed in *Austin Republican,* August 28, 1869.

chances of the Republican party in Texas, while a moderate administration might give it increased strength and respectability. Their action did not move many Democrats but it placed another obstacle in the way of the Hamilton party.[1]

On October 1, General Reynolds issued his order for revising the registration lists and for holding the general election, which was to commence November 30 and close December 3. The registration was to begin November 16 and run for ten days, and the registrars were given the same powers they held under former orders. The provisions relating to the method of holding the election will be noted further on.[2]

No objection was to be found to the directions for registration, but objection was very speedily made to the registrars appointed. In most counties, especially in the populous and important ones, Davis men alone were selected, though in a good many instances military officers were placed at the head. It was seen at once that this was giving the radicals an unfair advantage. Before Reynolds's order was issued, Jas. P. Newcomb, again editor of the *San Antonio Express,* had declared it necessary for the commander to appoint only radical Republicans, and no others, to these places, in order that " a proper registration " could be had; they should be able to reject applicants, as did those appointed by General Griffin, " even when they were technically entitled to register, if they were known to

[1] There was thought at the time to be some significance in the fact that both E. J. Davis and J. G. Tracy were in Brenham at the time Hamilton Stuart was nominated. Tracy was hobnobbing with the Democratic editors.

[2] General Orders, no. 174, in *Ann. Cyclop.,* 1869, pp. 676-7; and in *Austin Republican,* Oct. 4, 1869.

be opposed to the government." [1]   Since such men as Newcomb insisted that all who were not radicals were rebels and therefore " opposed to the government," this could mean but one thing; and it was given even a more sinister aspect when Reynolds afterwards, in the face of this brazen declaration, appointed this same Newcomb the head of a radical board of registrars for Bexar County.

When the registration began complaints were plentiful. For convenience, the old registration lists were accepted and only new names added.   The most frequent complaint was that all applicants who testified that they had been refused before, were rejected at once, no matter what the trouble had been.   Many claimed they were refused for no other reason than that they were Hamilton men.   In Bexar County, in addition to the usual complaints of unfair rejection, it was later shown that about one hundred names were struck off illegally after registration had closed.   Undoubtedly many of those who complained were legally ineligible, and there would have been dissatisfaction and accusations in any case; but the mere fact that in a close, exciting campaign, the boards were in the majority of cases drawn wholly from one side, often composed of persons of equivocal character, and given sole authority to appoint challengers,—in fact, that complete power over the registration of the voters was given to *one* of the factions, is enough of itself to justify grave suspicion of both actual and premeditated fraud.

During the later stages of the campaign Reynolds began a general removal of Hamilton's friends from the higher state offices.   In October W. R. Fayle, judge of the criminal court of Harris and Galveston counties, was removed

[1] The whole article is quoted in *Tri-Weekly State Gazette*, Sept. 6, 1869.

on the ground that he had caused a white jury to be returned for the trial of J. G. Tracy, Davis's campaign manager, indicted for homicide,—though it had not been customary in that district to return mixed juries. A former jury had been packed for acquittal, according to the statement of Tracy's friend, the prosecuting attorney, and the judge's sole object seems to have been to get an impartial jury. Tracy went to see Reynolds, who issued the order of removal and appointed a new judge, Dodge, a personal and political friend of Tracy. It was charged by Judge Fayle himself that the sole motive for his removal was to prevent harm to the Davis cause.[1] D. J. Baldwin was suspended from the office of district attorney for no other apparent reason than that he was a friend of Hamilton.[2] Joseph Wadsworth was removed from a similar position for the same reason. C. Caldwell was removed from the supreme court for no other cause than being one of the aggressive Hamilton leaders; and his colleague, the venerable A. H. Latimer, candidate for lieutenant-governor with Hamilton, was virtually thrust off and treated in a most insolent manner.[3] To his place was appointed Moses B. Walker, an ex-colonel in the United States Army.[4]

[1] *Flake's Bulletin,* quoted in *Austin Republican,* Nov. 2, 1869; *Ann. Cyclop.,* 1869, p. 676.

[2] He had been imprisoned during the war as a Union man; his successor was an ex-Confederate officer. *Ann. Cyclop.,* 1869, p. 676; *Houston Union,* Nov. 20, 1869.

[3] He had offered his resignation, to take effect Dec. 30; Reynolds informed him it would take effect Nov. 30. Resenting the affront, he asked that his resignation take place at once. The court was in session and Reynolds refused and ordered him not to leave town. *Austin Republican,* Nov. 2, 5, 11, 1869.

[4] Federal army officers were appointed to several judgeships and district-attorneyships. One was made mayor of Brenham.

4. *The Election*

On Tuesday, November 30, the election began, with the country in a state of suppressed excitement. In counties where there was any reason to apprehend disturbances, Reynolds had stationed detachments of soldiers to guard the polls. The polling places were in the county seats and the registry boards were the officers of election. The methods employed in the registration had not increased the confidence of the people in a fair election, and it was found that the provisions of Reynolds's recent order were far from assuring it. The vote was by ballot; but it was ordered that no mark should be placed upon the ballot by the registrars, except to designate " colored " voters. The customary precaution of numbering the ballot so as to make it correspond to the voter's number on the registry list, in order to detect a fraudulent change of ballot, was omitted. This left the ballot box completely at the mercy of the registrars. It was also ordered that if any disturbance arose the polls should be closed by the board and not re-opened until ordered by the military commander.

In general the election passed off more quietly than had been anticipated. The returns came in very slowly, but it soon became evident that the vote for Hamilton would prove to be unexpectedly small. A large proportion of the whites had not voted, either because they would not support any Republican candidate, or else because they feared, as the Davis party insisted, that Hamilton's election would not be acceptable to the administration and would therefore defeat the reconstruction of the state. But little more than half of the registered whites went to the polls at all, while a large percentage of the negroes voted.[1] Since

[1] The revised registration lists showed: whites, 78,648; colored, 56,-905; total, 135,553.

most of these last were controlled for Davis by means of the
League the race for governor was rendered very close.
Both sides claimed victory, but reports obtained from military headquarters gave Davis a majority which rose and
fell until it settled to about 800.

In the meantime came a deluge of accusations of fraud
from various parts of the state. Some of these pertained
to registration and have already been noticed. In Navarro
County, claimed for Hamilton, with a voting population of
over one thousand, no election was held at all, because the
chairman of the board, a non-resident, had taken away the
list of registered voters and never returned.[1] In Milam,
also said to be a Hamilton county, the election was stopped
on the morning of the second day on pretext of disturbance near the polls, and no returns were made at all. The
ballot-box of Hill County was taken into an adjoining
county and counted by one member of the board alone, who
returned a majority of 149 for Davis. Returns from El
Paso gave Davis 339 and Hamilton 122, though 277 voters
afterwards made affidavit that they had voted for the latter.
An examination of the ballots by the local district commander showed that they had been tampered with, and he
advised General Reynolds that an investigation should be
had.[2] It was charged and admitted that in a number of
counties the officers of election failed altogether to swear to
the correctness of the returns. The conservatives were
clamorous for Reynolds to make an investigation into these
fraud charges and to order a special election in Milam and
Navarro, as he had indicated he would do. If this should
be done they were confident of success. But Reynolds re-

[1] He was a son of J. H. Lippard, a candidate for the state senate
from that district, and it was said that Navarro was not a Lippard
stronghold.

[2] Mills, *Forty Years in El Paso; Austin Republican*, Dec. 2, 11, 21, 22,
23, 1869; Jan. 11, 21, 24, 1870; Hamilton's *Memorial.*

fused to do anything.[1]   The returns were accepted as sent in; and the question as to Milam and Navarro was dallied with awhile and then in some form referred to the President.   The President's action may be guessed at from the fact that the special election was never ordered.[2]   A protest of the conservative leaders was sent to Grant, but availed nothing.

On January 8, General Reynolds issued the following:

Special Orders, No. 6, Austin, Texas, Jan. 8, 1870.

The following appointments to civil office are hereby made, the persons appointed having been elected to the positions designated:

Edmund J. Davis to be Governor.

J. W. Flanagan to be Lieutenant Governor.

A. Bledsoe to be Comptroller.

G. W. Honey to be Treasurer.

Jacob Keuchler to be Commissioner of General Land Office.

The present incumbents will continue to discharge the duties of their respective offices until their successors appear in person and duly qualify.[3]

[1] Hamilton and his friends always believed that he had been deliberately and fraudulently counted out by Reynolds. Just before the election one of Reynolds's staff officers, Colonel Hunt, a warm personal friend of Hamilton, warned him that there was a move on foot at headquarters to make the election of Davis sure, " if he had to be counted in." The course openly pursued by Reynolds before, during and after the election, seemed to justify the warning and established the belief in his guilt.

[2] During this time the Hamilton party seemed to be entirely in the dark as to Reynolds's intentions, while the leaders of the other party were in frequent consultation with the General. For running comment of a partisan, but one on the ground and generally reliable, see files of *Austin Republican* for this time.

[3] The candidates on the Hamilton ticket had been:

A. J. Hamilton for governor.

A. H. Latimer for lieutenant governor.

A. T. Monroe for comptroller.

Jas. W. Thomas for treasurer.

Joseph Spence for commissioner general land office.

Five days later another order was issued making appropriations for the salaries of the state officials for the year 1870 as fixed by the new constitution. On January 11, General Orders no. 5 again gave out the results of the election without stating the vote for any of the candidates.[1] In addition to the Davis ticket, already named, the four Congressmen-elect were declared to be G. W. Whitmore, J. C. Conner, W. T. Clark and E. Degener from the 1st, 2nd, 3rd and 4th districts respectively.[2] The vote for the constitution was 72,466 to 4,928 against it. It was learned at headquarters that the official returns for governor were:

Davis	39,901
Hamilton	39,092
Stuart (Dem.)	380

Davis arrived at Austin about a week after his appointment and took up his duties as "provisional governor." He would not become actual governor until Congress should accept the constitution and readmit the state. Jas. P. Newcomb became his secretary of state. J. G. Tracy hurried to Austin for the purpose of establishing a paper there as the administration organ, purchased the *State Gazette* which he renamed the *State Journal,* and installed Newcomb as its editor.[3] Hamilton's friends called a consultation at Austin

---

[1] Copy in *Exec. Corres.*

[2] Conner was a Democratic carpet-bagger who had been stationed in that district for some two or three years as a captain in the U. S. army. His home was in Indiana.

[3] The record of this pair of spoilsmen and their business associates is worth noting. Tracy, ex-Confederate, ex-Democrat, and radical of eighteen months' standing, was postmaster at Houston, publisher and editor of the *Houston Union,* enjoying with the *S. A. Express* the exclusive patronage of the U. S. Government in Texas, chairman of the Republican executive committee, and was soon to be public printer. His partner in the *Union,* Quick, with identical war and political re-

for February 7, for the purpose of devising measures for bringing the election frauds to the attention of Congress, but the evident hopelessness of such a contest and the disinclination of many of the party leaders to carry the fight further led to the abandonment of the program.[1]

cord, was postmaster at Brownsville. Newcomb had been thriftier. He was editor of the *S. A. Express*, alderman of San Antonio, notary-public, assistant assessor of internal revenue, secretary of state, and editor of the *State Journal*. For business purposes the new combination was nearly ideal and drew from the *Republican* the remark that "with Tracy to make out the bills, and Newcomb as secretary of state to approve them, these gentlemen ought to do a right driving business." Siemering, part owner of the *Express* and the *State Journal*, had been a lieutenant in Duff's Partisan Rangers, that terror to Union men in west Texas during the war.

[1] It was in anticipation of this contest that Hamilton prepared his *Memorial*, an excellent summary, from the point of view of the conservative Republicans, of the election and of General Reynolds's relations thereto.

CHAPTER XI

The Final Act of Reconstruction

General Orders no. 5, of January 11, had contained the list of legislators-elect, and directed them to assemble at Austin on February 8, as prescribed by the Act of Congress of April 10, 1869. By General Orders no. 21, February 5, directions were given for the organization of the two houses. A stringent oath, based upon but amplifying the disqualifying clause of the Fourteenth Amendment, was prescribed, and the seat of any member failing to take it was declared vacant. Reynolds explained that the oath was required by the act of April 10, 1869, but in fact it copied the one passed in December for the second reconstruction of Georgia, and the commander had no authority whatever for exacting it in Texas.[1] By the same order a temporary speaker of the house was appointed, and all cases of contested seats were to be referred to military headquarters. The reason assigned for this close surveillance of the legislature was that any organization of the state government, prior to the ratification of the constitution by Congress, could only be provisional, and he must be responsible for its acts. The houses were ordered to transact no business until all members had taken the required oath, but to adjourn from day to day. Business was delayed in this way for three days, but those who hesitated at last came forward, convinced that if not debarred by the Fourteenth Amend-

[1] See Fleming, *Doc. Hist. of Reconstruction*, 488-491. Also *Flake's Bulletin*, Feb. 11 and *Austin Republican*, Feb. 8, 1870.

ment they were not debarred by this.   The first appointeee of Reynolds having declined, J. P. Butler was designated speaker.[1]   On February 10, Ira H. Evans, of Corpus Christi, an ex-officer of the United States Army, a townsman and close personal friend of Governor Davis, was elected permanent speaker.   On the same day General Reynolds informed the two houses that certain cases of contested seats, not arising under the reconstruction laws, should be acted upon by the bodies concerned.   Of these, one was in the senate and eight were in the house.   The others, about ten, were reserved for the decision of a military board.   In each house the radicals had a slight majority over both Democrats and conservative Republicans, and therefore controlled the committees on elections.[2] These made short work of the contests; the radical contestants were seated in nearly every instance.[3]   Several of those who lost their seats were leading Hamilton Republicans, as A. J. Evans in the senate and M. L. Armstrong in the house.   Practically all business pertaining to the executive was transacted by the military commander, as Davis consistently regarded his own powers as provisional governor too limited to justify any action of his own, even to sending messages to the two houses.

[1] Butler was the man who had spoken so bitterly and insultingly of General Reynolds in the Galveston convention, May 10, 1869. He was a carpet-bagger.

[2] In the Senate, radicals 16, conservatives 3, Democrats 11; in the House, radicals about 46, conservatives 8, Democrats about 36.

[3] One case that seems particularly flagrant was the unseating of Nelson Plato (Dem.) of the Brownsville district. He was not served with notice of a contest until the legislature convened; but was called before the committee, given no time in which to collect evidence, and immediately deprived of his seat by jamming through the majority report which threw out the vote of Cameron County.

There were only two matters in particular which the legislature was required to attend to at this provisional session: to ratify the Fourteenth and Fifteenth Amendments to the Constitution of the United States, and to elect United States senators. The amendments were submitted on February 11, and three days later were overwhelmingly adopted, practically without opposition. The election of the senators was not so easily disposed of. Rumor had been busy with the names of a number of candidates, of whom the most prominent were General J. J. Reynolds, Governor Davis, Morgan Hamilton, J. W. Flanagan, L. D. Evans, and J. P. Butler. Unexpectedly to himself, perhaps, violent opposition developed against Reynolds. He was bitterly attacked by the press for becoming a candidate before a body he had helped so much to constitute through manipulation of the voting, whose election he had declared without making returns, whose organization he had supervised and whose contested seats he himself had decided.[1] It was plain to see, also, that some of his late allies had no desire to elevate him at the expense of themselves, and that there was a strong undercurrent of feeling against him at Washington. Just before the radicals went to caucus for deciding upon their candidates, he withdrew his name. Davis had pledged himself to retain the governorship. This left M. C. Hamilton and the lieutenant-governor the most prominent candidates of the majority party. In the caucus which settled the choice there were a few who bitterly opposed Hamilton, because of his letter on the Houston convention. On February 22, Hamilton and J. W. Flanagan were elected by decisive majorities, the former for the short term to expire March 4, 1871, and also for the suc-

[1] *Flake's Bulletin*, Feb. 11; *Houston Telegraph*, Feb. 14; *Austin Republican*, Feb. 8 and 16, 1870.

ceeding term to 1877, and the latter for the term ending in March, 1875. The Democrats gave their votes to General Horace Boughton.

On February 24, after adopting resolutions complimentary to General Reynolds, the legislature adjourned, to be called by Governor Davis in regular session after the readmission of Texas to representation in Congress.[1]

Early in March Benjamin F. Butler reported a bill from the Reconstruction Committee for the admission of the Texas senators and representatives to Congress. It went through with no opposition and almost without debate. Certain conditions, however, were provided: one, that each member of the state legislature should within thirty days take the oath implied by the third section of the Fourteenth Amendment or vacate his seat; another, that the constitution of Texas should never be so amended or changed as to deprive any citizen or class of citizens of the United States of the right to vote as recognized by the constitution adopted, except as punishment for crime; a third, that it should never be lawful for the said state to deprive any citizen of the United States, on account of race, color, or previous condition of servitude, of the right to hold office under the constitution and laws of the state, or upon any such ground to require of him any other qualifications for office than such as were required of all other citizens; and finally, that the constitution of Texas should never " be so amended or changed as to deprive any citizen or class of citizens . . . of the school rights and privileges " secured by this constitution. The act was at once approved by President Grant, March 30, 1870.

Immediately the senators and representatives from Texas

[1] One other thing it was thoughtful enough to do. Tracy was elected state printer.

were sworn in.[1]   As soon as the news reached Texas, E. J. Davis dropped the qualifying term " provisional " from his official title.   The final act of reconstruction was performed on April 16, when General Reynolds issued a general order or proclamation remitting all civil authority in the state " to the officers elected by the people."

Legally, the reconstruction of Texas was now complete. After nine years, tumultuous with political and social revolution, she was back again in the Union with her sister states,—not on terms of perfect equality it is true,[2] but unmanacled, at any rate, and free to work out the new problems that confronted her.   The first of these was to endure as best she could the rule of a minority, the most ignorant and incapable of her population under the domination of reckless leaders, until time should overthrow it. Reconstruction had left the pyramid upon its apex; it must be placed upon its base again.

[1] There was some controversy over the admission of J. C. Conner (Dem.), representative from the second district; but there was no doubt of his majority in the election, and he was finally admitted to his seat.

[2] Dunning, *Essays*, 351.

EPILOGUE

CHAPTER XII

Radical Rule and its Overthrow

1. *Policies and Legislation*

Partly through a natural feeling of relief at the restoration of civil government, and partly through the promises of Davis in the recent campaign that his policy would be moderate, progressive, and for the enforcement of law and order, the new administration was at first greeted with general expressions of good-will. Even the *Austin Republican* announced that the friends of A. J. Hamilton would thenceforth recognize and support the organization of which Governor Davis was the leader. However, the true spirit of the governor's "progressive" plans was not revealed until after the legislature met in called session on April 26th.

In his message to that body the governor complained of the continuance of lawlessness in many parts of the state and recommended that an act be passed for the enrollment in a militia of all able-bodied men between the ages of eighteen and forty-five, except those who should pay a tax for the privilege of exemption. This militia was to be called out only in the event of a general resistance to the laws. For the apprehension of individual offenders or of those acting in small bodies, he recommended a system of state police reaching into every county. Both militia and police should be under the control of the governor, whose power should be reinforced by a provision enabling him to establish martial law in any troublesome district.

It was not long before an elaborate militia bill was reported in the lower house and speedily carried over the ineffective resistance of the minority. It contained all the features called for by the governor's message. All able-bodied men between the ages of eighteen and forty-five were divided into two classes: the " state guard ", composed of all volunteers enrolled, armed and regularly drilled in each county; and the " reserve militia ", consisting of all those not enrolled in the guard. The governor was made commander-in-chief and empowered to appoint and commission all general, field, company, and staff officers, and to control the organization of both branches of the militia. He was also given full power to call into active service the military force of the state

in time of war, rebellion, insurrection, invasion, resistance to civil process, breach of the peace, or imminent danger thereof, . . . [and] . . . whenever in his opinion the enforcement of the law is obstructed within any county or counties, by combinations of lawless men too strong for the control of the civil authorities, to declare such county or counties under martial law and to suspend the laws therein until the legislature shall convene and take such action as it may deem necessary. . . . The expense of maintaining the state guard or reserve militia, called into active service under this section, may, in whole or in part, in the discretion of the governor, be assessed upon the people of the county or counties where the laws are suspended.[1]

When the bill went to the senate, the eleven Democrats and three conservative Republicans, headed by Senators Bowers and Webster Flanagan, gave the fifteen radical or administration Republicans a long, hard fight. Flanagan offered a substitute that differed from the administration

[1] Gammel, VI, 185-190.

measure chiefly in these points: the militia officers were to
be elected by the enlisted men or the lower officers; the
force was to be called out only by the local civil authorities,
the district judge, justice of the peace, or sheriff; and no
provision was made for the declaration of martial law
or for quartering troops or assessing expenses upon any
county. With a majority of one vote, the radicals at length
defeated the substitute, on June 21st; and then, in violation
of an agreement, moved the previous question. Twelve of
the minority then withdrew, ostensibly for consultation,
thereby breaking the quorum. They were immediately arrested, but, with the exception of four who were necessary to a quorum, were, despite their protests, wholly excluded from their seats. The original bill was passed within
a few minutes afterwards.[1] A few days later, Alford, one
of the senators released in order to secure a quorum, was expelled by the " rump " on the ground that he had resisted
arrest.

Taking full advantage of this happy situation, the radical
senators kept their fellow-members under arrest for more
than three weeks, and during that time disposed of a number of administration measures as fast as they could be
rushed through the lower house. One of these, carrying
out the recommendation of Governor Davis, provided for
the organization of a state police, to consist of some two
hundred and fifty men headed by a chief of police, but completely under the control of the governor.[2] This measure
attracted less public attention and met with less opposition
than the militia bill, evidently because it conferred no extraordinary power upon the executive; but it was to prove

[1] *House Journal,* pp. 6, 135, 175; *Senate Journal,* 63, 98, 122, 209-227,
247-249, 252, 261.

[2] *House Journal,* 104, 210, 312-14; *Senate Journal,* 170, 251, 275,
278-79; *Gammel,* VI, 193-195.

the more dangerous of the two. Another act, passed at the instance of the governor with the laudable intent of diminishing homicides, put restrictions upon the indiscriminate carrying of dangerous weapons.

The determination of the radical majority to fasten the hold of their faction upon the state in every way possible was manifested in a series of acts vesting extraordinary powers in the governor. He was given complete control over the registration of voters, and he was empowered to appoint to a number of offices which the constitution made elective. These included not only all vacated offices, but those to which, for certain reasons, no elections had been held. For instance, the form of the various judicial districts had first to be determined by the legislature; but even when that had been done, no election was allowed for district attorneys or clerks, and Davis was authorized to appoint them instead. An even more flagrant violation of the principle of local self-government was the extension of the executive's appointing power to the governing bodies of towns. New charters were granted to a number of cities and towns, and in the case of every one of importance the governor was allowed to appoint the mayor and board of aldermen who were to control the other officials. The explanation of this remarkable arrangement was that the charters were drafted by local radical politicians, who feared that under the unrestricted suffrage then existing they could not carry a municipal election.[1] Not content with these partisan measures the radicals also passed an act postponing

---

[1] In Galveston when the citizens and newspapers protested against the charter backed by Ruby and others, the *State Journal* had the temerity and bad taste to taunt the press and the citizens with being " at the mercy of the governor ", and to threaten them with punishment at his hands in the matter of appointments unless they ceased their attacks upon his administration.—Issue of July 15, 1870.

until 1872 the regular elections, which for representatives in Congress should have been held in the fall of 1870 and for state offices in 1871.[1] The nominal purpose of this change was to make the state and Congressional elections coincide; but the effect really desired was to extend one year longer the lease of power of the radicals elected in 1869. The *State Journal,* the official organ, frankly avowed that the purpose was to prevent the offices from falling into the hands of the enemies of the administration.[2] By another act the governor was authorized to designate in each judicial district a newspaper that should be the official organ and do the public printing for that district. No public notice could be legally advertised except in this organ. The governor was thus enabled to reward " loyal " papers and to establish a chain of organs that would " radiate civilization into the darkest corners of the state ". A number of sheets that otherwise must have sunk were thus kept afloat; and in a few cases Democratic journals were willing to accept the patronage on the terms required.

However, not all the important acts of this session were for the building of a party machine. The laws of the late provisional and military governments were declared in force until superseded by new ones, and all state and county officers were authorized to act under them. The governor's message had given especial attention to the frontier, and one of the first measures enacted provided for raising and equipping twenty companies of rangers for service against the Indians; while a later act authorized the sale of $750,000 of seven per cent. state bonds for the maintenance of the new force. An attempt was made to organize a general system of public schools under a state

[1] Gammel, VI, 302-313.
[2] Issue of July 15, 1870.

superintendent of education, the schools of each county to
be managed by the county police court; but popular hostility
to the admission of negroes to the public schools, coupled
with inefficient management by the courts, rendered the
plan in large measure a failure.

The subject of state aid to railroads occupied much time
and attention. No less than fifty-two bills were introduced
for the incorporation or relief of as many railroad companies. The two most prominent of these bills were for
aiding the International and the Southern Pacific, both
trunk lines. The latter had first been chartered in 1852,
and again in 1856, and had built into the state some forty-
six miles before the war. It was now proposed to renew its
forfeited land grants and in addition to donate to the company $16,000 of seven per cent. gold-bearing state bonds
for every mile of road built. The bill passed with little
opposition in either house, but was vetoed by Governor
Davis on the ground that the new constitution forbade any
grant of land except to actual settlers, and that the terms
of the proposed bond issue were unsatisfactory. In his first
message he had favored liberal charters to railroads, but
had opposed the old practice of granting subsidies. The
senate repassed the bill, but in the house it failed of the
necessary two-thirds by three votes. The International bill
was more successful. It carried no land grant, but donated
$16,000 of eight per cent. bonds for every mile of road, and
attempted to protect these bonds by a provision that the
bonded debt of the state for internal improvements should
never exceed twelve millions of dollars.[1] This was the
only railroad subsidy that received the governor's approval.
Rumor had much to say of improper influences at work to
secure the passage of these bills; but conclusive proof is

[1] Gammel, VI, 606-612.

lacking, and the crying need for railroads, especially for trunk lines, affording outlets to the north and east, would partially account for the strong support given them by members of all parties.

2. *The Growth of the Opposition.*

Long before the legislative session closed, a widespread and powerful opposition had begun to gather against the radical policies. The conservative Republicans, who at first had manifested a willingness to accept the result of the recent struggle by aligning themselves with Davis's administration, found their advances repulsed or coldly accepted and made the subject of the irritating sarcasm of the administration journals. Though continuing their support half-heartedly for a time, they were soon hinting at the necessity for a conference of the Hamilton Republicans.[1] In the meantime the radicals were rapidly presenting the opposition with issues upon which to organize. The militia bill precipitated a most acrimonious discussion, that was further embittered by the arrest and temporary exclusion of the opposition minority in the senate. Not a newspaper, except those dependent upon administration patronage, favored the bill. Governor Davis's significant declaration that "a slow civil war" was going on in Texas; the eagerness with which the administration organs exploited every opportunity to picture the state as overwhelmed with lawlessness; and the submission to the legislature by Newcomb, secretary of state, of a report to the same effect—were all regarded as evidences of a radical scheme to subject the state to military power.

Although, as we have seen, the state-police act did not arouse much opposition at first, the operations of the force that was immediately organized under it further inflamed

[1] *Austin Republican,* June 14 and 28, 1870.

the feeling against the radicals. It can not be denied that a certain necessity existed for some measure of this kind; for a number of districts were still infested by desperadoes against whom the local officials seemed powerless. Nor can it be denied that the new police, able to concentrate at any point and unaffected by local considerations, did much valuable service in cleaning out infested regions. But they did not confine themselves to these legitimate and praise-worthy services. Some of the worst desperadoes in the state took service in the police, and under the shield of authority committed the most high-handed outrages: bare-faced robbery, arbitrary assessments upon helpless com-munities, unauthorized arrests, and even the foulest murders were proven against them.[1] Undoubtedly the governor and his adjutant-general, Davidson, had been grossly imposed upon; and they willingly removed the worst offenders when the evidence of their guilt became overwhelming. That, however, did not make the police popular; for they were used so often to enforce the arbitrary will of the governor, that they became the very emblems of despotic authority. Nor did the fact that many of them were negroes lessen the irritation and uneasiness that their presence always pro-duced.

The manner in which the governor exercised the extra-ordinary if not wholly unconstitutional appointive powers vested in him by the legislature constituted another griev-ance. Although many of his appointments, especially to judicial offices, were excellent, others were of a more than doubtful character, due partly to a lack of good material

[1] Especially notorious were Captains Jack Helm and C. S. Bell, who were in the habit of arresting persons against whom they had a grudge and killing them for "attempting to escape." For accounts of particularly atrocious murders, see the *Austin Daily Republican*, Nov. I and 18; also Oct. 10, 12 and 25; and *Tri-Weekly State Gazette*, Oct. 12 and Nov. 25, 1870.

within the radical ranks, and partly to the fact that those best qualified frequently refused to accept office under a radical administration.

But the heaviest indictment against Davis was that he had built up in the interest of his faction an essentially one-man power; for he had so shaped the laws and the administration, that his power over the people of Texas was as truly military as that wielded by the recent commanders of the Fifth Military District. In actual fact the liberty and life of every citizen lay in the governor's hands. It is not easy to prove that Davis consciously intended to abuse this power; on the contrary it would seem that what others regarded as an abuse he considered a necessary extension of authority. It must be remembered, in justice to him, that he viewed his administration not solely as a return to local self-government, but as a continuation by the state of the national process of reconstruction. He knew that his party was a minority of the voting population of Texas, and he had no confidence in the disposition of the white majority to abide by the laws, especially those establishing the civil and political rights of the negroes, unless overawed by military power.

By midsummer the two wings of the Republicans were openly at war again, and the Democrats were planning to take advantage of the growing hostility to the radical régime. However, the rapid and spontaneous development of the spirit of opposition outran the slower if more methodical organization of party, and was generally manifested in mass meetings that bore no party affiliation. Some of the more astute politicians, indeed, were not anxious to draw party lines at this time lest it should divide and weaken the anti-radical forces; hence a movement was early set on foot to unite the conservatives and the Democrats on a liberal platform under which " dead issues ", such as negro suffrage, should be buried. A considerable body of extreme Democrats, however, bitterly opposed any fusion and demanded a straightout Democratic organization and platform, with none of the old issues eliminated.[1]

On July 9th a group of prominent men representing all parties, including several legislators who had been elected on the radical ticket, met at Austin to organize the opposition. A week later they issued a public address, reviewing and condemning in the strongest terms the Davis policies, and presented in the name of the people of Texas a petition to Congress for a guarantee of a republican form of government.[2]

Whatever Governor Davis had gained earlier by the adhesion of former conservatives and Democrats, was now offset by defections in his own party. He quarreled with the comptroller, Bledsoe, over the manner of endorsement of the new frontier bonds,[3] with the result that they were placed on the market without the signature of either the comptroller or the treasurer. Their validity was questioned, they could not be sold, and it became impossible to pay or equip the companies raised for the protection of the frontier; the United States refused to accept the services of the rangers or to furnish them supplies; the Indians raided unchecked, and the blame was laid on the governor. United States Senator Morgan Hamilton had from the first opposed Davis's frontier policy and had much to do with dis-

[1] The most important Democratic journals advocating fusion were the *Houston Telegraph* and the *Galveston News;* the *State Gazette* led the opposition to it. For an able argument for fusion, see a speech of W. M. Walton in *Austin Republican,* Oct. 4, or *Tri-Weekly State Gazette,* Oct. 12, 1870.

[2] *Austin Republican,* July 14, 26, 27, 28; *Tri-Weekly State Gazette,* July 25, 1870. Among those participating were J. W. Throckmorton, B. H. Epperson, J. L. Haynes, W. M. Walton, and Webster Flanagan.

[3] *Supra,* p. 299.

crediting the bonds in the New York market; and now the administration journals attacked Hamilton viciously and drove him into the anti-Davis camp, whence he retaliated with a scorching letter against the printing law. His colleague, J. W. Flanagan, who had brought so much strength to the radical ticket in east Texas the year before, balked at the militia and police bills and was soon numbered with the anti-administration forces.[1] Nevertheless the governor persisted in his policy and in his methods of enforcing it; he continued the arbitrary use of the state police, and displayed an unnecessary readiness to try the experiment of martial law, which only increased anger and apprehension.[2] In the special elections ordered for the last of November to fill vacancies in the legislature it was clear enough that a reaction against radicalism had set in, for the Democrats and conservatives captured several districts that had gone for the radicals the year before.[3]

In some districts the conservatives and Democrats had agreed upon a fusion policy, in others they had not been able to agree;[4] but as it became clear that the conservatives

[1] *Austin Republican,* July 14, 16, 18; Aug. 2, 27, Sept. 6, 8, 10, 30, 1870; *State Journal,* Aug. 4, 1870.

[2] In commenting upon an order of Davis that persons arrested by the police for attempting to evade the quarantine regulations of Houston be tried by court martial, the *Austin Republican* said: " The attempt to try a citizen by martial law is a naked usurpation and one that no citizen of this State will submit to. General Davis may order a dozen courts martial, if it may please him to be guilty of so much folly, but he will never try any man in Texas by his courts. The day that E. J. Davis attempts to execute the findings of any court martial against any citizen of this State will be the blackest day in the calendar of his life."—Oct. 11, 1870.

[3] Two of these counties, Houston and Cherokee, were threatened with martial law because of alleged intimidation of voters. *State Journal,* Dec. 17, 18, 28, 1870.

[4] At Seguin a fusion convention, December 9, nominated John Hancock for congress.—*Austin Republican,* Dec. 24, 1870.

were too weak to stand alone, that they would not go back to the support of Davis, and that Davis himself would never be able to stem the current of reaction setting so strongly against him, the anti-fusion Democrats were able to carry through their plans for an outright Democratic organization. On November 22d a call was issued for a state convention of the party to be held in Austin on January 23, 1871. " This call may result in the inauguration of a popular movement in which all good citizens may join," said the conservative organ, which urged its friends to " stand and wait ".[1]

When the convention met the liberal element was in control; and, though the cardinal principles of the Democracy were reaffirmed, the platform adopted made no mention of " dead issues ", but invited " all good citizens, whatever may have been their past political preferences ", to help drive from power the radicals, whose objectionable and extraordinary measures were condemned seriatim. A thorough state organization was planned, with general and county committees; and provision was made for the establishment in Austin of a central party organ, which made its appearance in July as the *Democratic Statesman.*[2] The conservative Republicans generally appear to have acceded to the one-sided alliance; for the *Austin Republican* accepted the platform, though without enthusiasm—" the people of Texas care nothing for party or for party names." A week later this organ of the helpless Jack Hamilton faction ceased publication.

In the meantime the Twelfth Legislature had met for what it was pleased to term its first regular session. The governor informed the houses that the work of reorganiza-

[1] *Austin Republican*, Nov. 28, 1870.

[2] *Austin Republican*, Jan. 26, 1871 ; *Ann. Cyc.* 1871, pp. 734-735.

tion had been largely performed, that the people generally were aiding the officers in re-establishing order, and that an improved condition of affairs was manifest. More than ninety thousand citizens had been enrolled in the militia; objectionable persons had been removed from the state police, and this force, though small, had made 978 arrests during the previous six months.[1] No further radical legislation of a public character was recommended and none of moment was enacted at this session. Notice was taken, however, of Morgan C. Hamilton's quarrel with the administration, and a resolution was passed declaring invalid his election to the United States Senate twelve months before for the full term beginning in 1871, on the ground that the legislature had then been without the proper authority. General J. J. Reynolds, still stationed in Texas, was elected to the place; but Hamilton contested the seat and won, the Senate rejecting Reynolds.[2]

The worst measure of the session, and perhaps the worst ever passed by any Texas legislature, was one granting to two parallel railroads, the Southern Pacific and the Memphis, El Paso and Pacific, $6,000,000 of thirty-year eight per cent. state bonds, under the sole condition that the roads unite at a point about halfway across the state. It was provided that these bonds might later be exchanged for public land at the rate of twenty-four sections for every mile.[3] Since the roads were already claiming sixteen sections under an old act they ran a good chance of getting a total gift of over twenty-two millions of acres. The governor sent in an indignant veto message, exposing the character of the grant and showing that it would entail an an-

---

[1] *Senate Journal,* 12th Legislature, 1871, pp. 23-39.

[2] *Cong. Globe,* 1st sess. 42nd Cong., pp. 4, 168, 169.

[3] A " section " is six hundred and forty acres, a square mile.

nual tax upon the people heavier than was demanded for
the support of the state government; but his veto was over-
ridden almost without discussion. In counting up the
charges against Davis's administration, not a suspicion can
rest against his financial honesty, of which this veto message
is an enduring monument.[1] An effort was made by some
of the more scrupulous radicals to repeal the act postponing
the general state elections to 1872, but in caucus the majority decided in favor of the postponement, and Speaker
Evans, who refused to be bound thereby, was removed and
W. H. Sinclair elected in his stead.[2]

The legislature adjourned May 31st to meet again on
September 12th. Meanwhile, preparations were making for
the Congressional campaign. In each of the four districts
radical-Republican and Democratic candidates were named
by their respective conventions, and the excitement attending
this first battle under an unrestricted suffrage was intensified by factional disturbances within the ranks of each
party. The unprecedented expenses of the state, the ab-
normal tax rate, and the prospect of another session of
legislative extravagance could not fail to prove effective
weapons against the radicals; and a group of prominent
citizens of both the anti-radical parties issued a call for a
state taxpayers' convention to be held at Austin to protest
against exorbitant public expenditures.[3] The call met with
a ready response. County taxpayers' meetings were held
in all parts of the state, delegates were selected and a
widely representative body met at the capital on September
22d. Ex-Governor E. M. Pease was elected president, and
committees were appointed on general business, to gather

---

[1] *Senate Journal*, pp. 1217-1222. For the act, Gammel, VI, 1623-1628.
[2] *House Journal*, 1474-82; *Daily State Journal*, May 9, 10, and 12, 1871.
[3] *Democratic Statesman*, August 12, 1871.

tax statistics, and to confer with the governor. Davis, however, refused to recognize the convention in any way and headed a counter-demonstration of several hundred negroes.[1] The report of the committee on statistics disclosed that the rate for state taxes alone had risen from fifteen cents in 1860 and in 1866 to two dollars and seventeen and one-half cents on the one hundred dollars valuation, exclusive of that levied to pay interest on the bonds donated to the International and the Southern Pacific railroads, which would equal about sixty cents additional, and exclusive also of a two-dollar poll tax.[2] The convention did much to consolidate the opposition and to direct it upon a most vulnerable point of attack.

As the election drew near and it became evident that the result would be close, the excitement increased. Governor Davis issued on August 9th an election order, designed to secure peace and decorum at the polls, but so unnecessarily

---

[1] *Democratic Statesman*, Sept. 23, and 26, 1871.

[2] The rate per $100 valuation was made up as follows:

General property tax, state	$0.500
" " " county	0.250
Roads and bridges	0.250
School-houses	0.125
Special school tax	1.000
Frontier-bond interest	0.050
Total	$2.175

The poll taxes were:

For schools	$1.00
" roads and bridges	1.00
Total	$2.00

There were also occupation and license taxes. Because of the questionable validity of the one per cent. school tax the committee advised the people to refuse to pay it. See reports in full in *Democratic Statesman*, Oct. 3 and 5, 1871.

stringent as to aggravate still further the feeling against him.[1] The election took place at the county seats, from October 3rd to 6th. The polling booths were surrounded by armed militiamen and state police, many of them ne-groes, and the voters were required to deploy in single file through a narrow plank lane under the eyes of Davis's offi-cials. Nevertheless, the Democratic candidates for Congress were all successful. In the first district, W. S. Herndon defeated G. W. Whitmore, 16,172 votes to 11,572; in the second district, J. C. Conner defeated A. M. Bryant, 18,285 to 5,948; in the third, D. C. Giddings beat Wm. T. Clark by 23,374 to 20,406; and in the fourth, John Hancock was successful over E. Degener by 17,010 to 12,636 votes.[2]

Notwithstanding the precautions taken, or perhaps be-cause of them, serious disturbances amounting to intimida-tion occurred in several counties, and in others the cry of fraud was raised by both sides. The board of state can-vassers threw out the votes of several counties, but changed the result only in the third district, where Clark was de-clared elected over Giddings. The latter contested the seat, however, and after a long struggle obtained it, despite the efforts of Davis, who seems to have been actuated by a private grudge against him.[3] Limestone and Freestone counties, where there was the greatest disorder, Davis de-termined to punish with severity; they were declared under martial law, issuance of the writ of *habeas corpus* was

---

[1] The order is printed in the *Daily State Journal*, Aug. 10, 1871; also in *Comprehensive History of Texas*, II, pp. 191-192.

[2] *Ann. Cyc.*, 1871, p. 736. Whitmore, Clark, and Degener, Repub-licans, had been elected in 1869. Conner, Democrat, was the only in-cumbent retained.

[3] *Cong. Globe*, 2nd sess., 42nd Cong., p. 3385. Giddings was seated on May 13, 1872. For this contest consult index to proceedings of this session under " Contested Elections, Texas."

prohibited, an assessment of $50,000 was levied upon Limestone, and state troops were quartered there.[1] The legislature, however, which was again in session, called upon him for the reasons for his action, and on November 6th passed a resolution disapproving it as unnecessary and uncalled for, because the courts were unobstructed and the legislature in actual session.[2] Ten days later the governor revoked his proclamation. This was by no means the first time Davis had made use of the power the militia law granted him. Earlier in the year Walker and Hill counties had been subjected to this treatment, because of local disturbances; and in the former a man was tried and condemned to the penitentiary by military commission.

Disagreements between certain of the administration officials gave no end of satisfaction to the Democrats. Governor Davis and Comptroller Bledsoe had been quarreling ever since their induction into office, but at last on one point they agreed. Bledsoe refused to countersign the International Railroad bonds, asserting his belief that their issuance was unconstitutional. Davis had always opposed them, but the treasurer, G. W. Honey, took the opposite view, and a lively quarrel ensued. In May, 1872, while Honey was away, Davis declared that he had vacated the office of treasurer, appointed B. Graham to the position and with the aid of the state police took possession. Honey tried to regain possession, but the governor prevented him, alleging that a shortage in accounts of the office had been discovered. The question was fought out in the courts; the missing money was shown to have been lent to a local bank, but Graham was retained in the treasurership. In

---

[1] Proclamation of October 9th in *Daily State Journal*, Oct. 11, 1871.

[2] *Ann. Cyc.*, 1871, p. 732. For the evidence adduced by Davis, see *House Journal*, 12th Legis., adjourned session, pp. 191-211; *Daily State Journal*, Oct. 13, 1871. The evidence was strong, but wholly *ex parte.*

November, Adjutant-General James Davidson, head of the police force, absconded with about $30,000 of the state's funds. The opposition did not fail to charge the governor with responsibility and complicity in the defalcation, but not the slightest proof of personal dishonesty on the part of Davis was found. It seems true, however, that he arbitrarily and needlessly allowed unbonded officers who were in his confidence to handle large sums belonging to the state, and to that extent made Davidson's defalcation possible.

Toward the middle of 1872 public attention was centered once more upon national politics. The Texas Republicans met in convention at Houston in May to nominate candidates for Presidential electors and Congressmen at large, and to select delegates to the national convention of their party. The platform endorsed President Grant and instructed the delegates to support him for renomination; denounced the nomination of Horace Greeley by the Liberal Republicans at Cincinnati; and applauded the measures of Governor Davis's administration, especially with regard to public free schools, internal improvements, and the defence of the frontier. The Democrats, who met in Corsicana in June, re-affirmed their platform of the previous year, denounced the Republican administrations in state and nation, expressed approval of the action of the Liberal Republicans, and promised to support whatever course the Baltimore convention should take. On state matters they promised support to the public schools and protection to the frontier, but condemned the granting of money subsidies by the state to private corporations.[1] Some of the extreme Democrats refused to follow the lead of Greeley and accepted O'Conor as their Presidential candidate; and the split in the organization was here and there

[1] *Ann. Cyc.*, 1872, p. 765, 766.

carried into the local campaign now being hotly waged for control of the new legislature. Another question, a sectional one, that involved some political trading, was the selection of a state capital.

There should have been no doubt of the result; for the Congressional election of the year before had shown that the Democrats had a clear majority in the greater part of the state. Moreover, a number of radicals had become dissatisfied with Governor Davis, whom they now regarded as responsible for the increase of Democratic strength, and as too great a burden for the Republicans to carry. The election was held November 5th to 8th. Greeley received a majority of 19,020 over Grant; all the Democratic nominees for Congress were successful; and the Democrats secured a decided majority in the legislature.

3. *Election of 1873 and the End.*

The end of Republican rule was now in sight, provided the Federal government should not interfere. With an unfriendly legislature the governor would find his policies greatly hampered if not wholly blocked, and in another year his present term would end. The Democrats indulged in threats of impeachment, but when the Thirteenth Legislature met, January 14, 1873, the idea had been abandoned. Davis's message was mild and conciliatory, but the Democrats had a program to carry out: they promptly repealed the public printing law and the state-police act, and so amended the militia act as to deprive the governor of any extraordinary powers derived therefrom.[1] The " enabling act " under which Davis had appointed officers whom the constitution made elective, the registration and election

---

[1] Gammel, VII, 456, 468, 493. A new act was passed to regulate public printing, but it carefully avoided the bad features of the former one.

laws, and the school law were either repealed or shorn of their objectionable features. In every case, except the three last named, the governor withheld his consent, and the new act passed over his veto or became a law by his failure to return it within the constitutional five days. Another act of importance provided that the next general election for governor and all other state and county officers should be held on the first Tuesday in December, 1873; and to this the governor assented. The rest of the work of the Thirteenth Legislature need not be detailed; sufficient it is to say the members have been styled the " liberators of Texas."

Preparations were now making for the final struggle. In August the Republicans held their state convention in Dallas, dominated by Governor Davis; they nominated him for re-election, offered a liberal platform, and denounced the acts of the recent legislature. The Democrats held a large and enthusiastic convention in Austin early the next month and nominated Judge Richard Coke and R. B. Hubbard for governor and lieutenant-governor. The lengthy platform expressed confidence in the outcome of the elections; congratulated the people upon the repeal of the " oppressive, odious and unconstitutional acts " of the radical Republicans; promised that the government should be administered in no retaliatory spirit, but in the interest of every citizen regardless of color, station, or politics; offered encouragement to immigration and to railroads, and protection to the frontier; and advocated the calling of a constitutional convention.[1]

As the time of election approached the greatest excitement prevailed. As in 1869, the chief reliance of Davis was upon the negro vote, and the old organization of the Loyal League, which had been zealously kept up during all

[1] *Ann. Cyc.*, 1873, pp. 737-739. The constitutional convention was held in 1876 and adopted the constitution now (1910) in force.

this time, was made the most of. To everyone, however, except Davis himself, the result was never in doubt. Stubbornly refusing to believe himself beaten, he carried the fight into those eastern counties where the heavy black population had made radicalism most hated and himself denounced and threatened as the chief exponent of negro domination. But his personal courage did not avail him. The whites were determined that E. J. Davis should never again rule over Texas, that radical-carpetbag-negro domination was to be ended. It was in a sense a revolution. There is no shadow of a doubt of fraud and intimidation at this election. " Davis negroes " were in many communities ordered to keep away from the polling places, while white men under age were voted. On the other hand negro Democrats were threatened by Loyal Leaguers.[1] The total vote was surprisingly large; 85,549 votes were cast for Coke and 42,663 for Davis. All the new state officials were Democrats, as were the great majority of the legislators and the county officers.

But the radicals were not done. Even after making liberal allowance for irregularities at the polls, there was no question that the verdict of the people was against them; but that alone would not have mattered, for theirs had always been a minority rule. It was now determined to have the courts set aside the election, and then, if necessary, to appeal to Grant for assistance. A test case was provided in a *habeas corpus* proceeding before the state supreme court to release from the custody of the sheriff one Joseph Rodriguez, a Mexican, charged with voting more than once in the election. The constitution provided that " all elections . . . shall be held at the county seats of the several

[1] These statements have often been made by Democrats who knew of the circumstances.

counties until otherwise provided by law; and the polls
shall be open for four days . . ." [1] It was well known that
the four-day period was intended to apply only so long as
the elections should be held at the county seats; and when
the last legislature provided for holding them in the various
precincts, only one day was allowed. But the radicals now
made the point that the two clauses above quoted, because
of the semicolon that separated them, were wholly distinct
provisions, and that the recent election had been an illegal
one because not held for four days. The court sustained
this view, Rodriguez was released, and the election was declared void.[2] Moreover, Davis announced that he would
not give up his office until April 28, 1874, four years from
the date of his inauguration, or until a successor should be
legally elected and installed, and by proclamation ordered
the recently-elected officers and legislators not to attempt
to exercise their functions.[3]

The Democrats had no thought of yielding to the court
or the governor. At the proper time the newly-elected state
officers and legislators arrived in Austin, and on January
12th, the night before the legislature was to convene, a
conference of the Democratic leaders was held. It had been
discovered that Davis had planned armed resistance and
that a body of negro militia was at hand to prevent the
Democrats from taking possession of the capitol. Late
that night the Democrats took possession of the upper
stories of the building; the negro militia held the lower. In
the meantime Davis had telegraphed Grant for military as-

---

[1] Art. 3, sec. 6. See Gammel, VII, p. 399.

[2] *Ex parte* Rodriguez, 39 Texas Reports, pp. 709. This is known
among lawyers as the "semi-colon decision"; and so odious has it been
that no lawyer likes to cite any opinion delivered by this court. See
Comprehensive History of Texas, II, 201.

[3] *Ann. Cyc.*, 1873, pp. 739-740.

sistance, but the President wisely refused. Next morning the two houses convened and sent a joint committee to Davis, who declined to recognize the legislature. The secretary of state, Newcomb, refused to give up the election returns, until Davis so far yielded as to allow them to be taken under protest. This was done on the 15th. The votes were counted and Coke and Hubbard duly inaugurated. Davis still held out; he ordered another company of militia to his aid, the Travis Rifles, but it obeyed the command of the new Democratic adjutant-general, McCulloch, instead; and he appealed once more to the Federal government and was again refused. During all this time Austin was full of greatly-excited armed citizens, who were with difficulty restrained from attacking the negro militia. Finding it useless to resist further, Davis gave in on the 17th and retired. Coke took possession, and the radical régime was at an end.[1] Thus, nine years after the close of the Civil War and nearly four years after Texas had been readmitted to the Union, the state was once more really in the hands of her own people.

The administration of Davis was responsible for more of the bitterness with which the people of Texas have remembered the reconstruction era than all that happened from the close of the war to 1870. In fact the word reconstruction recalls to most people first of all the arbitrary rule of this radical governor; and certainly the name of no Texan has gone down to posterity so hated as his. But after all, Davis has not been fairly judged. He was self-willed, obstinate, pig-headed almost beyond belief; a most intense and narrow partisan, who could see nothing good in an

---

[1] The account here given is taken from that of O. M. Roberts in the *Comprehensive History of Texas*, II, pp. 201-207, and *Ann. Cyc.*, 1873, pp. 739-741. A slightly different account is that of T. B. Wheeler in the *Quarterly of the Texas State Hist. Ass'n.*, XI, pp. 56-63.

opponent and nothing evil in a friend. Surrounded by a group of the most unprincipled adventurers that ever disgraced a government, he suffered from their advice and their acts. Yet his administration was his own and he guided it with the iron hand of a martinet; he had no regard for the popular will, he consulted no desires but his own, and he was absolutely devoid of tact. But, apparently without scruples in matters purely political, Davis was personally honest. He never descended to the vulgar level of greed and dishonesty so common to his satellites; it can not be shown that he ever diverted one cent of public money to his own pocket. More than that, he strove to give the state an honest financial administration and to save it from spoliation and bankruptcy; and of this his vetoes of railroad subsidies is proof enough. It is true he caused the expenditure of great sums in other directions, and there was much scandal in the handling of the funds, but in this last Davis was not personally implicated. And it may be said of his policies with regard to police, internal improvements, and the schools, that it was not so much the end he had in view as the methods he employed that aroused resistance and hatred. In many respects he was the best of the faction that nominated him for governor in 1869; but no man could have been worse fitted by temperament for the delicate task before the local Republicans at that time. When circumstances demanded the most painstaking moderation in order to overcome the effect of the Congressional policy, E. J. Davis and his radical associates succeeded only in plunging the Republican party in Texas into irretrievable ruin.

BIBLIOGRAPHY

1. MANUSCRIPT SOURCES.

Executive Correspondence.—Letters to the governors, filed in the office of the secretary of state, Austin. Voluminous; the best source for general conditions.

Reconstruction Correspondence of Generals Griffin and Reynolds. Filed with the above, but in separate boxes; contains letters, copies of orders and other official documents not accessible elsewhere. Many are concerned with the Freedmen's Bureau.

Executive Records.—Register books, containing governors' proclamations, copies of important letters, and reports from other heads of administration; and the letter-books of the secretary of state.

No records of this period remain in the offices of the attorney-general, treasurer, and comptroller, all having been consumed in the great fire of 1881 which destroyed the old capitol building.

Johnson Papers, in the Library of Congress. Contain a great many valuable letters to President Johnson on affairs in Texas, from both sides.

Roberts Papers, in the History vault, University of Texas. Letters to O. M. Roberts; also fragments of an autobiography, pamphlets and a few newspapers.

2. PRINTED SOURCES.

Newspapers.—The Texas State Library and the Swante Palm collection at the University of Texas contain the most extensive files. Few however, are complete. These may be supplemented by files in the Carnegie libraries at Houston and San Antonio and in the offices of the *Galveston News* and the *San Antonio Express.* The newspapers that have been most useful are: the *Southern Intelligencer* (R) [1], the *State Gazette* (D), *Flake's Bulletin* (R), *Galveston News* (D), *Galveston Civilian* (D), *Houston Telegraph* (D), *San Antonio Herald* (D), *San Antonio Express* (R), *Texas Republican* (D), *Austin Republican* (R), *Houston Union* (R), *Houston Times* (D), *State Journal* (R), *Democratic Statesman* (D). Nearly all of these are fairly complete. Fragmentary files of others are also to be found.

The Townsend Library, a vast collection of clippings from the principal New York papers, in the Columbia University Library, covers

[1] R means Radical or Republican; D means Conservative or Democrat.

the civil war and reconstruction and contains many references, not always accurate, to affairs in Texas.

Pamphlets.—Throckmorton's *Address to the People of Texas*, reviewing and defending his administration, is in the State Library; the constitution proposed for "West Texas," and the *Proceedings* of the Tax Payers' Convention are in the library of the University of Texas; A. J. Hamilton's *Memorial* was lent by Mrs. W. W. Mills of Austin.

Public Documents.—Gammel, *Laws of Texas*, vols. v, vi, and vii; contains all the legislative acts and resolutions, and the constitutions of 1866 and 1869. The *Convention Journals* of 1866 and 1868-69 contain full accounts of the proceedings, except the debates. The *House and Senate Journals* of the 11th, 12th and 13th Legislatures. The *Official Records, War of the Rebellion*, give by far the fullest information concerning the war and are valuable for the "break-up" also. The various Congressional publications are indispensable; the *Congressional Globe*, the House and Senate *Executive Documents, Committee Reports*, etc. Richardson, *Messages and Papers of the Presidents*, VI. United States *Statutes at Large*, XIII and XIV. Fleming, *Documentary History of Reconstruction*, vol. i. Texas Supreme Court Reports, vols. 30-39.

Books and Periodicals.—There is no satisfactory general account of Texas during this period. The best is by O. M. Roberts in the *Comprehensive History of Texas*, vol. ii, a collaborative work edited by Dudley G. Wooten. A few pages each are given in the histories of the state by John Henry Brown, Thrall, and Geo. P. Garrison. Scanty references are in John H. Reagan's *Memoirs*, and F. R. Lubbock's *Six Decades in Texas*. R. H. Williams, *With the Border Ruffians*, an unreliable account of conditions about San Antonio and on the Rio Grande during the war, barely reaches this period. W. W. Mills, *Forty Years in El Paso*, has a few helpful sketches. *A Pioneer History of Wise County*, by C. D. Cates, contains some material of local interest and value. E. L. Dohoney's *An Average American* reflects conditions in East Texas. Of value for railroad problems and legislation is C. S. Potts, *Railroad Transportation in Texas* (University of Texas *Bulletin*, no. 119, 1909). Professor Dunning's *Essays on the Civil War and Reconstruction* contains valuable chapters on the process of reconstruction in the south, with several references to Texas. The *Texas Almanac*, 1857-1873, is full of valuable statistics. Appleton's *Annual Cyclopædia* for these years frequently gives concise information and documents not easily accessible elsewhere. In the *Quarterly* of the *Texas State Historical Association* have been published three helpful articles: "The Ku Klux Klan," by W. D. Wood, vol. ix, pp. 262-268; "Reminiscences of Reconstruction in Texas," by T. B. Wheeler, vol. xi, pp. 56-65; and "The Experiences of an Unrecognized Senator," by O. M. Roberts, posthumously published, vol. xii, pp. 87-147.

INDEX

A

Ab initio, doctrines of, 95–98, 176–180, 206–211, 264.
Alexander, Wm., attorney-general, under A. J. Hamilton, 59; under E. M. Pease, 173; resigns, 178.
Amendments to the Constitution of the United States, thirteenth and fourteenth, rejected, 118–120; fourteenth and fifteenth, adopted, 290.
Amnesty, oath of, 58.
Andrews, Gen. C. C., district commander, 78.
Apprenticeship law, 122–123.
Armstrong, James, delegate to convention of 1868, 200.
Armstrong, M. L., 258, 289.

B

Bacon, W. P., 161.
Ballinger, W. P., peace commissioner, 37.
Bell, Judge James H., secretary of state, 59, 264, 265.
Bennett, A. J., 259.
Bledsoe, A., comptroller, 285, 304, 311.
Bowers, state senator, 296.
Branch, A. M., representative to Congress, 117.
Brenham, burning of, 127.
Burford, Nat. M., speaker eleventh legislature, 115.
Burnet, David G., elected to U. S. Senate in 1866, 115.
Burnett, J. R., 245, 263.
Butler, J. P., 289–90.

C

Cave, E. W., secretary of state, 20.
Caldwell, Judge C., 150, 174, 189; delegate to convention of 1868, 200, 206, 214, 217, 240, 242.
Chilton, Geo. W., elected to Congress, 117.
Civil authorities, relations with military, under Hamilton, 77 ff.; under Throckmorton, 126–138, 149 ff.; under Pease, 183–187.
Clark, W. T., elected to Congress, 286.
Coke, Richard, Judge, 61; nominated governor, 314; takes seat, 317.
Committee of public safety, 17.
Conditions in Texas during war, 21 ff.
Confederacy, admission of Texas to, 21; break-up of, 27 ff.; property confiscated, 41; status of acts *de facto* of, 103–105.
Congress, representatives to, in 1866, 117–118.
Conner, J. C., 286.
"Conscript Law," 21.
Conservatives (Democratic), in election of 1866, 108 ff.; in eleventh legislature, 114 ff.; 167, 173, 188, 194, 197–199; (Republican) appeal to Congress, 261 ff.; opposition to Radicals, 301 ff.; fusion with Democrats, 305.
Constitutional convention of 1866, 85 ff.; work of, 89 ff.; of 1868, 200 ff.
Constitution of 1866, validity of, 176–180; of 1868, reports of committees on, 225–228, work on, 251–257; printing of, 255,260.
Cotton, trade during war, 24; confusion about, 41–44.
Courts under provisional government, 59–61.

D

Dalrymple, W. C., delegate to convention of 1866, 86.
Davis, Col. E. J., expedition against Laredo, 26; delegate to convention of 1866, 89, 93; delegate to convention of 1868, 200; president of, 201 ff.; 249, 258–9, 263, 272; campaign for governorship, 273 ff.; governor, 285 ff.